Global
Business Ethics

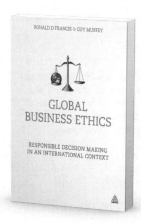

Global Business Ethics

Responsible decision making in an international context

Ronald D Francis
Guy Murfey

KoganPage

LONDON PHILADELPHIA NEW DELHI

First published in Great Britain and the United States in 2016 by Kogan Page Limited

2nd Floor, 45 Gee Street
London EC1V 3RS
United Kingdom
www.koganpage.com

1518 Walnut Street, Suite 1100
Philadelphia PA 19102
USA

4737/23 Ansari Road
Daryaganj
New Delhi 110002
India

© Ronald D Francis and Guy Murfey, 2016

ISBN   978 0 7494 7395 2
E-ISBN   978 0 7494 7396 9

British Library Cataloguing-in-Publication Data

A CIP record for this book is available from the British Library.

Library of Congress Cataloging-in-Publication Data

Francis, Ronald D. (Ronald David), 1931- author.
  Global business ethics : responsible decision making in an international context / Ronald D. Francis, Guy Murfey.
     pages cm
  Includes bibliographical references and index.
  ISBN 978-0-7494-7395-2 – ISBN 978-0-7494-7396-9 (ebk)   1. Business ethics.   2. International business enterprises–Moral and ethical aspects.   I. Murfey, Guy, author.   II. Title.
  HF5387.F7364 2016
  174'.4–dc23
                                                                                                    2015027326

Typeset by Graphicraft Limited, Hong Kong
Print production managed by Jellyfish
Printed and bound in India by Replika Press, Pvt Ltd

CONTENTS

Online resources to accompany this book are available at
www.koganpage.com/GBE

PREFACE

The statement 'in this rapidly changing world' is so commonly used now it has become a cliché. The community now accepts the pace of change as routine and this is dangerous. The cumulative effect of our improved computers, our complex machines and our understanding of the natural world including our own biology is massive to the point of being incomprehensible. We have eminent people such as Stephen Hawking (physicist) and Elon Musk (technology entrepreneur) calling for an ethics committee to rule over Artificial Intelligence projects, and we have Ray Kurzweil (director of engineering at Google) making statements that not only will the world change, our existing world will effectively cease to exist (Cellan-Jones, 2015, Schultz, 2015 and Zolfagharifard, 2015). Now is not the time for the world community to be treating business as 'business as usual'.

There are real risks, greater than we have ever known. The time to resolve them is not after they have occurred; that will be too late. The traditional mechanisms that we have relied upon for centuries to make adjustments between business and social responsibility will not work in this situation. One of the crucial determinants of our future will be the morality of the executives that are overseeing these changes and the ethics of their corporations. This book is an attempt to give a short but comprehensive understanding of the key issues in global business ethics and assist business students and business people to work through ethical problems.

Among the issues it canvasses is that it is a subject that should be of international significance, and as such it recognizes such approaches as Confucianism, Sharī'ah law, and the substantial cultural differences that commonly occur.

Here the stance adopted is that of noting that the intention to be ethical is a critical component. If a legalistic approach is taken it is quite possible to subvert the good work of ethics. Loopholing may be commonly used but, it is argued, it is contrary to the spirit and intention of being ethical.

If we disagree with the law then the proper action is to try to change it. In this we need to recognize that laws may be ambiguous, but that the problem is in the nature of the wording of the law, and therefore this work recognizes that definitions may be soft rather than hard.

We have included a brief account of the various approaches to ethics that theorists have contributed. We also include vignette cases, solved cases, discussion points and, importantly, issues of ethical gradualism and of the quantification of ethical matters. Finally it is noted that the authors would welcome feedback and suggestions for improvement.

ACKNOWLEDGEMENTS

This work, as will be obvious, owes much to others. Among the people we wish to acknowledge and thank are my colleague Ray Elliott for his kind permission to use the case of the different perspectives, to be included in the workbook. We also acknowledge the published authors of scholarly works as well as all the journalists, activists and other writers committed to ethical corporate behaviour. This work also takes in some material from various other books on ethics by the first author. This present work is, it is hoped, seen as an international research-based study that presents information and guides not to be found elsewhere.

We are greatly thankful for the ready and kind help given by Kogan Page, particularly by Jennifer Hall, Lucy Carter and Philippa Fiszzon. We give due praise and thanks to all of the mentioned and unmentioned helpers. It is sincerely hoped that this work will find favour in both the marketplace and in academia.

We also gladly acknowledge the kind permission of the publishers, Bloomsbury, of the Lloyd book *The 'Nice' Company* for their granting permission to quote.

No acknowledgements would be complete without serious mention of two significant others. One is my co-author, Guy Murfey, who took on this task and did it splendidly. The other is my wife, whose unfailing support and encouragement was instrumental in bringing this work to fruition.   *Ronald D Francis*

I would also like to specifically thank my wife Josephine and my sister Judith for all their help researching, proofreading, referencing, sounding out ideas and overall moral support. Both were unstinting, patient and generous every day through the writing (and Judith managing the help between chemotherapy treatments). Thanks to my other sister Gail for all her great contributions and for keeping a lot of stuff ticking over while resources were sucked into the manuscript. To Tim Dunlevie for Saturday morning walks that generated controversy, fleshed out concepts and looked for truth. My daughter Julia gets a special mention for her research into 'native advertising' and her general passion for journalistic integrity. Thanks to my son Nathan and his continuous flow of ideas and comic relief. Thanks to Jack Chatziyakoumis, Russell Walley, Peter Dybing, Veli Fikret, Ron Kugler and Brendan Myers, whose brains I picked for their keen insights into corporate life (and Jack for 30 years of BBQs). Thanks to Peter Antonenko, who rang pretty much every second day to make sure I was coping. Thanks to Carol Watts for her friendship, support and frequent reminders of how the real business world operates. Thanks to Fay, my late mother; we all miss her terribly. Thanks to my godmother Gen, who always believed I could write a book. Special thanks too to Ronald for giving me the opportunity to participate in a really great project.   *Guy Murfey*

PART ONE
The necessity, justification and research into cross-cultural business ethics

PART ONE

Background to ethics

Introduction

This chapter is to introduce the necessity and justification for ethics in business. It canvasses some salient issues in business ethics, and provides cases for consideration. In this it invites readers to consider the issues involved in being ethical. It should be kept in mind how extensive a subject business ethics is. The spectrum to be covered ranges from the philosophical view of how to formulate ethical principles that cover the range of issues encountered in business, down to recognized standards for international corporations.

It deserves the strongest possible emphasis that it is now a global world. As such we are compelled to be aware of different cultures having different values. To that end, matters like Sharīʿah law, Confucianism, and cultural practices are important for understanding the modern business environment. These factors, as well as the international efforts to address the ethical conduct of corporations, are fundamental drivers of this work.

This chapter concludes that there is a substantial argument in favour of being ethical, and that includes long-term considerations.

Purpose of the book

The Chief Executive Officer of a large accounting organization, ignoring corporate hierarchy, calls a Senior Associate to provide glowing feedback received from a client on a recent and difficult contract negotiation. The Senior Associate was, however, a last-minute replacement due to an unexpected illness and actually had no substantial role in the work, or in the resolution. The initial work on this contract was undertaken by a person who is now absent due to a serious illness and is likely to be away for months. Should the Senior Associate correct the CEO and attribute the work to the absent colleague?

This brief story is so familiar in its theme it is almost a cliché; however, it is unfortunately all too common in the corporate world. Importantly it illustrates so clearly the nature of dilemmas. No-one who hears this story is in any doubt about its intent. We know instantly and intuitively what is wrong. This book attempts to make that intuition more explicit. Feelings alone are no guide: presumably tyrants, psychopaths, and ideological maniacs are all convinced of the rightness of their feelings. It is by the use of reason that we come to moral understanding.

It is not implied here that ethics and the law are two separate realms of discourse. Rather it is argued that they occupy complementary functions along the same dimension of being concerned with human values, and of providing remedies and improvements to derelictions of behaviour.

Key learning points

The key learning points of this introductory chapter are:

- The necessity for business ethics.

- The advantages of being ethical.

- The importance of corporate governance.

- The need for strong ethical guidelines.

- The role of goodwill.

The chapter also explores:

- Early attempts at ethics in business and commerce.

- The Marlow Declaration.

- The means and ends debate.

- Whether ethics is a luxury.

Moral versus aesthetic values

Throughout the text it is recommended to distinguish what is moral from what we find attractive. We might be offended by being asked to admire the ornate architecture of a business premises, but there is nothing moral in it. On the other hand a person might be compelled to adopt a particular viewpoint about conducting a business that is at odds with that person's values: that is a moral question. The main point here is that it is important to distinguish the aesthetic from the moral.

The necessity for business ethics

All senior business people should have an interest in business ethics, firstly, because it is highly likely they have a legal obligation to do so. In the wake of corporate failures in the 1990s most governments introduced suites of legislation, regulations and regulatory bodies that require publicly listed companies to have and report on their ethical conduct codes. There are also implications for the extent and amount of punishment that may be meted out to a company when some unlawful act occurs. A demonstration that the company is fundamentally ethical and the event was an anomaly can substantially mitigate the potential consequences (discussed elsewhere in the book).

The variations between jurisdictions can have implications for global companies. Note that one of News Corporation's most serious concerns coming out of the phone hacking scandals in the UK was the potential that the behaviour would have implications for its extensive US operations where the laws provide for prosecutions under the Foreign Corrupt Practices Act.

A business leader's interest in ethics should not stop there. Their corporation may perform the required steps – have a code, train staff in the code and have some form of compliance activity – but yet behave in a way that is unethical while adhering to the law. There are many contemporary examples of this throughout this text. A business executive should take an interest beyond box-ticking, burdensome administration because lawful yet unethical behaviour can cause severe harm to their organization and the community. A 'box-ticking' mentality is likely to be at odds with ethical behaviour. It is as if once the box is ticked a person can then turn off the ethical switch. Having done the 'right thing' they are then absolved from behaving ethically.

There may have been nothing unlawful about banks loaning money to people who were a dubious credit risk. However, when the practice became large scale and ultimately collapsed under the weight of unviable borrowings, it caused the Global Financial Crisis. Millions of ordinary people lost their savings or had them reduced, the values of property collapsed, and business and consumer confidence was shattered. It was only the intervention by governments on a massive scale that prevented the disaster becoming a catastrophe. The frequently cited defence for these unconscionable acts has been that it was lawful and that a corporation's duty is to its shareholders; to optimize profit.

Technology has been driving an increasingly global world. A call centre in Mumbai can easily take a call from a consumer in Dallas. Video conference calls connect boardrooms in London and Hong Kong. Information flows in great currents through optic fibre cable beneath the world's oceans. The phones in our pockets have more computing power than the Apollo spaceships and connect us together all day every day. This revolution has been dissolving borders and national distinctions that have been the basis of our traditional social order.

In the past, companies identified with a nation even if they operated in multiple countries, and looked at least in part to the social wellbeing of its home country. In the new world order large multinationals are borderless entities chasing the best tax deal or cheapest workforce. The borderless world has increased the opportunity to legally avoid taxes and shift work to jurisdictions with fewer legal restraints in such areas as employment conditions. These actions deprive nations of the revenue they need and workers of the jobs that are the foundation of their quality of life. Again, the many executives maintain that they are compelled to take these actions, that their duty is to their shareholders and profitability.

This blurring of national lines has created opportunity but has arisen in parallel to rapidly advancing mass media and a greater sense of social responsibility in the wider world community. In brief, these changes mean that inappropriate behaviour such as exploiting foreign workers for the sake of profits can damage a company's reputation before they even have a chance to respond. This public exposure of this type of behaviour has probably had a beneficial effect.

Lawmakers play an important role, discussed at various points throughout this work, but to make government the sole keeper of social responsibility is to ignore history and reality. The law nearly always follows behind social convention and change. It could not have been expected to have anticipated and legislated for social media before it existed. How many other changes are nations facing as the technology evolves exponentially? Not only is the rate of change increasing but the degree of the change is more significant.

Innovations like drones, self-driving cars, and 3D printing of human organs are growing in impact. Automation of manufacturing and clerical functions is extinguishing vast numbers of jobs for unskilled and semi-skilled workers. Some of these changes have been and will be profound and some will have the capacity to inflict great social harm. It was and is inevitable that our business leaders will be in the better position to see and assess these changes as they are occurring well before the lawmakers, and even public opinion, can catch up. The decisions our business leaders make could have the most significant effects on everyone's future.

To take Milton Friedman's approach is to say morality is unrelated to business: to wrap questionable action in the cloak of 'duty to shareholders' is a convenient rationalization. Did the businessmen who sold the poison gas, Zyklon B, used to kill prisoners in Nazi concentration camps, have to explain to their shareholders that it was good for the bottom line? At the time, the sale of this product was completely lawful. Business always has a moral dimension.

In this increasingly complex world the ambiguity of situations has increased. As the information base becomes more complex the balance of decisions becomes increasingly hard to make. In such complicated and fluid situations there is a counter-vailing need for a set of guiding principles.

The commitment to ethical behaviour needs to be supplemented by explicitly teaching it, and we need to foster a business climate in which ethical behaviour is seen to be the norm.

Among the challenging ethical problems business encounters are:

- If I don't have to pay tax in the countries where I do business, should I? And if so how much?
- What are the impacts on the consumers of the product?
- What are my responsibilities to suppliers? Do I drive a hard bargain without regard for their profitability?
- Do I need to be concerned about the employees of a subcontractor in a developing economy?
- What are the environmental impacts of this decision?
- How do I balance my values with the very different values of a business partner from another culture?
- How much do I sacrifice profit for something that is perceived as a social good? What is the balance between profit and responsibility to the wider community?
- How do I create a culture of integrity and set standards for employees?
- How do I deal with informers (whistleblowers) who are ethically right but an embarrassment to the company?
- How do I deal with a problem of ethnicity in the workplace without seeming to be racist?
- Under what conditions is it all right to accept gifts?
- How should I deal with sexual impropriety by employees?
- If national espionage is acceptable does that make it all right to indulge in industrial and commercial espionage?

One of the essential aspects of ethics is consistency. Codes of ethics need to be of fixed quality. It is not appropriate to have a series of codes of increasing leniency from which to select. A person might imagine an organization containing several subgroups. The 'corporate flagship' might run the 'best' ethical set with 'lower' subsets being run according to more lenient standards. Such an exercise would turn ethics into expedience. It would be preferable to have the entire organization aspiring to the most developed set of standards. The Walmart example in the following box is a demonstration of the inconsistencies that can occur between the value set of the corporation in its home country and that of a subsidiary in a country with greater opportunity for corrupt practices.

The direct cost of unethical behaviour

Walmart

Walmart's Mexican subsidiary is a major component of the company's operation. In 2012, *New York Times* reporters discovered that corruption was endemic to the subsidiary. The principal example of this conduct was the building of a retail complex that opened in 2004, close to Teotihuacán pyramids, one of Mexico's important historic sites. For a number of reasons related to managing traffic around the town and the sensitivity of the site, the zoning for the area was to be residential. The site had significant appeal to the Walmart executives who bribed the official responsible for the zoning map, thereby clearing the blockage. The construction caused a number of protests at the time and bribery in those situations was assumed but nothing was proved until 2012.

Unlike the stereotypical image of Western companies having to succumb to inappropriate demands of a corrupt foreign culture, the reporters discovered that Walmart's agents were aggressive in their use of bribery. Worse still, it was revealed that head office had been made aware of this activity several years before and had started and then stopped an internal investigation. Unsurprisingly Walmart became the subject of a Federal investigation by both US and Mexican governments, and several investor lawsuits. The cost of dealing with these investigations and a 30 per cent increase in compliance costs is estimated to be close to US$460 million.

SOURCE: See Walmart in recommended reading

Advantages of being ethical

There are two compelling reasons for a business to act as ethically as possible: one reason is that it is, in the longer term, commercially advantageous; the second reason is that it is the right thing to do. In the immediate sense it is the responsibility of corporation officers to apply their often significant power appropriately to improve the community overall while ensuring levels of profit. In terms of our future, it is of crucial importance that our corporations are ethical. As has been noted in the fore-word the exponential change in our technologies might bring significant benefit but they are also a significant risk. There are ample existing examples of where a new technology can result in overwhelming wealth and control very quickly. Within a few short years the major technology corporations have surpassed traditional manufac-turing and resource organizations that have dominated business for decades. This process is accelerating, one discovery, one innovation at a time, and disruption ripples through business and our communities. Taken in concert profitability and responsi-bility have an overwhelming persuasive power.

Those organizations that adopt an ethical stance gain several advantages. These include the staff knowing that they are operating openly and honestly. Also, it is good for their business reputation in both the medium and the long term. Committing themselves to a code could be a powerful defence in any court case in which a com-pany might be accused of improper behaviour. These tangible and intangible reasons for ethical behaviour in business have benefits that are both commercial, and bear upon the quality of life.

There are many barriers to the introduction of ethics into corporate entities. Among those barriers are:

- that it is complicated;
- that it is not profitable; and
- that it is a luxury that businesses cannot afford.

One of the major points of this work is to help understand and remove those barriers where possible. It is argued here that the lack of attention to ethics is very costly, a view supported by persuasive argument.

It needs emphasis that this is not a legal text; but it is useful to draw attention to the complementary nature of ethical codes and legal principles, as is done in the chapter on legal issues. In order to make this book useful in learning, example cases are included, as well as decision trees, diagrams, references, and a comprehensive end-of-book index.

The overall purpose of the book is to provide a concise guide and resource for those interested in business ethics. This is a text to assist business students and busi-ness leaders to better understand this complex topic. Although there are many books in this field of business ethics this work attempts to set out a guide that is more global in reach.

Business courses at technical and academic institutions address such issues as ethics, and it is in these places that views, attitudes and opinions are formed. This early learning sets a tone that could persist throughout a working life. This book will act as a guide for developing and fostering a consideration of ethical principles, and act as a force in developing ethical issues as normative behaviour.

Corporate governance

Corporate governance includes efficient decision making, appropriate resource allocation, strategic planning, and so on. In its moral sense good corporate governance has come to be seen as promoting an ethical climate. It is both morally appropriate and consequentially appropriate because ethical behaviour achieves desirable commercial outcomes.

As it stands, corporate governance should set a proper example of good intent, and provide for those lower in corporate hierarchies the clear message that it is 'do as I do' rather than 'do as I say'. Middle and lower management find it hard to be ethical when it seems that those at the top of the corporate hierarchy have no commitment. The message of sincerity will always filter down, and no amount of deception will foster the view that a board is ethical when it plainly is not.

Additionally, the commitment to ethical corporate governance by a board will enhance the prospects of an ethical infrastructure within the organization. That ethical infrastructure is a manifestation of the commitment, a means of preventing and resolving ethical problems, and a demonstration of sincerity.

The issue of corporate governance had its genesis in several sources. The pressure to improve corporate governance was, however, impelled by the corporate greed of the 1980s and has received significant renewal in the light of the Global Financial Crisis. Considerable learning has emerged from the failures of major corporations. Typically, those failures involved:

- inappropriate remuneration policies (there was significant focus on short-term results rather than long-term sustainability);
- insufficient independence of board members and others with oversight responsibility (CEOs were given considerable freedom of action with minimal scrutiny);
- inadequate reporting (there was insufficient visibility of performance and conflicts of interest);
- minority and foreign shareholders disproportionately impacted; and
- a lack of comprehension of risks in certain decisions.

Together these failures resulted in high levels of corporate risk taking that had severe consequences for the world's economy, the effects of which are still being worked through. It is as a result of the public scrutiny of these kinds of events that various institutes of company directors, semi-government and government agencies have been created.

The notion of ethical corporate governance has a focus on leadership: 'the tone from the top'. Mergers, leaner organizations, and accountability have all had their impact. In such a changing world it is imperative that we have some fixed values. Impulsive action is the enemy of good commerce, and it is by the adoption of such values that we put certainty into our transactions. Trade winds are winds that are good for trade in that they blow constantly and in a known direction. We knew, with some degree of certainty, that sailing ships would get to their destinations on time.

Undue emphasis on purely commercial aspects of any enterprise will most often produce a counter-reaction. Good corporate governance requires commercial insight and commercial courage; but no less than that it requires adherence to the principles of honesty and integrity. Not only does this ethical attitude preserve reputational advantages but it may also be seen as a high-level form of corporate risk management. It is also intimately tied to having worthy corporate visions and aspirations. It is worth noting that managing borders in an increasingly borderless world generates complications – a point addressed by Hansen and Papademetriou (2013).

With the increasing globalization of the economy the need is yet more pressing to be ethical in governance. Confidence in the integrity of corporations is vital to continued manufacturing and servicing, and the institution and monitoring of an agreed code of conduct enhances confidence in commerce. Firm and clear corporate legislation can do much, but so can the 'softer' principles that invest our understanding of ethical dealing, and enhance the quality of human relationships.

It is argued that good governance enhances stakeholder value, company morale, and productivity. Corporate governance can be defined as the bodies and procedures that govern the policies and operations of organizations. Such precepts would necessarily cover such issues as directors' benefits, insider trading, and conflicts of interest.

Among the points to be made is that self-regulation will seldom be an adequate substitute for governmental regulation. Such self-regulation does, however, monitor the performance of members of associations, and serves as a means of developing rules that potentially helps shape future laws. When the Chinese formulated their language they recognized that the word 'crisis' had two distinct elements, and created two discrete symbols to reflect those meanings. The first element was 'danger', the second was 'hidden opportunity'. Ethical issues should be seen as challenges rather than obstacles; as opportunities to improve our understanding and interconnectivity. Corporate governance meetings commonly set the standards for ethical behaviour. As such it is worth noting that a knowledge of the rules of such meetings is vital (see, for example, Francis and Armstrong, 2012).

Ensuring corporate values are applied internationally

Banamex

In 2014 the highly profitable Mexican subsidiary of Citibank, Banamex, was defrauded of US$500 million. Initially, according to Citibank's own investigation, it appeared that there was no collusion with the staff of the company, although a number of senior people were dismissed for not ensuring adequate controls over the loan at the core of the incident. Shortly afterwards, however, 11 former Banamex employees were arrested. The CEO who was viewed as crucial to Banamex's success eventually resigned as a result of this and other scandals that came to light. Citibank was fined US$2 million by Mexican authorities and has also pulled out of six Latin American countries as part of its post-GFC restructure.

The investigations continue, and as an example of how investors are holding companies accountable for unethical behaviour, the Oklahoma Firefighters Pension and Retirement Fund successfully sued Citicorp to gain access to documents over its Mexican operations.

SOURCE: See Banamex in recommended reading

Questions of proper functioning are formalized in various ways. At a more formal level some stock exchanges require listed companies to disclose, in their annual reports, their policies on corporate governance practices. Almost all jurisdictions and international organizations have, as a result of the GFC, considered that failures of corporate governance were a principal cause. The work undertaken by the Organisation for Economic Co-operation and Development (OECD) is an exemplary case of what has been happening across the world although there are different approaches. The organization has developed a set of guidelines that can assist both member and non-member nations as well as corporations by providing benchmarks. These were set down in 2004 but are currently undergoing review. (A link to the complete version of the guidelines is cited in recommended reading.)

What principles should underpin corporate governance?

OECD Principles

The OECD concluded that there were six basic principles that should be incorporated into the governance of corporations. Specifically 'the corporate governance framework should:'

1 '... promote transparent and efficient markets, be consistent with the rule of law and clearly articulate the division of responsibilities among the different supervisory, regulatory and enforcement authorities.'

2 '... protect and facilitate the exercise of shareholders' rights.'

3 '... ensure the equitable treatment of all shareholders, including minority and foreign shareholders. All shareholders should have the opportunity to obtain effective redress for violation of their rights.'

4 '... recognize the rights of stakeholders established by law or through mutual agreements and encourage active co-operation between corporations and stakeholders in creating wealth, jobs, and the sustainability of financially sound enterprises.'

5 '... ensure that timely and accurate disclosure is made on all material matters regarding the corporation, including the financial situation, performance, ownership, and governance of the company.'

6 '... ensure the strategic guidance of the company, the effective monitoring of management by the board, and the board's accountability to the company and the shareholders.'

The overall significance of corporate governance is that ethics must start at the top, and be constantly fostered there. Without ethical leadership there will be no ethical following. The purpose of business has been defined in various ways. It may be held that its purpose is to create goods and services to meet human needs – not to make money for its own sake. Put another way it could be said that it is to make a profit while behaving ethically. This point of view has been well expressed by Estes in his book *Tyranny of the Bottom Line* (Estes, 1996).

In that work he noted that companies originally were not there exclusively for profit. Indeed the royal charters given were for purposes additional to profit – the extension of empire, aggrandizement of the emperor nation, as well as the motives of bringing good to less-favoured places. The accounting procedures used to inform far-away investors have come to have a life of their own, and unreasonably dominate measures of corporate success. Estes' solution is the simple one of adopting more appropriate and more diverse accounting procedures.

Triple bottom line reporting originated with the East India Company, and found its way into the literature through Estes (1996). A more recent account is given in Elkington (1999). Recasting this argument we might say that financial accounting is one of the reporting criteria, the other two being sustainability and social justice.

There is a persuasive argument that all of these criteria are to the benefit of long-term profit, and add economic value to the organization. Among the conclusions drawn by Henriques and Richardson (2004) is that while the triple bottom line complicates matters it is worth the effort.

On this view, the creation of profits for shareholders, and creation of jobs, are necessary conditions for success but not its purpose. The purpose of industry is to serve human needs – market is the servant, not the master, of human needs. According to Adam Smith the essence of capitalism is that the two should co-exist for the benefit of each other.

The need for strong ethical guidelines

The recession of the late 1980s and more recently the Global Financial Crisis have shown the need for firm ethical guidelines for business. The reputation of all business is tarnished with each corporate failure. While not all company collapses are due to unethical behaviour (such issues as poor banking practices, union difficulties, bad management, the chasing of high profits, and high interest rates are also implicated), an ethical judgement is made on those collapses.

Ethics involves employee issues such as fair wages, safe working conditions, work morale and industrial relations. It also involves shareholder issues such as a fair and reasonable return on invested capital, regularity and security of payment, and knowledge of honest dealing. There are also company issues such as being a good neighbour, being a patriot, making proper and productive use of natural resources, quality of goods and services, honest advertising, fair pricing, and safe products. This list may be extended to include:

- relationships between organizations (eg rival companies, suppliers);
- relationships between unions and employers;
- individuals within the organization;
- relationships between organizations and the community at large;
- issues such as ethnic discrimination in the workplace;
- the clash of principles in cases of international contracts; and
- issues for firms with foreign subsidiaries.

The need for guidelines is a recurring theme throughout the text.

Early attempts in industry and commerce

Within the past two centuries, at least in Western culture, there have been several attempts to introduce ethical dealing into business. Treating individuals as deserving of ethical consideration led some industrialists and social philosophers to treat commerce as not being confined to profitable outcomes. As it turned out, the fair treatment of workers was profitable, although that did not seem to be the main motive for its institution. The 'New Lanark' venture of Robert Owen is an example. In the early 18th century he bought a textile mill in Scotland in which workers were treated in a dignified fashion, paid well, and encouraged rather than criticized. The results were increased productivity and increased profit.

Prominent Quaker families, such as the Cadburys and the Frys, have contributed much to the ethical commercial environment; they have also contributed to social issues, such as prison reform. Socialist philosophers such as Prince Kropotkin, Charles Fourier and Comte Saint-Simon have expounded the merits of social co-operation, as was also exemplified in the British Cooperative Society chain of shops (which stemmed from Robert Owen). These earlier attempts have had a chequered history. More recently there have been successful attempts to value and profit from co-operation: the Credit Union movement is one good instance. The whole socialist movement had its genesis in ethical concerns about equity, balance, human worth, and the quality of life.

Goodwill

Goodwill is a critical asset of business, regardless of size. It is marketable and often forms a significant part of the value of the business for the purpose of sale or raising capital. Better businesses understand that it is important to take a holistic view to maintain and increase the value of their goodwill. These companies understand that all their relationships play a role: their relationships with their clients, with their suppliers, with their staff and with the community as a whole. A business that can create an image of having a good service attitude, of being friendly and responsible, will generate wealth.

Friendliness in particular is highly rated by many companies because it evokes self-confidence, openness and co-operation. It is much more highly prized than an organization that is perceived as aggressive, intensely competitive and prone to political infighting. Previously, companies might have thought that the value of friendliness should be interpreted as a symptom of a lack of discipline and might have preferred their corporate personality to be characterized as tough, hard headed and resolute. That attitude is now changing. To put this another way, collegiality across all business relationships has commercial value.

Ethical behaviour is integral to goodwill. An organization cannot provide good service, be friendly and responsible without being ethical. Just as in our personal relationships, business relationships without a good underpinning of values will eventually be seen for the sham that they are. It has to be recognized that in commerce, a business person must deal with people whom they do not like and have difficulty relating to. A good reference here is Brinkman and Kirschner (2003) with their appropriately titled book *Dealing with Difficult People*.

The importance of relationships to 'goodwill' regardless of scale

'United breaks guitars'

At a stopover at Chicago's O'Hare airport in 2008, a passenger seated near musician and songwriter Dave Carroll drew his attention to baggage attendants throwing his guitar. When he was able to retrieve his instrument it had been broken. He attempted over 12 months to obtain compensation for the $3,200 worth of damage. United repeatedly refused to acknowledge responsibility or pay for the damage.

In frustration over this unconscionable action Mr Carroll wrote a song 'United Breaks Guitars', recorded it and made a video which he posted to YouTube in 2009. The video went viral. It has had in excess of 14.5 million views (United tried to get Mr Carroll to take down the video after 150,000 views). He refused, arguing that the money was no longer the issue. It is thought that the video has caused millions of dollars of damage to the brand.

SOURCE: See United Airlines in recommended reading

The Marlow Declaration

Concern over motives and relationships is not new. In Britain in the early sixties a document called the 'Marlow Declaration' was produced. A copy of that document was obtained many years ago by one of the authors, and is mentioned here (Brown *et al*, 1964).

That document held that ethics is a unity, and indivisible. It also held that the purpose of industry was to fulfil human needs, and not the other way around. The essentials of business include fair wages, security, status, comradeship, scope for self-development and fulfilment. Good safe working conditions are part of the package, as is pride in skill, a sense of 'belonging', and value to others of the work done. In addition to the principles already mentioned it is desirable that organizations be good neighbours, taking a constructive interest in local and national affairs. The document advocated a balance between the proper and productive use and development of resources, both human and material.

The original Declaration was drafted and circulated by 18 men at Marlow in Buckinghamshire: their origins included the churches, the boardroom, trade unions, and the teaching profession. They came together because of their common conviction that our generation has within its grasp a great opportunity to shape a new society sustained by the rightness of its purpose and based on the justice of its institutions.

Among the points that they made was that the golden age is not past: qualities such as justice, ability, integrity still have strong currency. The continuation of human effort is both current and required. To this end actions, including business actions, must be based on clear ethical principles, and become a part of custom and practice. Among the principles that they addressed and endorsed were the importance of community, balanced with the notion that responsibility is always based on the individual. Their second point concerned social responsibility in which developing values enrich all of our lives, and is an obligation placed upon all of us.

The declared goal of the Declaration was to direct public opinion towards society getting a better understanding of the nature of individual and economic realities within which it must function. It held that the most valuable asset of any organization is best measured by the skill, knowledge, loyalty, enthusiasm and goodwill of those whom it employs, and those with whom it does business.

To that end aspects such as education, technical training, safety, induction, stress, and redundancy are all critical aspects. To this should be added the proper use of leisure, and of early retirement. There is an indivisibility of work/home life, each of which has a significant impact on the other. Consultation and negotiation are also both vital to a successful enterprise.

A final point by the Declarants was that authority is a trust. Leaders do so by force of example, and thus have a strong influence on people's lives: to that end they must be held accountable. Further, such leading by example should bring attendant humility. The leader must be the servant of those they presume to lead. It is a demonstration that they do not just hold power for its own sake.

'Ends justifies the means' debate

Ethical codes are designed to produce particular ends. They are, therefore, goals to be achieved, although sometimes sight of the goal is lost. It may seem unethical to cause harm to others; however, societies are always balancing benefit versus risk. For example, road deaths could be stopped tomorrow by banning cars. This does not occur because we accept the relatively small number of people who lose their lives or are maimed as an acceptable cost in exchange for the amenity that cars bring to the community. The use of cars justifies road deaths – the end justifies the means. That is not to say that societies do not strive to mitigate the harm by implementing speed restrictions, drink-driving laws and better roads.

Is ethics a luxury?

Ethics may be seen as a luxury affordable only by the well established. Like someone starting a new business with a severe liquidity problem, a hard-pressed executive of a major global company might need to adopt some dubious strategies in order to survive in his role. Many would consider that only when the economic environment is benign might an organization have the luxury of forgoing an immediate return, and of taking the long-term ethical view.

Companies that operate with substantial goodwill (and, for example, offer unconditional money-back guarantees for their products or services) gain incalculable benefit over companies that do not. It takes many years to build up a good reputation, and it is of enormous financial benefit to the companies that continue to maintain their good name.

Although individual transactions may be forgone, other customers will continue to use such companies because they know that if a poor purchase has been made it is easy to exchange or get a refund. The basic issue here is whether or not a business wishes to foster a continuing relationship; it would be as well to behave as if the business had such a relationship in mind. At the highly practical level there are issues of ethics and gullibility. Two recent examples are online frauds (like the 'Nigerian scam'), and the advertising of fraudulent schemes. For an account of threats and counter-measures see Fernandes (2013). We do need to recognize that internet fraud may take any one of several forms, including identity theft and finance. For an account of financial matters see Ngai *et al* (2011).

Conclusion

This chapter focused on the importance of business ethics, and commenced the discussion of the potential issues as well as corporate governance. These issues will be discussed in more detail throughout the book. This chapter has also considered early attempts and justifications for being ethical in business. It has explored the 'ends justifies the means' debate and whether or not 'ethics is a luxury'.

Background to ethics

1 Should a code of ethics be fixed or flexible to adapt to circumstances?

2 What are the benefits of ethical behaviour?

3 How does corporate governance fit into the ethical framework?

4 What is goodwill? Why is it significant from an ethical perspective?

5 What do we mean by 'the ends justifies the means'?

6 Is ethical conduct a luxury?

CASE STUDY Outsourcing to shift risk

Joan is the CEO of a manufacturer of cast iron steel pieces for specialized equipment. The manufacturing process is hazardous and despite considerable effort accidents continue to happen. The risk officer has sourced an overseas manufacturer who can produce the pieces and has developed a strategy that will shift the workforce to other less hazardous work. From the risk officer's perspective this is an ideal solution; company employees retain their jobs and a dangerous process is eliminated. There will also be notable savings in insurance. Joan, however, is concerned because she is aware that the overseas manufacturer is not governed by the same OHS regulations. It is highly likely that the risks for the overseas workers will be considerably greater.

Is there anything ethically wrong with the proposal?

Should Joan feel uneasy (at least in a business sense), and what is the basis of that unease?

If Joan were to learn that the community to which the work is going will have a significantly improved quality of life, does that make a difference to the ethical view of the transaction?

Factors to consider

This is not an uncommon scenario for CEOs. Outsourcing hazardous work and low-skilled work has significant appeal. *Prima facie* it protects local workers, lowers insurance and is usually cheaper. However, as a number of large corporations have learned, there is a risk to thinking that responsibility stops at the border. Ethically questionable behaviour can have its ramifications. This is a common theme throughout the examples and much of the content of this book. Companies operating 'within the law' but outside the perceived values of the community can find powerful and unexpected sanctions applied. Equally true is that companies that think ethically and react ethically to difficult situations have averted disaster and usually maintain their brands' reputations.

What can Joan do? Presuming she has been fully informed by the risk officer of the benefits of shifting the work from an internal perspective, Joan should spend some time finding out any missing facts. She should undergo her own investigation. She should find out whether there will be workers at risk in the outsourced country. She should look at the supplier company and ensure they have a responsible approach. She should find out if there are laws to protect workers and whether those laws are enforced or overlooked. If the company and the country are known to be unethical she should take that into consideration. Many CEOs use the test of 'how would this look on the cover of the newspaper?'

Joan could of course take the chance, bet that it won't attract public attention, or that if it does it won't be serious. The pressure of the 'bottom line' is a persuasive force. If she makes that choice though she will have at least fully informed herself of the risk.

Perhaps it is open to her to engage more deeply with this country to ensure better working conditions (that is now a very common response but usually after the fact rather than before). Communities in developing countries can have their lives improved by engaging in the global economy. There may be a significant public relations win if the arrangement began on an ethical basis. The maths of such an exercise may show that to do all those steps to put in the effort needed deprives the company of most of the benefit it initially sought, and negates the idea. Certainly Joan will need to explain to her shareholders why she is spending the money in the way she is.

Joan, by completing her investigation, then has a much clearer view of her position in terms of making the decision. She has taken into account more than the legal dimension of the question, including the values of any decision. She will have an answer when the shareholders ask her why she did or did not pick up the offer.

Recommended reading

Banamex

Economist (2014, June) Banamex: Tabasco sauce; Citibank's former jewel is spattered with scandal, *Economist* [online] http://www.economist.com/news/finance-and-economics/21603444-citibanks-former-jewel-spattered-scandal-tabasco-sauce

Fox News Latino (2014, October) Citibank closes shop in six Latin American countries as part of its slim-down effort, *Fox News Latino* [online] http://latino.foxnews.com/latino/money/2014/10/15/citigroup-mexican-subsidiary-banamex-rocked-by-second-fraud-scandal-year/

Reuters (2014, October) Mexico regulators fine Citi unit $2 million over loan scandal, *Reuters* [online] http://www.reuters.com/article/2014/10/16/citigroup-banamex-idUSL2N0S91OF20141016 [accessed 30 January 2015]

Van Doorn, P (2014, February) How did the fraud against Citi's Banamex work? *The Street* [online] http://www.thestreet.com/story/12462191/1/how-did-the-fraud-against-citis-banamex-work.html [accessed 30 January 2015]

OECD

OECD corporate governance principles [online] http://www.oecd.org/daf/ca/corporategovernanceprinciples/31557724.pdf

United Airlines

Carrol, D (2009, July) United breaks guitars, (SONG & VIDEO) *YouTube* [online] www.youtube.com/watch?v=5YGc4zOqozo [accessed 2 February 2015]

Cosh, C (2009, August) A man and his guitar, *National Post (Canada: The Financial Post)* [online] http://www.financialpost.com/scripts/story.html?id=f9065720-c55a-4612-84eb-e168fd37ed1f&k=15437 [accessed 2 February 2015]

Jamieson, A (2009, July) Musician behind anti-airline hit video 'United Breaks Guitars' pledges more songs. *Daily Telegraph* [online] http://www.telegraph.co.uk/travel/travelnews/5892082/Musician-behind-anti-airline-hit-video-United-Breaks-Guitars-pledges-more-songs.html [accessed 2 February 2015]

Walmart

Fox, E J (2013, December) Wal-Mart knew about Mexico bribery in 2005, say lawmakers, *CNN Money* [online] http://money.cnn.com/2013/01/10/news/companies/walmart-investigation/ [accessed 30 January 2015]

Haner, J and McKinley Jr, J C (2012, December) The bribery aisle: how Wal-Mart got its way in Mexico, *New York Times* [online] http://www.nytimes.com/2012/12/18/business/walmart-bribes-teotihuacan.html?hp&_r=0

Harris, E (2014, June) After the bribery scandal, high-level departures at Walmart, *New York Times* [online] http://www.nytimes.com/2014/06/05/business/after-walmart-bribery-scandals-a-pattern-of-quiet-departures.html

Justification for ethics

02

Introduction

The purpose of this chapter is to address the question, 'why should corporations and their leaders and employees be ethical?' There would be many in the world community that would see no need to justify ethical behaviour, that good behaviour is a reason in its own right. The religious underpinnings of many of our communities see 'goodness' as requiring nothing more than faith. There are, however, sound and well-substantiated reasons why a corporation or an individual would act ethically even though their own value system would have taken them in another direction. The worst of CEOs, who would be willing to exploit workers or resources or convention, would hesitate if they were conscious of a risk like a strike, a consumer boycott or a long-term investigation.

Key learning points

This chapter will discuss the reasons why corporations should be ethical. Specifically these are:

- Ethics is rational.

- Ethics is profitable.

- Ethics helps companies maintain their relationship with shareholders.

- Ethics can facilitate opportunities.

- Ethics assists in the management of privacy issues.

- Ethics is core to the sustainability of the financial system.

This chapter will also look at decision-making processes, specifically discriminant analysis.

Ethics is rational

Ethics must have a rational as well as an emotional basis; some ethical values may be captured by our intellect while others may not. Reason can tell us how to arrive at conclusions from other statements; it can also tell us the consequences of certain courses of action, but it cannot tell us what values we should adopt. Expedience (or mercy) may sometimes seem more acceptable than principle. We might, for instance, excuse the widow who steals to feed her children. Severe circumstances could be mitigating, but would we make the same judgement in a business decision?

For example, a sales representative, to secure a critical contract in a certain nation, arranges a 'consultancy fee' to a third party who is likely to have a conflict of interest; it is clear that there is a family relationship between the third party and the contracting party. This is a breach of the corporation's 'code of conduct' and would normally result in immediate dismissal. When challenged by the corporation's compliance officer, the sales representative argues that she has not received any personal benefit from the transaction and that the contract was essential to the ongoing viability of the organization. The application of the principle 'without fear or favour' is not as easy on the conscience as it might seem. Our admiration of personal and family loyalty might not extend so readily to company loyalty.

Ethics is profitable

Business ethics, like education, may seem costly, but not as expensive as the alternative. We do not admire the cheating entrepreneur, those defrauding the public, and those shifting funds to tax havens. Profit at any price is no longer an acceptable edict. The argument from Dickensian times, that the economy would suffer if children were not permitted to sweep chimneys, is no longer tenable: exploitation is not admirable in any of its forms and increasingly the limits of corporate responsibility are widening.

As was noted in the previous chapter, and a theme that will recur throughout this text, the community expects corporations to take care of their workers, both locally and in the developing world. A company can no longer outsource these duties to subcontractors in countries with little or no effective protection and announce it is 'not our problem'. The same can be said for environmental issues.

It is interesting to note that many business people have the idea that ethics is admirable, but is a luxury that is contrary to corporate objectives. It is also believed to be something that is an intrusion into serious business actions, and that it is difficult to implement and maintain. What this section does is attempt to rebut the idea that ethics is a cost; it is quite the reverse. Another theme throughout this book is that ethical behaviour and long-term profit are essential companions.

The twin issues of profit and responsibility affecting commerce are commonly seen to be opposed. These issues, it is argued here, have much more in common than in opposition. Plainly those in business are there primarily to serve corporate ends, where such measures as profit and market share are critical. Corporations also seem to be driven by quite reasonable concerns such as long-term reputation and the desire to contribute to the general economy.

This contrast of perspectives between profit and ethics is more apparent than real. Corporations with a good reputation do benefit by having fewer problems recruiting and retaining good staff; they do not lose their best people to competitors. Losing a good staff member depletes corporate resources, often significantly. Corporations all-too-commonly undervalue the corporate knowledge their employees hold in their heads. Losing a staff member also benefits the competition, and is thus a double loss. The boost to morale by being ethical should also help to:

- lessen absenteeism;
- improve productivity;
- reduce pilfering; and
- reduce theft such as the padding of expense accounts.

Managers should take note of the ethical approach embedded in the Japanese leadership style where these issues are effectively non-existent (see index for Leadership, Japanese and American styles).

In the marketplace repeat business results from a reputation for fair trading, and therefore saves on advertising. Corporations with a genuine commitment to ethical policies prevent most of the problems that commonly beset annual general meetings. Organizations with ethical commitment largely avoid the problems that happen to disreputable organizations. Similarly, a well-regarded organization should have fewer problems with raising venture capital, drops in share price, loss of market share, or any of the conventional indicators of unsuccessful commercial activity.

If a problem were to occur, the evidence of ethical commitment by an organization could act as a substantial defence against accusations, justified or otherwise, were a case to go to court. This is evident in some court judgements in which good intent is mentioned. On this view ethics is good risk management. A high-integrity ethical code also supports the reputation of an organization. A firm commitment to ethics, as evidenced by objective pointers, supports an argument that a breach was an aberration. After the breach it demonstrates remorse, and that the organization is sincere in its intention not to re-offend. The commitment to an ethical code goes beyond specifics, and addresses a broader range of conduct in that it shows a commitment to good citizenship.

Empirical studies have examined the connection between being ethical and being profitable; two Canadian studies have confirmed this. One study used a rating system and found that the corporations with the highest score on social responsibility over the long term also made the most money (Grensing-Pophal, 1998). Secondly, a study by Bastien (1997) found a correlation between responsible performance and long-term profit. It is interesting to note that it was a topic of serious concern some time ago, but recently has failed to attract much attention.

The balancing of profitability and ethics is a rich subject. Barraquier (2011) for example, has analysed managers' behaviour when confronted with the dilemma of legal compliance and ethical demands. In this model the balancing between profit and ethics is determined by a three-stage process. Her conclusion is that the process generates four decision outcomes. They are fraud, crisis, competition, and innovation. Clearly all of those concepts have implications. Corporations in crisis, when faced with such dilemmas should take these four strategies into account. Which one of these strategies dominates will be determined by commitment to whichever strategy is the natural preference. It is well to bear ethical considerations in mind, especially in the light of both ethics for its own sake, and also for its implications for long-term profit. The tension between organizations, managers and profitability will be discussed in further detail in Chapter 4.

The issue of dropping profits creates tensions. One of the basic problems is that in an effort to save money a corporation might consider cutting service, thereby reducing sales of goods and services. The falling profitability may however be reversed by taking more innovative approaches such as giving more local autonomy to managers, being open and honest in dealing, cutting inessential costs, and giving staff a greater say in the running of the business.

Corporations are problem-solving machines that should make better use of their collective creative energies in difficult times instead of opting for blunt short-term measures.

Lo (2009) referred to the long-term (rather than short-term) benefits of sustainability in general, apart from the short-term profit motive. The conclusions drawn were that sustainable firms perform better, but sustainable firms are outperformed when the marketability model is used. This is explained in terms that counterstrike strategies count in terms of profit for some sectors of the economy, but that investors do not currently favour sustainability as much as they should. For more about counterstrike strategies see Choi and Perez (2007). It was noted by Crane and Matten (2010) that corporate citizenship and sustainability in this age of globalization require special skills that include knowledge of other cultures, ethical leadership, and business acumen. These are all achievable.

Organizations that do not regulate themselves invite regulation by outside agencies, maybe in a form that is less well informed, and less palatable than self-governance. One example of a related initiative that seems to work well is the 'quality audit review' of accounting practices used by many accountants. It is becoming increasingly obvious that inattention to ethics will incur compliance costs, which can exceed the cost of instituting an ethical infrastructure. This is in terms of money but also in terms of reputational damage.

Burton and Goldsby (2009) subjected the notion of profitability and ethics to a philosophical examination. They proposed that a moral floor exists at which conformance to ethics will not generate rewards. Rising above that level does not benefit the corporation. Similarly there are activities that the marketplace will punish if the corporation drops below a certain level of ethical activity.

Corporations can be thrown into crisis and how they respond is crucial. Snow Foods and Tylenol, both discussed elsewhere, provide examples of the right and wrong ways to address a crisis. In brief, Snow Foods tried to cover up a problem which not only poisoned record numbers of customers but destroyed what, until then, had been a dominant market brand. By comparison, when a malicious individual put poison into Tylenol, killing a number of people, Johnson & Johnson acted swiftly and comprehensively with a focus on saving lives and in the process saved their very valuable product because the public had confidence in the integrity of the management.

Here the principle is that the response should be immediate, it should show concern for people and the environment, and it should be ahead of legal requirements rather than driven by them. Whatever the truth of these incidents it is clear that a prompt and humane response is both ethical, and in the corporation's interests.

This array of arguments applies with greater strength in a global economy. The financial advantages of being ethical are apparent. What does deserve emphasis is the contribution that ethics can make to the enlargement of our general as well as our commercial understanding. It is a significant means of promoting international goodwill, and provides an acceptable forum for debates on values. The long-term benefits of being ethical are described by Reichheld and Teal as 'the hidden force behind growth, profits, and lasting value' (see Reichheld and Teal (2001) in recommended reading).

Ethics is mandated by law

As noted in the introduction, the vast majority of global businesses are obliged by law to have an ethical code, an ethical culture and usually are required to report. This will be discussed in more detail in Chapter 7.

Ethics helps companies maintain their relationship with shareholders

The investment landscape has changed dramatically in recent times with the rise of the institutional investor. Organizations, such as pension funds, are controlling very large portfolios and having a greater influence over corporations and their behaviour. This creates a tension between the larger and smaller shareholders, one that is becoming more apparent with the impetus from various shareholder associations. Smaller shareholders do not have the same kind of direct say that a major investor does. The right of minorities to have a say is an important principle.

Both the institutional and smaller shareholders (although more so the smaller shareholders) have resorted to adverse publicity to highlight their concerns. Bodies representing smaller shareholders have also been able to exert some influence on corporations' behaviour. Institutional investors can take a more direct approach to expressing their concern. Typically the type of concerns that investors raise are:

- the ways in which directors are appointed and reappointed;
- the salaries received by directors and senior executives;
- the issuing of bonus shares to senior executives;
- performance-linked rewards; and
- the ethics of some of the company's activities.

It is a commonplace observation that the profitability of a corporation and the remuneration to directors and other principles are not sufficiently related. Shareholders' motives are variable although principally shares are bought for a fair return on capital. They can, however, buy shares as a way of showing approval of what the corporation is trying to achieve, or because of the feeling that the investment is making a contribution to the national economy. Shareholders may be concerned about advertising, and how it may affect both profitability and the public profile of the corporation. If the purpose of a corporation is to make a profit it does not follow that the profit should be made at all costs.

Progressively the joint interests of larger and smaller investors are coming together to require corporations to be both profitable and ethical. In other words, the apparent conflicts of interests (larger and smaller investors, secrecy versus openness, different stakeholders, etc) are slowly being reconciled. The unnecessary tensions, the time-wasting disputes, the adverse publicity, and the reputational damage that flow from such unresolved conflicts all work to the detriment of good corporate governance. Put another way, this reconciliation of policy differences, and the reduction of unnecessary secrecy, is good corporate risk management.

Shareholders are not just interested in profit

The problem for Hershey's in Africa

West Africa is the major producer of cocoa (producing just over 70 per cent of the world's output). West African cocoa is grown on small farms, where the farmers themselves are extremely poor and children are often the main source of labour. The work is often heavy, long and exposes the workers to pesticides that can have a serious effect on long-term health. Using children in this manner is a breach of international conventions. A number of aid agencies have raised this as an issue and have been looking to raise public awareness given the popularity chocolate has in the Western marketplace. These agencies are demanding corporations certify that the cocoa used in their products is not grown or processed using child labour.

Hershey Corporation is a manufacturer and distributor of confectionary. It purchases significant amounts of cocoa as part of the manufacturing of its chocolate products. A Louisiana pension fund, an investor in Hershey's, has sued, seeking records about senior management's knowledge of the supply chain. Specifically, the fund is seeking to ascertain whether the company is using cocoa grown and produced using child labour. The corporation is resisting giving access to its confidential documents and was initially successful. This decision was however overturned in a Delaware court.

As of February 2015 Hershey's chocolate is still not recommended on the Food Empowerment Project's Chocolate list.

SOURCE: See Hershey's Chocolate in recommended reading

Ethics can facilitate opportunities

Globalization has provided unprecedented opportunity and been a major spur of economic growth, creating an overall lift in the standard of living. Many hundreds, if not thousands, of corporations have been able to find new markets or reduce costs by accessing developing economies. In turn corporations have grown, as have profits. However, with economic opportunities come criminal ones, as well as opportunities for unethical profit. This applies strongly to operations in developing countries.

Sadly many of the countries have struggled after their independence from colonial powers. The overwhelming majority have had difficult political and economic times. They have been governed by dictatorships, oligarchies and theocracies, often changing rapidly as individuals and interest groups vie for power. Corruption and inequity are endemic in many countries. Corporations operating in developing countries are confronted with a tension of values and even laws, creating dilemmas that sometimes may seem insurmountable. For example:

1 If someone has to be bribed to do business at all in that country, how does a corporation do business without breaching the ethics or the laws of its home country? There is a growing raft of legislation worldwide, like the US's 'Foreign Corrupt Practices Act' (1977), which mandates severe penalties for this conduct.

2 If the substantial saving on costs by outsourcing labour risks a consumer backlash for the treatment of the workers in the developing economy, is it worth it?

For many corporate officers the decision to engage in unethical behaviour usually produces a short-term gain. However, if the behaviour is revealed, there are likely to be staggering costs as the corporation defends itself from government inquiry, litigation from its shareholders, damage to its brand and consumer backlash. In more than one example in this text, the costs have run to hundreds of millions and in one instance billions of dollars. This could have been avoided if the corporations had had ethical cultures.

Cheap foreign wages can be more expensive than they first seem

Apple suicides

Foxconn is a large Taiwanese corporation that manufactures electronic goods for a number of major organizations including Apple Corporation. On 11 January 2012, 150 Chinese employees at a mainland Foxconn factory complex threatened a mass suicide in protest of working conditions; 12-hour days, six-day working weeks, a significant number living in dormitories on site, isolated from their families. The workers were talked out of their suicide pact but they received international attention and Apple was at risk of significant damage to its brand. Apple, rather than distancing itself, became involved in investigating the allegations. It took further steps within a few weeks which included:

- joining the Fair Work Association (the first electronics corporation to join);

- publishing a comprehensive list of its suppliers;

- working with Chinese labour rights activists; and

- allowing independent monitoring of its suppliers' factories.

The matter, however, has been ongoing, with a recent undercover investigation by the BBC alleging that Apple has not significantly improved working conditions. Apple disputes that it is unethical and asserts that it has been acting harder than any other corporation to improve working conditions.

SOURCE: See Apple suicides in recommended reading

The other important opportunity that globalism creates is the chance to make the world better. Shaw (2009) argued against the notion that capitalism is characterized by greed. The hope for an improved society is exemplified in the notion of corporate social responsibility. This emerging trend is an instance of how capitalism promotes welfare as well as prosperity.

Suppose we were to have to deal with businesses in cultures in which the competitive advantage is seen to be gained by tyrannical social policies and inequitable labour laws. Should corporations simply not deal with them? That is a doctrine of retreat that, in the long run, affords no relief. One of the reasons that reputable institutions are admired is because of the relative absence of corruption. Education, business practices, political stability, and social cohesiveness are all enviable qualities. It is the ethical stance of these processes that makes them admirable.

Ethics is essential for business record keeping

Information about money matters is crucial to business. We must be able to trust the integrity of financial reporting if we are to make any sensible business decisions. While legal and innovative approaches to auditing are commendable, ones that are devious and with the intention to subvert proper accountability are to be deplored. Whether or not the presentation of information is 'creative' is a matter of fine judgement.

Further, there is always the danger that accountants may lose control of the ethical presentation of accounting information. Both the labelling of information, and its inclusion and exclusion are areas of concern. There is a story of London auditors who, at the beginning of this century, had a simple technique of checking books. The chief auditor would go to the company accountants and have them swear on the Bible that the accounts were an accurate representation of the company's financial position.

Professional motives and national interest may not always be the same. One instance is the immediacy of reaction to 'information'. For example, brokers are paid a commission on the shares they buy and sell for their clients. That impulse to immediate activity may not be in the best interests of the shareholders. A takeover bid might push up the value of the shares, but to the benefit of brokers. Buy-and-sell activity is not concerned with long-term performance.

Ethics assists in the management of privacy

With the massive growth of technology, corporations are collecting and using data as never before. So vast is this information that the professionals in this field speak about 'mining data' rather than collecting data. It is a valuable asset to know what a consumer's interests and preferences are. The old mass-marketing model is dissolving. Unprecedented knowledge about and access to a potential customer is available and for sale to corporations.

As well as the ability to target advertising to the individual, it can be directed to their specific needs and wants, at a specific time. It is possible for an analytics program monitoring the internet to know that a person is searching for a car or a holiday, sell that knowledge to an auto or travel company and then fill that individual's computer screens with ads for those items. This tailored advertising is very effective. This is the business model of the new giants of the economy like Google and Facebook.

Similarly vast amounts of data are collected to make financial decisions such as the purchasing of shares or to assess credit risks or for selection and recruitment exercises. The majority of the internet generation are acutely aware that their Facebook pages could be viewed by prospective employers.

The management of information by computers also poses an escalating threat as new opportunities for misuse surface. These include:

- improper data entry to computers;
- stealing from files;
- the introduction of computer viruses; and
- illegal data matching.

This latter point is a recently developed and serious threat to personal privacy. Single items of information about an individual reveal something, but the matching of data from different sources may reveal far more than is acceptable. There are two difficulties here; one is that the subject is unlikely to know that any conclusions are being drawn about him or her; second, some of the basic 'information' may be of dubious authenticity.

The ethical question is how far to take this development before it is an intrusion into confidentiality and privacy. This issue is one of critical contemporary morality. The right to personal privacy is one that is more tacitly than expressly agreed – but is no less real. Intrusions may take many forms, some examples being the collection of irrelevant information, improper selling of information, computer data matching, surveillance, and improper publication. Social media provides an opportunity for employees, consumers or any aggrieved individual to make unwarranted accusations, and do damage before comments can be removed, leaving the company open to liability or damage to brand.

Businesses have previously been tested in regard to managing privacy in the workforce on the issue of whether or not work colleagues, or employers, should be notified if an employee is HIV positive, or has AIDS. Here the issue was the preservation of medical privacy balanced against the potential risk to fellow workers and to victims.

For some, such as first-aid workers and hospital employees, the risk of infection may be real; in other cases, where there is virtually no risk, a notification can cause unnecessary discrimination.

Breaches of personal privacy may be reduced by providing criminal penalties for those gaining, disseminating or using information illegally. Rendering such actions illegal makes breaches riskier, and prevents their use by formal organizations. In other words, the use of sanctions increases the risk to offenders, and reduces the payoff to users. The scope of application of such a prohibition to all cases will be debatable. From journalism to national security, from credit organizations to research, there are many arguments for exemption from strict rules of privacy.

Proactive action by corporations to establish cultures of ethical behaviour through the use of well-crafted and lived codes (including tests like 'the need to know') can help insure a corporation against breaches of the law, exposure to litigation, exposure to public criticism and harming the morale of their organization.

Ethics is core to the sustainability of the financial system

In the introduction to this text the example of the Global Financial Crisis (GFC) was given. The crisis, the most serious since the Great Depression of the 1930s, was the result of unethical conduct. At the core was loaning money to persons who were a bad credit risk for short-term gain. Financial institutions chasing higher returns progressively engaged in this practice until, like all artificial schemes, it collapsed under its own weight, almost taking the world economy with it. The GFC serves as a good example of how crucial ethical behaviour is to the system as a whole. Angel Gurría, OECD Secretary General in 2009, speaking about the causes of the GFC specifically stated that 'financial innovation sacrificed business ethics for the sake of extraordinary profit' (Gurría, 2009). Widespread unethical behaviour is a detriment to the sustainability of a nation's (and the world's) economy.

A key is that public confidence in the system is a necessary feature. As Carlo V di Florio, the Director of Compliance, Inspections and Examinations for the US Securities and Exchange Commission (SEC), stated 'Ethics is fundamental to securities law' (di Florio, 2011). Who would invest in stocks and securities if they believed that there was a good chance that the entity may be engaged in questionable practices that would eventually reduce their investment to zero? What is the cost of a loss of trust between organizations, between corporations and massive pension funds, between the public and those they entrust with their savings and investments? The raft of government legislation across the world about corporate governance is directed at restoring that trust in the securities markets.

Big returns, growing dividends, contented shareholders, and fat bonuses are all compelling reasons in the short term to push risky conduct. It is even more difficult for a corporation to resist when shareholders perceive that the competition is doing much better because it is engaging in unethical conduct. It is a courageous company that spurns that behaviour in those circumstances. However, all those short-term benefits look like the 'siren song' they are as the scheme unwinds.

It devalues and often destroys corporations, ripping retirement saving up, making headlines that demonize businesses, ruining careers and escalating government intervention. It creates a greater burden on the community generally with higher unemployment. This is quite apart from the loss of skill and input to the economy as a whole. It is a waste of human resources, a burden to taxpayers and generally damaging to the social fabric. If a long-term view is taken, the conduct can be seen for what it is, ultimately dangerous and unsustainable.

The forms of unethical conduct are manifest and limited only by the creativity of the business people deploying the inappropriate strategy. Throughout this text there are many examples of unethical corporate behaviour all of which, if a large enough portion of the business community were to engage in them, would place the very system itself at risk.

To name some key examples:

1 the use of overseas jurisdictions, complex structures and transactions to avoid paying tax;

2 failure to provide a safe working environment for employees (or the employees of a subcontractor, in circumstances where the work is sent overseas);

3 failure to have systems in place to ensure consumers are not harmed;

4 failure to take responsibility and immediate action when public health and safety is at risk as a result of an incident;

5 outsourcing environmental responsibilities to subcontractors in developing economies without the legal constraints and corporate scruples of developed economies;

6 using the legal system tactically to damage or undermine a competitor or another aggrieved person with legitimate claims;

7 bribing government officials (particularly in developing economies);

8 using the liquidation provisions to illegitimately avoid payment to creditors;

9 shifting borrowing costs to suppliers by failing to pay them promptly; and

10 participating in the black or shadow economy.

A single business engaged in a single instance or a small number of questionable transactions appears harmless. It is easily rationalized. However, when the question is asked 'what if all businesses did this?' the behaviour seems less harmless. It is not necessary to look too far to see the damage; the GFC is just the most recent example. It is not melodramatic to say that the cumulative effect of unethical behaviour is dangerous for a community. The social contract between business and the community deserves respect not only in its own right but because it is important to stability.

Exploited workers and their families can eventually tire of corrupt systems and growing inequalities and push back in unexpected ways. History is littered with the bodies of elites who presumed their entitlement at the expense of the mass around them. To use a contemporary example, Europe, as a consequence of the GFC, is seeing the rise of more extremist parties, particularly in Spain, Italy and Greece where there has been greater unemployment and financial havoc. These scenarios continue to play out.

There are serious threats to the community generally by the unethical corporation; principal amongst them is the penchant for corporations not to pay taxes. Perhaps this is only a relatively few companies now, and perhaps it won't spread to other industries. Perhaps it will never be widespread but what happens if every company accepts it as business as usual, something they ought or must do for their shareholders? What happens to the programmes of government those taxes are used for? What happens to the social contract between the community and business?

How important is the fair payment of tax to the social fabric?

Starbucks, Amazon and Google

Starbucks, Amazon and Google, along with many other large corporations, have been increasingly challenged by concerned people for their failure to pay enough tax. This failure is not illegal. These corporations use elaborate international structures and transactions to shift profits to low-taxing countries. The executives of these organizations have argued that there is nothing inappropriate with this behaviour; in fact many would argue they are obliged to do so given they have a responsibility to their shareholders to maximize profit. This response, particularly in a period where many countries are introducing austerity agendas, has resulted in a public backlash. For example, Starbucks outlets have been picketed and many of their sites have been boycotted. This has had management suggest that they will reconsider their tax position.

The core issue is what social harm is caused when the biggest taxpayers avoid their responsibilities? This point is discussed again in Chapter 7.

SOURCE: See Starbucks, Amazon and Google in recommended reading

Discriminant analysis and decision making

Throughout the text there are a number of case studies and questions raised, and it is therefore useful at this point to introduce a discussion of decision making. This will start the process of building a framework for working through ethical dilemmas, whether this is about how corporations have dealt with issues in the past or how hypothetical cases might be approached. Good decision making is a process.

Too often the rationale for business decisions is a 'gut reaction.' Rarely are 'gut reactions' good decisions. A professional that believes a good decision comes not from understanding of all the factors but their own instant impulse is deluding themselves and it is a sign of ignorance. Good business people use processes that gather and filter information to make the best decision they can. At the end of that process, particularly where the options are closely balanced, they may still have to make a judgement call but that is different to a 'gut reaction'.

Making ethical judgements parallels making judicial decisions. As has often been remarked, the difficulty is not so much getting the facts (although that can sometimes be a problem) but, rather, what to do with them. On consideration, so many of life's decisions are of that kind. Information is known or available, but what to do with it is the really difficult question.

We have a limited amount of information that we find useful, and need to give some kind of weighting to what is known. In medical diagnosis the signs and symptoms are not all of equal value. It is one of the tasks of clinical diagnosis to assess the importance of such signs and symptoms (a sign is what is observed, a symptom is what is felt). That point is no less true of business diagnosis, of commercial research findings, and of ethics cases.

The technique of discriminant analysis is a good example of the quantification of this issue, for example in a case where it has been alleged that an employee has breached confidentiality by accessing restricted data. An independent person, a systems administrator, is selected to investigate the leak. The investigator starts by looking at where the relevant data is held (it may exist in multiple places) and the persons who have access to those places.

It is common, particularly for larger organizations, to have systems that can trace each individual's access and the time of access to computer stored data. The investigator will then look at each piece of information, when the access was made and by whom. They will assign a weight to each piece of information and its role in the total picture. Together that allows the investigator to form a view. It is the collective information that yields the judgement based on probability. This is an approach that professionals must use all the time to deal with imperfect information whether in questions of ethics, process or policy.

Conclusion

This chapter looked at the reasons why business should conduct itself in an ethical fashion. The discussion went beyond the metaphysical to examine the evidence that it is not only desirable but necessary for businesses to act ethically. Ethical businesses are profitable, maintain relationships, use opportunities and are generally operating on a more solid foundation than unethical businesses. This chapter also looked at the importance ethics has in the maintenance of the current financial system and social order. It concluded with an examination of decision-making processes to assist in engaging with the examples and case studies throughout the text.

Focus questions

Justification for ethics

1 Why would you consider an ethical decision rational rather than emotional?

2 How would you explain to a business person that ethics is profitable?

3 What role do shareholders play in the social responsibility versus profitability debate?

4 Give an example of a dilemma commonly faced by a company operating in the developing world.

5 Why are accurate records important?

6 What are the privacy issues facing business today?

7 A company shifts its profit to a low-tax jurisdiction and increases the value of the shares. What are the risks?

8 What is discriminant analysis?

CASE STUDY   Does an end justify a means?

Miguel is a process analyst for a large multinational firm. He has been assigned to analyse a particular clerical function undertaken in one of the branches. Miguel undertakes interviews, prepares process maps, looks at the technology, seeks out 'best practice' for the function in the industry as a whole and undertakes other information-gathering activities.

Halfway through the process Miguel is called in by his manager, ostensibly to discuss progress. At the start of the conversation his manager asks if he would treat the conversation as confidential and proceeds to tell him that it would be highly desirable that the report recommend the function be outsourced. Miguel had to that point not considered that a necessary or desirable option.

His manager goes on to explain that the work area has a highly toxic culture. It has had a history of bullying, favouritism, sexual harassment, abuse of conditions, and excessive unplanned absences. No one issue or one person has been sufficiently serious enough to terminate jobs. The area is also heavily unionized so there is a need to find a rationale as bullet proof as possible to close that area.

Should Miguel provide the recommendation his manager wants?

Would Miguel's answer be different if he was aware that his manager had made this type of request to other analysts?

Factors to consider

Employees should be prepared to confront Miguel's situation. A corporation may have a problem that is hard or impossible to solve directly so it looks to more expeditious resolutions. A situation with a staff member or a bothersome section that might take months of expensive action to resolve might be removed easily by a convenient restructure. Many an internal and external consultancy is brought in to lend authority and substance to an outcome sought by an executive. Most consultants would be acutely aware that in many of their commissions their recommendations should necessarily align with that of the person paying their bill or their wages.

Miguel could take a number of approaches to this dilemma. He might simply look to his own values and reject fabricating a story to achieve an outcome.

In the alternative, he might take a broader approach and weigh the factors. He might have good cause to participate in this charade. He should consider:

1   The substance of the claim (perhaps he has seen evidence of the behaviour?).

2   The quality of his manager's argument (perhaps it is actually not as difficult to resolve this situation by other means?).

3   The integrity of his manager.

4   Miguel's relationship with his manager (crucial in an employee's 'day-to-day' work life and overall career).

5   Is the outsourcing argument sustainable (if the report is to be scrutinized by others, is it an argument that can stand up or would it appear obvious that there is another agenda?).

6 His own career (cultivating the good opinion of his manager would be important but if the matter could easily be disclosed as a sham, he might opt to think of his reputation in the long term).

Miguel might decide to comply or not. The important issue is that he turns his mind to all the relevant considerations and makes a decision based on the evidence to hand and a proper weighting of each element. There are risks but Miguel is deciding with a proper awareness of them.

Recommended reading

Reichheld, F F and Teal, T A (2001) *The Loyalty Effect: The hidden force behind growth, profits, and lasting value*, Harvard Business Press Books, Cambridge, MA

Apple suicides

Bilton, R (2014, December) Apple 'failing to protect Chinese factory workers' *BBC News Business* [online] http://www.bbc.com/news/business-30532463.

Cooper, R (2013, January) Inside Apple's Chinese 'sweatshop' factory where workers are paid just £1.12 per hour to produce iPhones and iPads for the West, *Daily Mail Australia* [online] http://www.dailymail.co.uk/news/article-2103798/Revealed-Inside-Apples-Chinese-sweatshop-factory-workers-paid-just-1-12-hour.html

Guglielmo, C (2013, December) Apple's labor practices in China scrutinized after Foxconn Pegatron reviewed, *Forbes* [online] http://www.forbes.com/sites/conniegulielmo/2013/12/12/apples-labor-practices-in-china-scrutinized-after-foxconn-pegatron-reviewed/.

Williams, R (2014, December) Apple goes to war with the BBC, *Telegraph* [online] http://www.telegraph.co.uk/technology/apple/11303052/Apple-working-conditions-Tim-Cook.html

Hershey's chocolate

Anti-Slavery International (2004) The cocoa industry in West Africa: A history of exploitation, *Anti-Slavery International* [online] http://www.antislavery.org/includes/documents/cm_docs/2008/c/cocoa_report_2004.pdf

Feeley, J (2014, March) Hershey investors suing over child labor can pursue files, *Bloomberg* [online] http://www.bloomberg.com/news/articles/2014-03-18/hershey-judge-says-shareholders-can-seek-child-labor-files-1-

Food Empowerment Project (2015, February) Chocolate List FEP website, *Food Empowerment Project* [online] http://www.foodispower.org/chocolate-list/

International Cocoa Organization (2012) Production of Cocoa Beans, *International Cocoa Organization* [online] http://www.icco.org/about-us/international-cocoa-agreements/cat_view/30-related documetns/46-statistics-production.html [accessed 2 February 2015]

International Labour Organization (2005, February) International Programme on the Elimination of Child Labour (IPEC) *International Labour Organization* [online] http://www.ilo.org/public//english//standards/ipec/themes/cocoa/download/2005_02_cl_cocoa.pdf

International Labour Organization (nd) ILO Conventions and Recommendations on child labour, *International Labour Organization* [online] http://www.ilo.org/ipec/facts/ILOconventionsonchildlabour/lang--en/index.htm

World Vision (nd) World Vision Factsheet: Chocolates bitter taste – forced, child labour in the cocoa industry *World Vision* [online] http://campaign.worldvision.com.au/wp-content/uploads/2013/04/Forced-child-and-trafficked-labour-in-the-cocoa-industry-fact-sheet.pdf.

Starbucks, Amazon and Google

Bergin, T (2012, October) Special Report: How Starbucks avoids UK taxes, *Reuters* [online] http://uk.reuters.com/article/2012/10/15/us-britain-starbucks-tax-idUSBRE89E0EX20121015

Barford, V and Holt, G (2013, May) Google, Amazon, Starbucks: The rise of tax shaming, *BBC News Magazine* [online] http://www.bbc.com/news/magazine-20560359

Cowell, F A and Gordon, J P F (1988) Unwillingness to pay: tax, evasion, and public good provision, *Journal of Public Economics*, **36**, pp 305–21

Institute of Business Ethics (2013, April) Tax avoidance as an ethical issue for business, Business Ethics Briefing 31, *IBE* [online] http://www.ibe.org.uk/userassets/briefings/ibe_briefing_31_tax_avoidance_as_an_ethical_issue_for_business.pdf

Cross-cultural issues in business ethics

03

Introduction

Core to understanding ethical decision making in global business is an appreciation of cultural influences. This includes the customs and values of the communities involved as well as the customs and values of the participating organizations. It is important to remember the interactive and dynamic nature of these factors rather than thinking of them as a mere catalogue. The purpose of this chapter is to explore the cultural issues as they relate to business ethics. It is not about organizational culture, which will be covered in the following chapter. This chapter will also discuss the opportunities cultural difference provides to re-examine and improve our own values. It will also provide some of the groundwork for addressing ethical problems to be discussed and worked through in Chapter 9.

Key learning points

This chapter will discuss the principal theoretical model (Hofstede) for assessing business ethics across cultures. It will also cover national and environmental factors that influence ethical decision making in cross-cultural situations. Specifically these are:

- Geography (eg climate, population density, natural resources).

- Social institutions (eg media, family, religion, government, education).

- Dominant cultural values.

- Economy and economic systems.

- Public opinion, political systems and the law.

- Language.

- Industry norms.

This chapter will also examine how we can learn from other cultures, including:

- The interaction of foreign culture and ethics.

- Forms of social control.

- Taking a different culture's perspective.

Hofstede's model

One of the most significant contributions to cultural differences has been given to us by Hofstede, Hofstede and Minkov (2010). Hofstede in 1965 was in the unique position to analyse cultural differences as he was the head of personnel for International Business Machines (IBM). At the time, as now, IBM was a very large and prestigious company with 117,000 staff located in over 50 countries. With the employees of IBM as a sample group he developed a survey to identify cultural differences. The unprecedented amount of data collected between 1967 and 1973 was distilled into a model of cultural differences centred around four dimensions:

Individualism-collectivism continuum. In an individualistic culture you would expect the members to be more self-oriented, looking to their own interests and that of their immediate families. In the collectivist culture people consider that they are members of a wider group, an extended family or a tribe or some other collective, like a business.

Power distance. This dimension is about how the members of the society view themselves in the business hierarchy. In a community with a high 'power distance', leaders are given very high status and are considered to be very important. In low 'power distance' countries there is a more egalitarian mindset. The status of the manager is not considered significantly greater than that of the workers themselves.

Masculinity-femininity continuum. Some cultures are male oriented and consequently adopt more masculine strategies in the workplace. They are aggressive in their approach, driven by monetary reward, competitive and expect that women will act in a traditional way. In a society that is orientated towards the feminine side, members are less competitive, more co-operative and are more accepting of women in non-traditional roles. Feminine cultures have a greater concern for the wider social good.

Uncertainty avoidance. Members in a community with a high 'uncertainty avoidance' rating have a greater need for stability, structure and certainty. Typically there is greater corporate loyalty and an expectation that the corporation will return that loyalty. The members are also likely to be insecure, less tolerant of deviance and more aggressive in the workplace. In a community at the low end of the 'uncertainty avoidance' scale, the members are more open to diversity, accepting of difference and less risk averse.

Studies have shown that Hofstede's model has high validity, having been replicated in numerous studies in different countries and different workplaces over the past 50 years.

Later Hofstede added two additional scales with similar extensive and exhaustive analysis: people in over 90 countries were surveyed to establish the 'Indulgence self-restraint' dimension (although these newer scales are not as extensively represented in the research):

Long-term versus short-term orientation (formerly referred to as 'Confucian dynamism'). This dimension relates to a culture having either a short- or a long-term focus. In a culture where a long-term approach is taken, business people place a greater emphasis on cultivating relationships and building a market position; family and business often fuse. The social as well as the commercial elements of their businesses are important for their personal satisfaction. Cultures with a short-term orientation split their business and family lives and look for quick results.

Indulgence self-restraint. This refers to whether the members of a particular culture do or do not feel inhibited by the social expectations of their community. In the indulgent culture members feel that they can live life as they choose while those in the self-restraint culture believe that they are more bound to live by the community's rules.

The dimensions all influence a business person's values and therefore how they approach ethical problems. It is important to recognize that there is a difference between an individual and their society. The statistical analysis is about 'trends' not absolute rules but it is instructive in understanding cultural differences. It is also important to note that culture is only one aspect of building a picture of what influences individual values and behaviour.

Hofstede's work is often the starting point for research into cross-cultural ethical behaviour and is referred to throughout this chapter, particularly in the section discussing dominant cultural values.

National and environmental factors

A comprehensive review of the past 25 years of literature into cross-cultural business ethics identified eight major national and environmental factors that influenced ethical decision making (Strubler *et al*, 2012). The purpose of this survey was to assist researchers and business people to understand and manage cross-cultural dilemmas. These factors and the research relating to each are discussed in the following sections.

Geography and environment

Climate, population density and natural resources have an important role to play in the makeup of a culture and therefore its ethical behaviour. Communities such as those in the Pacific Islands, where natural resources are limited and tropical storms are common, tend towards a more collectivist culture through necessity. They are more inclined to support one another and share what they have, including food and labour. Similarly, in Asia where the staple is rice and the process of harvesting requires co-operation with your neighbours, the culture also tends towards the 'collectivist' end of Hofstede's model.

If we compare these two regions with US geography and culture, we see that natural resources are more plentiful and the weather is more suitable for their agriculture. Wheat is the staple crop, and does not require the co-operation demanded in the harvesting of rice. The United States is a culture that is well noted for its almost fierce sense of the individual, and this gives them a higher rating on the 'individualistic' culture scale. Of course these factors are not operating in isolation. US religious and political beliefs are crucial factors but environment has always had a facilitating role.

Environmental factors are not only part of the background to the creation of culture but they also influence decision making in a more immediate sense. (This is discussed in 'Industry norms' on p 53.)

Social institutions

The social institutions of a community (such as family, government, education, religion, and the media) are the avenues through which societies' expectations are known. Many of these expectations will be unwritten; the members of the society will know from a young age what is expected of them. A country's social institutions are an important component of the value system that underpins a business manager's decision-making process.

Intuitively most of us would accept that our values and decision-making processes would be influenced by those groups that we spend most of our time with; family, friends, work colleagues. Research into ethics supports this (Ferrell and Gresham, 1985).

The more that we interact with a group that is unethical the greater the likelihood our own decisions will be unethical. It is not a difficult leap of logic, and a frequent theme of literature, that a person working in an immoral group will struggle to maintain their own ethical standard. What is interesting, however, is despite the individual not living up to their own values the research found that their values did not necessarily change even though they were not behaving ethically.

Government provides one of the important formal expressions of society's expectations on its members by drafting laws (Svensson and Wood, 2008). Western society holds a belief that capitalism is an important instrument to improve the society overall and therefore structures its rules to facilitate business. There is, however, a constant tension about the amount and extent of regulation. It is unlikely that any society would accept that business should be completely free to regulate itself. There have been ample demonstrations of the harm that can be caused by businesses that take only a 'pragmatic' approach. This issue and some high-profile examples are discussed in more detail in 'Public opinion, political systems and the law'.

The increase in university education has had a slow but profound influence on ethical decision making in management (Svensson and Wood, 2008). There is a worldwide trend to allow greater access to tertiary education. In recent decades the traditional catchments of universities that tended to favour wealthy individuals have shifted. In the interests of equality many societies have decided that intellect rather than money and social status should be more of a determinant in gaining access to higher education. Tertiary institutions have seen increased numbers of students who are disabled or are from minority or low socio-economic groups. These students have a heightened sense of social justice as they are likely to have been at the receiving end of social injustice. This change has produced a professional group with a greater sense of community responsibility and they influence the conduct of business whether as business owners, employees or clients.

Wines and Napier (1992) cited a number of studies that have looked at the relationship between religion and management values. The nexus between these value systems has not been substantiated in America, but outside the United States there may be a significant relationship. In one study the value system of the individual managers enabled the researcher to pick whether a participant in the study was a Catholic or Muslim in 70 per cent of instances. In a further study it was shown that regions with a strong Buddhist presence had a greater resistance to industrialization. This suggests that religious beliefs have an influence on the decisions of managers when confronted with an ethical dilemma.

Media has been a growing and influential determinant of ethical behaviour in cross-cultural settings (Svensson and Wood, 2008). It would be hard to imagine a CEO at this time not being aware of the potential consequences for damage to the corporate brand in the event of an ethical misstep in a developing country (or in their own communities). Nestlé, Citibank (boxed example follows) and Apple (see Apple suicides in Chapter 2) have all been subject to negative media attention because of conduct or alleged conduct in developing economies.

The Nestlé baby milk controversy is a long-running one. Nestlé, a Swiss food manufacturer, adopted a marketing strategy in the 1970s to sell infant formula to mothers in developing countries. The main problem was that the formula required sterile water and containers, which are much more difficult to come by in developing countries because of ignorance, illiteracy or just availability. Without sterile conditions the formula is a serious health risk and has the potential to kill the babies. When this became public knowledge the outcry resulted in a boycott of Nestlé in 1977 by American consumers which spread to Europe and other developed nations.

The range of concerned people and organizations has included actors, clergy, businesses, unions, local authorities, charitable organizations and everyday consumers in over 100 countries. Nestlé has run defamation litigation (against persons accusing them of murdering babies) as well as introducing procedures to mitigate any risk but still has not fully resolved this issue. The boycott was lifted but it has been reinstated at various times (see Nestlé Baby Milk in recommended reading).

Unwanted media attention

Citibank

Citibank, like many financial firms, has been progressing into developing economies where the potential growth in loans business is three times that of developed countries. There was an incident in 2011 where police alleged that a client of Citibank was beaten to death by Citibank collectors in a Citibank office. The company refutes this but the incident has brought worldwide attention to the circumstances facing Western firms operating in developing economies.

The central authorities in Indonesia do not set a high standard in regards to 'debt collection' activities. Much debt collection is outsourced to contract collectors who are paid on the basis of how much they collect which in turn leads to more aggressive tactics. Allegations of murder and the employment of contract thugs have been difficult to manage in the public arena despite strenuous efforts on the part of Citibank.

SOURCE: See Citibank in recommended reading

As previously mentioned, Apple has most of its products assembled in developing countries, notably mainland China, and the treatment of workers assembling Apple products has been brought into serious question after a threatened mass suicide (see 'Apple suicides' in recommended reading, Chapter 2.

As noted there, and as these examples show, there can be serious consequences for a corporation that fails to recognize that its customers can react detrimentally to inappropriate conduct. Products and services may be boycotted if the corporation is perceived to be immoral, greedy and insensitive, particularly towards vulnerable people in other countries. With the 24-hour news cycle, online news, Facebook and Twitter a corporation has no time to react. In this kind of environment, as Owen (1983) commented, unethical decisions 'are not only immoral but stupid'. The only defence is to be proactive and to build systems and processes to make judgements that are socially responsible.

Dominant cultural values

Vitell *et al* (1993) make a series of propositions flowing from Hofstede's initial framework, asking the question: what behaviours can we specifically expect from business people from each of the culture types? In countries that rated highly on 'individualism' (like the United States) the model and some research suggested that business people would apply their own standards rather than any formal or informal norms. The research stated that in the United States many corporations had written ethical codes; however, these were usually not even circulated let alone enforced. Vitell *et al* (1993) concluded that individuals in countries with high 'individualist' ratings were more likely to see themselves as the stakeholder with the superior claim. Again this was partially demonstrated in research showing a positive correlation between the desire for wealth and unethical conduct.

Behaviours in individualistic cultures

- Less weight given to codes of behaviour than personal views.
- More likely to give weight to self than other stakeholders.

The reverse would be true for 'collectivist cultures' where employees have a high level of loyalty to their corporations and are more likely to put the interests of the corporation, shareholders and other employees before themselves.

Behaviours in collectivist cultures

- More weight given to codes of behaviour than personal views.
- More likely to give weight to other stakeholders than self.

In the case of an individual from countries with a low 'power distance' rating such as the United States (where employees do not perceive the status of their superior as significantly different from themselves) there will be a greater inclination to obtain their ethical cues from their peers rather than from their superiors. This is distinct from the person from a country with the high 'power distance' rating such as France. In France an individual will more often favour their superior's ethical stance over their colleagues'. Similarly, in low 'power distance' countries the individual will favour the informal industry standard over the written code, while the person in the high-rated 'power distance' country will give more weight to the formal codes. Again, Vitell *et al* (1993) point to research that provides support for these propositions.

Behaviours in low 'power-distance' cultures

- More weight given to opinions of peers than superiors.
- Informal industry norms given more weight than formal code.

Behaviours in high 'power-distance' cultures

- More weight given to opinions of superiors than peers.
- Formal codes given more weight than informal industry norms.

In Japan, which is a high 'uncertainty avoidance'-rated country, it is expected individuals will be anxious about any behaviour that does not conform to the norms of society. Research on Japanese corporations supported this proposition, finding that there was a significant level of conformity (Vitell *et al*, 1993). Employees built up close relationships within the company and had an overall objective of serving the common good. As noted above in Hofstede's model there is an expectation that this loyalty will be returned by the corporation.

Given that the United States is recognized as a low-rated 'uncertainty avoidance' country the same study looked at US corporations for comparison. The researchers found there were significant levels of mistrust compared to levels in Japan. They also found, particularly where there were no ethical codes and/or where the situation was ambiguous, there was a greater acceptance of non-conformist behaviour; that is, more likelihood of allowing unethical behaviour.

Employees in countries where there is a high 'uncertainty avoidance' rating will be more likely to take into account formal codes, and less ready to recognize an ethical dilemma, but will be more ready to see the downside to any dubious decision making. Importantly they tend not to see themselves as the most significant stakeholder in a transaction. Whereas the individuals in the countries rated low on 'avoidance uncertainty' are less likely to take into account industry codes, less likely to perceive any wrongdoing in their questionable decision making and will view themselves as the most significant stakeholder. Japanese executives, for example, are more likely to resign if they are of the opinion their actions have had a negative consequence for the business whereas in the United States executives have to be expelled from their positions in the same circumstances.

Behaviours in high 'uncertainty avoidance' cultures

- High levels of conformity.
- High levels of trust.
- Formal codes given greater weight.
- More readily able to see the negatives of a poor ethical decision.
- More likely to give weight to other stakeholders than self.

Behaviours in low 'uncertainty avoidance' cultures

- Greater acceptance of deviant behaviour.
- High levels of mistrust.
- Formal codes given less weight than personal views.
- Less willing to accept the negatives of a poor ethical decision.
- Less able to recognize an ethical dilemma.
- More likely to give weight to self than other stakeholders.

The significance of the masculinity-femininity scale is that in masculine-oriented cultures the members are expected to be overly ambitious, very competitive and focused on monetary benefits. These characteristics increase the likelihood of unethical conduct. Japan and the United States have been classified as masculine cultures. By way of comparison Sweden has a more balanced approach where genders have similar social roles. There is a greater overlap of societal expectations.

This reduces the pressure to be ambitious, competitive and money oriented. It creates an environment where there is less likelihood of an unethical decision but there is also a greater awareness of ethical issues. For example, in a masculine culture the 'hard sell' would likely be the norm, even expected, whereas in a feminine-oriented culture the 'hard sell' itself could be seen as ethically inappropriate.

Behaviours of masculine cultures

- Overly ambitious.

- Very competitive.

- Focused on monetary benefit.

- Increased likelihood of poor ethical decisions.

- Less able to recognize an ethical dilemma.

Behaviours of feminine cultures

- Co-operative.

- Collaborative.

- Less focused on monetary benefit.

- Less likelihood of poor ethical decisions.

- More able to recognize an ethical dilemma.

Economy and economic systems

Tsalikis *et al* (2008) conducted extensive surveys in both China and India using the business ethics index (BEI) that originated in the United States to measure consumer perceptions of the ethical or unethical conduct of business. The BEI showed that China reported low levels of unethical business behaviour. Tsalikis and his colleagues noted, however, that China has had a planned economy and that all business decisions up until the 1980s were made by government.

In those circumstances it was hypothesized that the Chinese people may have difficulty knowing what ethical business conduct should be. There is also the consideration that the Chinese people have been socialized by generations of Marxist and Maoist ideology. This would orient the population towards a 'collectivist' mindset that would influence whether they saw a transaction as ethical or not. (See 'Behaviours in collectivist cultures' on p 47.)

The BEI for India, however, showed the population considered that there was a high level of unethical behaviour in business. This was consistent with a *Times of India* poll that reported 70 per cent of Indians saw business as a major corrupting force. Referring to an earlier study Tsalikis noted that business people saw unethical conduct as a necessary part of continuing to trade, but held the government responsible for it.

This attitude of Indian business people is not without foundation. The government of any country plays a greater role in the value system than merely the drafting of laws. How the government and its public service conduct themselves is a crucial factor. Take, for example, a revenue agency that is failing to collect sufficient tax because it is corrupt or chronically inefficient or starved of resources. Those businesses which act unethically by paying bribes, or by failing to remit the correct amount of tax because they know they are unlikely to be caught, have a commercial advantage over ethical businesses.

A business that is prepared to use a portion of the money gained from their non-compliant activity to undercut their competition, will contaminate the ethical environment. Depending on the extent of the commercial advantage, the ethical business will become unviable and close. The marketplace will only be left with individuals and organizations that are prepared to operate in an unprincipled way. A significant proportion of the economic collapse in Greece in the wake of the Global Financial Crisis can be attributed to the collapse of confidence in Greece's public sector, particularly their revenue office, which had become very inefficient and corrupt.

Public opinion, political systems and the law

In democratic countries, the political and legal systems play an important role in business values. Businesses only operate within the ethical boundaries that the public allow (Owen, 1983). Should business conduct be sufficiently unacceptable to the public then, through their elected officials, laws will be enacted to stop the offending behaviour.

For example, the early 2000s saw an increase in public concern in the United States about the conduct of corporations. This concern arose principally out of a number of corporate scandals, the most notorious examples being Enron (energy) and WorldCom (telecommunications). Both were large US corporations whose leadership used a number of illegal and unethical practices such as misleading reporting, use of accounting loopholes, artificially inflating revenue and depressing costs. In Enron's case this was to hide billions lost in bad deals.

For WorldCom it was to increase the value of shares to the benefit of the senior executives. When the truth was exposed these corporations collapsed, stockholders lost billions and a number of executives were gaoled. In Enron's case, Arthur Andersen – at the time one of the top five accounting firms worldwide, and who had been acting as the external auditor – was also effectively dismantled. These were at the time the largest corporate collapses in the United States.

There was a massive public outcry against this corporate banditry and the US government acted by introducing the Sarbanes-Oxley Act in 2002. The Act provides for the creation of a monitoring agency and creates a large number of obligations on company boards, company officers and external auditors. These range from the individual responsibility corporate officers must maintain over the accuracy of records to the independence of auditors, to the avoidance of conflicts of interests, as well as a range of other measures.

The Global Financial Crisis (GFC) of 2008 has led to significant political action to mitigate public anger at the behaviour of the finance sector whose practices were at the core of the crisis. There had been a strong ideological underpinning prior to 2008 that banks were, as far as practicable, best left to self-regulate. An abundance of bureaucratic controls was perceived as detrimental to the operation of the free enterprise system. Post 2008 there was outrage at the degree of freedom given to the sector. The GFC has resulted in a number of measures both introduced and still in development around the world.

Primarily, the measures look to address the capital and liquidity provisions governing banks because a key issue was the high levels of debt to equity that were in the long term unsustainable. Now banks are expected to hold greater levels of cash. The 'shadow banking' system that was previously unregulated is now regulated. There are more laws protecting consumers and deposit insurance rules changed. Collectively these responses are a significant shift away from a 'light touch' approach towards an interventionist stance (Davies, 2011).

These are, however, slender files in comparison to the laws and regulatory agencies created over the past couple of decades in response to business decisions that have been insensitive to social wellbeing. Business people need to be acutely aware of popular opinion. A public response may not even be rational; the sanction imposed could be unreasonably draconian if there is sufficient anger. It is worth reflecting that the Sarbanes-Oxley Act was bipartisan in its development and passed almost unanimously in the US Congress.

When the electorate is sufficiently angered politicians respond regardless of party lines. It is unlikely, but not outside the realm of possibility, that a business could be closed or, if the product or service is necessary, it could be nationalized (Owen, 1983). Business leaders need to be conscious of how their potential actions will be perceived by the community and should strive to regulate themselves in such a way that there is little risk of government intervention.

The force of public opinion cannot be said to be operating to the same extent in countries that are not democracies; however, even in non-democratic countries power still depends on the agreement of most of the population most of the time. Leaders in non-democratic countries are normally sensitive enough to a public outcry, particularly if it is unrelated to their hold on power, to take remedial steps.

Use of language

The study of business ethics like many other areas suffers from the vagaries of language; even within one culture one person's interpretation of 'good' is likely to be different to another's. The challenge becomes exponential when working across cultures and the spectrum of values. Theorists and researchers have been developing models to add greater precision to the language to improve the assessment of an individual's ethical code. One of these researchers, Connor (2006) cites Hartman's principles (Hartman *et al*, 2013) and later works and then applies this to examining ethics. This framework looks at not only what people value but how they value. The framework is divided into three parts:

- Intrinsic – the individual, their integrity and their sense of social responsibility.

- Extrinsic – what is visible and measurable, what a person is prepared to do to perform 'good deeds'.

- Systemic – how are the rules respected and how clear are they to the individual?

A useful series of questions flows from this structure for anyone tasked with investigating the ethical climate in a particular organization:

1 Does management have a clear vision for the organization and is it consistent with their understanding of the organization's realities?

2 Do the employees have a clear understanding of the vision and does it match their perception of the organization's realities?

3 Do management and staff share the vision?

4 Do management and staff share the perception of the organizations realities?

If the answers to these questions produce mismatches then there is a serious issue; however, management being made aware of this risk is a significant advantage. The leadership team is positioned to take remedial action potentially before there is damage to corporate reputation.

Industry norms

Strubler *et al* (2012) use the term 'industry norms' to refer to the corporation's operating environment (see p 43). First, does the corporation have access to the raw materials, labour and other resources it needs or does it operate in conditions of scarcity? Second, what are the conditions in the marketplace; are trading conditions relatively balanced or are they fiercely competitive? Researchers have hypothesized that you would expect that in situations of scarcity managers would resort to expedient and pragmatic means resulting in a higher instance of unethical and illegal behaviour. The results, however, have been inconclusive.

Business managers can be impacted by market forces other than scarcity of resources, including but not limited to:

- poor economic conditions;
- intense rivalry with competitors;
- purchasers with the influence to reduce margins on goods sold; and
- paradigm-shifting new technologies rendering products obsolete.

Where a business manager considers his corporation is in a survival situation, again it would be expected that they would be more likely to engage in inappropriate conduct (Morris *et al*, 1995). Moving on from the analysis of Strubler, Hofstede and Vitell, we might add some other considerations of our understanding of culture.

Taking non-verbal communication as an example, in addition to formal language there is also substantial scope for misunderstandings in non-verbal communication. The misuse of personal space, the use of particular words, attitudes to punctuality, and the provision of specific food items all carry the capacity for misunderstanding. What is seemly in one culture may be unseemly, or seem unethical, in another. Misunderstandings could be seen, by some, as insults (eg a Western beckoning signal in one culture may be seen as an obscene gesture in another). Later in this text some suggestions are offered for cross-cultural dealing. Despite extensive, and largely unsuccessful, attempts by psychologists, it is still not possible to formalize this non-verbal communication; all we can do is to try to understand.

Learning from other cultures

One of the singular merits of ethical consideration in a cross-cultural context is the way in which it forces us to confront our own values, to develop them, and to defend them. Cross-cultural comparisons afford an opportunity to examine the basis of our ethical codes. This section deals with the opportunities that working in a global environment across multiple cultures presents.

Societies have evolved a number of strategies to regulate themselves. In Western countries there has been rapid urbanization, massively shifting the populations away from smaller agriculturally focused communities. This shift has eroded the unwritten traditional customs and etiquette, making the West dependent on more formal means of control in agreed codes of conduct and agencies of control.

Many Asian and African developing countries often have highly effective yet informal means of social control. Progressively, and not necessarily for the better, a number of societies appear to be opting for an institutionalized means of coping with social problems, using the Western style. Tribal sanctions may still be better than formal policing. Translated to a business environment, an informal intra-industry code may be more effective in encouraging good behaviour than a set of official rules applied by an external authority. It is by the examination of issues such as informal control that we might come to an enhanced understanding of ethical substance, and of procedures that are effective in improving behaviour.

The interaction of foreign culture and ethics

Cultural values may collide on several issues. Among such are the notions of collective responsibility, attitudes to women, sexual orientation, disabled persons, religion, judgement about body shape, secret commissions, and loyalty to family over loyalty to principle. Among the important themes of business ethics is the need to reconcile the different values of different cultures, and to find principles that transcend culture; and the need to find means of teaching, encouraging and enforcing an ethical code in business.

Among the pertinent questions raised by the interaction of foreign cultures are: What is the difference between a bribe and an appropriate gift? What are permissible forms of professional criticism? Should the treatment of women in a subsidiary be different to their treatment in another country?

Often the tensions between cultures are viewed as unnecessary irritants to the objects of organizations (particularly from 'individualist' countries). Collectively though these differences are a resource that corporations can use to build harmonious networks within their organizations and with their clients.

> ### The importance of recognizing the reach of cultural values (body image)
>
> #### Walt Disney
>
> Walt Disney Corporation is the well-known film studio that has expanded into theme parks and merchandising from its films. In 2012 it released a computer-animated movie called 'Brave'. The movie was a shift from Disney formula in a number of ways, particularly how their heroines were portrayed. The main protagonist 'Merida' is independent. She is not looking for a prince to solve her problems; she solves them herself. Importantly she is portrayed with a more realistic body image. The film was given plaudits for the positive messages it was giving girls.
>
> In 2013, the corporation decided to induct Merida into their 'Princess Collection' and redrew her in their traditional style; with a thin waist, bigger eyes and neater hair. There was a considerable consumer backlash to the redrawn character (200,000 signatories to an online petition). Those protesting said that it undid the message that the film gave, now telling girls it was not alright to look normal, that they had to be good looking to be worthwhile. The new 'Merida' was removed from the Disney website.
>
> **SOURCE**: See Walt Disney in recommended reading

Taking a different culture's perspective

In the past, there have been some countries that have shown an interest in learning from other countries (such as Sweden), and other cultures (such as the Japanese). It is notable that current interest focuses on productivity and quality control rather than on ethical practices. Where other countries are seen to be more efficient, we might wrongly conclude that the advantages they appear to have derive only from efficient production and good management, rather than their strong ethical commitment.

It is difficult for people from one culture to appreciate how they are viewed by another culture. To some, the notion of the payment of a 'petty bribe' may seem inappropriate. As Dirk Bogarde noted in his autobiography, *Snakes and Ladders*, in one European country every transaction:

> from registering a car, leasing a villa, applying for a *carte de sejour*, receiving a parking ticket or obtaining a table in a restaurant was accompanied always by a flurry of paper money, or surrogate contracts. Nothing was above board, nothing ever seemed exactly what it was.

To those who live there it may not seem out of the ordinary, and may even be expected. There are many countries in which what Western culture would call a petty bribe forms an important subsidy to the income of that person; without that payment they may not be able to survive financially. It is not unusual for a bewildered westerner to be given 'change' when paying an Eastern European police officer to avoid a traffic infringement.

Standish's novel *The Silk Tontine* sets the scene in ancient China, where a picture is drawn of a young man of 'good' family who commits a serious offence for which the death penalty applies. The wealthy father of the offender buys a young man of an impoverished family to be executed in his son's place. What many find surprising is that the young man who is to be executed helps his family to gain honour and riches. The principle of family or cohort responsibility is not part of Western criminal law nor, very often, of ethical actions. Responsibility is more often personal than collective.

Ethics is essentially about human values. Since not all values are shared we are compelled to consider the issues we have in common, and those on which we divide. For instance, what may seem self-evident in one culture may be ethically unacceptable in another. Ethics affords an opportunity to discuss and resolve these human values.

Corruption

One of the major issues for business is the different levels of corruption throughout the world. Generally, there are a number of countries in the world where corruption is the exception rather than the rule, and others where the reverse is true. This presents a significant problem for business people not only in the countries with the corrupt practices but within their home countries. The United States, Europe and many other countries have specific provisions outlawing corrupt practices in foreign countries such as the US's Foreign Corrupt Practices Act. It should not just be presumed, however, that the representatives of Western corporations are in the difficult position of being compelled to work within a corrupt culture. As the Banamex case in Chapter 1 demonstrates, in some instances some subsidiaries see the inclination towards corrupt practices in their local environment as a business opportunity.

Transparency International (TI) is an organization founded by Peter Eigen of Augsburg, and now has a Secretariat based in Berlin. Its description is that of a coalition against corruption in international business transactions. Its main brief is to foster the use of openness and transparency as the best means of countering such corruption; it has the appropriate belief that corruption flourishes in secrecy, for which the antidote is transparency.

TI has also produced a corruption index, which sets out criteria of corruption, and the methodology used to derive the index numbers. A comprehensive account of how the index works and the results of the investigations is available (see Transparency International website in References).

On the 2013 Corruption Perception Index, Denmark and New Zealand scored best, both at 91 (where 100 is 'clean'). Next were Finland, Sweden, Norway, Singapore, Switzerland, Netherlands, Australia and Canada equal at 81. At the lower end are Syria, Turkmenistan and Uzbekistan, all at 17. Then follow Iraq, Libya, South Sudan, and Sudan. Bottom of the index (most perceived corruption) were Afghanistan, North Korea and Somalia, all scoring 8. The list covered 175 nations. It will be clear that corruption has differential consequences in different industries; they include agriculture, public service, real estate, manufacturing and, perhaps most importantly, overseas aid.

Conclusion

In this chapter we have addressed Hofstede's dimensions of cultural difference and reviewed the main national and environmental factors that have been identified as influencing ethical decision making. These elements form part of the structure for analysing ethical dilemmas in a globalized environment. This chapter also covered some of the opportunities in cross-cultural situations to build better values for ourselves. The organizational and other factors that complete the picture are discussed in the next two chapters. This material will also form part of the groundwork for 'Creating ethical cultures' and 'Investigating ethical issues'.

Focus questions

Cross-cultural issues in business ethics

1 What are Hofstede's dimensions? Describe each.

2 What role does geography play in determining the underlying values of a community? Provide two examples.

3 What are the main social institutions that influence an individual's moral judgement and why?

4 What are the dominant values in collectivist and individualist cultures?

5 How do economic forces influence a community's approach to business?

6 Describe the difference between intrinsic, extrinsic and systemic models.

7 How do economic forces influence a business manager's ethical decision making?

8 How can we use cultural differences to better develop our own ethical standards?

9 Is corruption an important issue for international businesses? If so, why?

CASE STUDY   Gifts

Stuart is a senior financier based in London. He had been tasked with arranging finance for the construction of a shopping centre in a major Asian city. He has been working closely with a number of the senior executives of an Arab development company that will eventually lease the shops. His role has involved a number of overseas flights at short notice, long hours, late night phone calls and the resolution of a number of crises over several months.

At the conclusion of the project he receives an excited phone call from his wife that there is a new Jaguar in the driveway, tickets for an expensive holiday and a note of thanks for all his work and her patience from his Arab colleagues. Stuart recognizes that this is a difficult situation not only in regards the appropriateness of keeping such expensive gifts but also the cultural dilemma. The giving of expensive gifts is common practice for his colleagues' culture so returning the gift risks insulting their generosity.

Does Stuart keep the gifts or not?

If Stuart doesn't accept the gifts, how will he explain it to his wife?

Would the answer be different if the gift was given prior to the commencement of the project rather than at the completion?

Factors to consider

Stuart's position is not that uncommon. Professionals employed in the global economy are routinely placed in situations where a 'gift' is given to them in a business context. There are a number of foreign cultures where the giving of often generous gifts is not unusual. It is also not uncommon in Western culture for a grateful client to give a gift. The gift giver may be a person with whom they are working closely or where there is a prospect of future work. The giving of gifts raises a number of issues. It may be meant or considered as a bribe. If it is not a bribe it may still be inappropriate. The gift may be perceived by others as a bribe, and could taint future dealings. If the gift is inappropriate it may, if returned or refused, offend the giver.

The receiver of the gift should first consider all the circumstances. Starting with quantum, a large and generous gift should set off alarm bells for the receiver. If it is a large gift given to anyone who is part of a decision-making process prior to the making of the decision it is highly likely that the gift is intended as a bribe. Remember also that bribery is often a common business practice in some countries, and as with the giving of gifts not altogether unusual in Western countries. These more obvious situations can quickly be resolved by an ethical professional. There are, however, more nuanced situations that require more attention.

As has been said earlier businesses are often built on personal relationships and sound business practitioners strive to cultivate networks. A gift given at the end of a project as an acknowledgement of the person's hard work and a job well done can either intentionally or unintentionally become the 'conflict of interest' of the future. What if you were to do business with that corporation again? No matter how objective the recipient believes themselves to be and no matter how genuine the giver of the gift is, any future transactions are contaminated.

Most Western corporations today have high expectations of their employees. Not only are 'conflicts of interests' prohibited but situations that may be perceived as a 'conflict of interest' must also be avoided. Even attending end-of-year functions of business associates is closely scrutinized. Any professional should be alert to the perception they are creating, be closely familiar with their corporation's codes of behaviour and if at all in doubt speak to their superior or relevant human resources area.

If the refusal of the gift is likely to cause offence to a client then it is also important to consult with your superior to address the situation. They may be confident enough to intervene and politely refuse on your behalf explaining the organization's policies or the matter may be enough of a concern to seek specialist assistance. The message is always to consult and consult early; it is inadvisable to try to resolve these situations alone.

Recommended reading

Citibank

Halpern, J (2004, August) Paper boys; inside the dark lucrative world of consumer debt collection, *New York Times Magazine* [online] http://www.nytimes.com/interactive/2014/08/15/magazine/bad-paper-debt-collector.html

Hayden, E (2011, August) The disturbing story of Citibank's debt collectors and a dead Indonesian, *The Wire* [online] http://www.thewire.com/global/2011/08/disturbing-story-citibanks-debt-collectors-and-dead-indonesian/41382/

Serrill, M (2011, June) Citigroup collides with death in Indonesia emerging market debt, Bloomberg News [online] http://www.bloomberg.com/news/2011-06-29/citigroup-collides-with-death-in-indonesia-emerging-market-debt.html

S, M (2011, April) Fraud and death in Indonesia, *The Economist* [online] http://www.economist.com/blogs/freeexchange/2011/04/financial_markets

Nestlé baby milk

Muller, M (2013, February) Nestlé baby milk scandal has grown up but not gone away, *Guardian* [online] http://www.theguardian.com/sustainable-business/nestle-baby-milk-scandal-food-industry-standards

Newman, M and Wright, O (2013, June) After Nestlé, Aptamil manufacturer Danone is now hit by breast milk scandal, *Independent* [online] http://www.independent.co.uk/news/uk/home-news/after-nestl-aptamil-manufacturer-danone-is-now-hit-by-breast-milk-scandal-8679226.html

Walt Disney

Child, B (2013, May) Brave director criticizes Disney's 'sexualized' Princess Merida redesign, *Guardian* [online] http://www.theguardian.com/film/2013/may/13/brave-director-criticises-sexualised-merida-redesign

Child, B (2013, May) Disney retreats from Princess Merida makeover after widespread criticism, *Guardian* [online] http://www.theguardian.com/film/2013/may/16/disney-princess-merida-makeover

Organizational factors in business ethics

04

Introduction

In the previous chapter it was established that the core to understanding ethical decision making in global business is an appreciation of cultural influences. This chapter continues the discussion of these influencing factors, specifically examining organizational culture. Chapter 5 discusses research into individual decision making, closing this part of the text: the necessity, justification and research for business ethics. In conjunction with the previous and following chapters, this chapter will also provide some of the groundwork for addressing ethical culture and issues to be discussed and worked through in Chapters 8 and 9.

Key learning points

This chapter will firstly examine the factors of organizational culture that influence ethical decision making. These are:

- The moral development of a corporation.
- Demonstrated ethics of leadership.
- Presence and enforcement of ethical codes.
- Culture, history and climate of an organization.
- The opportunity to act unethically.

This chapter will also examine other issues in relation to organizations and ethics:

- Organizations and ethics.
- Industrial relations.
- Emergent ethics.

The organization and ethics

In the wake of the unprecedented corporate failures of Enron, WorldCom and the GFC (which were driven by extraordinarily bad corporate behaviour), it is essential that consideration be given to the role of organizational culture. These failures did not occur in a vacuum; they took years to build up to the point where they were enormous in size and audacity. There are crucial questions that need to be resolved about the common values in organizations. These values need to be assessed, understood and ultimately channelled towards the ethical rather than unethical.

Turning again to the literature review into international business ethics and remembering that the cross-cultural factors discussed in Chapter 3 interplay with organizations as much as individuals, the review identified four major themes relating to organizational culture (Strubler *et al*, 2012). These themes and the research relating to each are discussed in the following sections.

The moral development of a company

There are two main and competing conceptual models relating to the moral development of corporations. The first utilizes Kohlberg's (1976) work on the development of moral sense in children (discussed in the next chapter) applying the idea of stages of development to corporations (Reidenbach and Robin, 1991). That study recognized that the model is limited as corporations and humans develop differently but considers it useful to assess and guide corporations and researchers.

The description of the model 'stages of development' gives an initial impression of corporations progressively working themselves up from the bottom of the table of an ethical hierarchy (see Table 4.1). The authors of this study were careful to note that this is not necessarily the case. Businesses move in and out of these different levels based on a range of factors such as the ethos of the company founders or a takeover by a different corporation at a different stage of moral development. Importantly, not all corporations move up the hierarchy, particularly those at the bottom (amoral companies); by their nature they rarely, if ever, advance.

The second model looks at corporations' 'modes of managing morality' (MMM). This approach focuses on a corporation's preferred method of resolving ethical dilemmas (Rossouw and van Vuuren, 2003). The authors of the MMM model argued that it is a superior methodology that eliminates most of the difficulties in the 'stages of development' approach, although there is a degree of alignment between the two models.

TABLE 4.1 Stages of moral development in corporations

Stage	Corporation type	Concern or profit compared to ethics
5	Ethical	Most balanced (profits and ethics equal)
4	Emerging ethical	More balanced (strong recognition of social responsibility)
3	Responsive	Some balance (recognition that social responsibility needs to be addressed but usually reactively)
2	Legalistic	Little balance (belief that compliance with the law is the only responsibility)
1	Amoral	Unbalanced (profit orientated only, even legal constraints might be ignored)

(Extracted from Reidenbach and Robin, 1991)

The 'stages of moral development of companies' model

Stage 1: the amoral company

This corporation is motivated solely by profit and is constrained only by the risk of being caught. Rules or social norms that can be ignored, circumvented or broken are fair game if doing so can bring a greater return. The ethos is 'survival of the fittest' and wider social considerations are viewed as weakness.

If the corporation discusses ethics it will inevitably be because they have been exposed in some public way and are trying to repair the damage rather than making a sincere attempt to correct their attitude. This attitude is readily rationalized as a necessity to be 'a step ahead of the competition'. The management would be very directive rather than collaborative; employees will be expected to obey rather than question.

Amoral example

Snow Brand milk

Snow Brand was a dairy product company in Japan with nearly half the market share. In 2000 approximately 14,000 people suffered food poisoning as a result of bacterial infection that occurred because of a failure in hygiene standards at one of their plants. The corporation behaved in a manner showing that they were more concerned about the financial damage to the organization than the health of their customers.

The corporation tried to create an impression that the problem was smaller than it was, by claiming that the valve (the site of the infection) was tiny and that the machine it was attached to hardly used. In fact it was used constantly. Osaka health authorities issued a product recall for two items and suggested that the corporation recall all its products. Management refused for a time, then agreed, then failed to actually complete the recall.

The incident, which was the worst case of food poisoning in Japan's history, resulted in the ultimate removal of the brand from the market place and convictions for two of the executives.

SOURCE: See Snow Brand milk in recommended reading

Stage 2: the legalistic company

This corporation's operating ethos is 'everything within the law'. Issues are resolved with reference to their internal legal group without questioning whether their action has any wider considerations. Even their internal codes will reflect this mode of thinking. Codes will be written and framed as rules to be obeyed with staff punished if they fail to meet the required standard. It is likely that in an effort to ensure control, these codes will increase exponentially until they are unworkable by an increasingly confused workforce. Examination of a company's written codes will readily inform any reviewer whether they fit into this category. The collective mindset is that they are meeting their requirements within the community by operating within a strict interpretation of the law.

Legalistic example

Ford Pinto

The Ford Pinto vehicle is an infamous case of corporate misconduct. The vehicle had a propensity to explode when involved in specific types of collisions to the rear end. When the corporation was made aware of the fault an actuarial calculation was made to compare the value of the recall (US $137 million) to the cost of paying out to persons injured in these collisions ($49.5 million). The Executive at the time opted to take the lower-cost option, effectively leaving a small number of their customers to be killed or seriously maimed to save costs.

The case is a landmark negligence matter that resulted in a massive punitive penalty for Ford. It created mass awareness of corporate misconduct even as the basis for mainstream films such as *Class Action* (1991) and *Fight Club* (1999).

When close attention is paid to Ford's defence, we see the language of the legalistic company. Ford argued that the car 'met all federal, state and local government standards concerning auto fuel systems' and then later stated that they acted immediately to recall the car when 'ordered to do it'.

The ethos of the corporation was focused on compliance with the law, not doing the right thing.

SOURCE: Reidenbach and Robin, 1991

Stage 3: the responsive company

This corporation recognizes that its responsibilities incorporate more than what is required by law. They will be seeking to strike a balance between profit and their social responsibilities, which include the communities they work in and their employees. They may have made this shift from Stage 2 as the result of a public mistake or costly event. The corporation at the responsive stage is, however, still reactive. Its actions are largely driven by the potential backlash from an unethical decision rather than a sense of obligation. Their codes are drafted in such a way that they include values and responsibilities but the core of the document will be to protect the company rather than the wider community.

Responsive example

Nike

In the late 1980s Nike developed strategies for shifting production from Korea and Taiwan (where wages and unionism were increasing) to Indonesia, Thailand and Vietnam (where wages and unionism were lower). As well as the very low wages in these countries, there were also a number of other abuses of staff. Nike's relocation strategy was made public by activists in 1992 and the brand was substantially tainted in the eyes of Western consumers.

The company faced embarrassing confrontations including protests at the Barcelona Olympics and challenges to their celebrity spokespeople including Michael Jordan. In an effort to repair the damage a diplomat was hired to investigate, but his report was considered by most people as too soft, and ultimately inflamed the situation.

In 1998 sales fell and their CEO determined that the company must take action. Over the next 10 years Nike:

- established the Fair Labour Association (which sets up maximum hours, safety and other working conditions);

- published all of its suppliers;

- audited 600 factories globally; and

- continues to publish a 'social responsibility report' each year.

SOURCE: See Nike in recommended reading

Stage 4: the emergent company

This corporation actively seeks to create an ethical culture. There is recognition throughout the organization that there is a balance to be struck between profit and the social good. Codes are written in a collaborative way and continuously refined as real-world experience tests their operation. The corporation ethos permeates training, selection, other procedures and policies. There are officers with the specific responsibility to check and review the decision making in the organization.

This might include roles such as a 'risk manager' who sits as part of the Executive, an ethics committee or an Ombudsman. The CEO will be visibly engaged with the ethics measures. There can be hotlines where officers can report inappropriate behaviour that bypasses the hierarchy. In an ideal world the hotline handlers would be independent of the company. Together these measures tell the organization that management is committed to their stated values. The corporation is still, however, not performing at an ethical optimum as there are still missteps and failures when the code is insufficient or misapplied.

Emergent example

Tylenol tampering

Johnson & Johnson (J&J) were the manufacturers of the painkiller Tylenol. The product was a cornerstone of their business. With 100 million users, Tylenol on its own was a sufficiently large enough product to put the business in the top half of the Fortune 500. In 1982 bottles of the drug were tampered with; some of the medication was replaced with cyanide and put back on chemists' shelves.

Several people were killed as a result of this criminal act. J&J's response to the crisis was instant. They immediately withdrew the product and engaged in a huge media campaign to warn the public. Their action, while extraordinarily costly, prevented any further deaths and ultimately saved the brand as people retained their trust in J&J.

Commenting after the event a senior executive attributed their action as consistent with their ethical code. This code had been embedded into their organization and focused on ensuring no harm to the public was their priority. The code was part of their culture and identity.

This shows an increasing awareness of ethical responsibility and is a significant step forward. This is something reflected in a number of major companies but these are not perfect systems; inappropriate behaviour still occurs.

SOURCE: Reidenbach and Robin, 1991

Stage 5: the ethical company

The morals and values of this organization are accepted by the workforce and incorporated into everyday decision making at all levels. The code is outward facing to the community as a whole. An important component is a proactive mindset. The corporation's officers consider their actions in advance against the value set. Considerations of profit, social benefit and social harm are processed in parallel.

The ethical company

TOMS Shoes

'TOMS Shoes' was set up in 2006 after its founder, travelling in Argentina, noticed that many of the children were without shoes. He resolved to assist and set up a footwear company that committed to giving one pair of shoes to a needy person for each pair of shoes purchased. The brand has been particularly popular. The social responsibility element has had special attraction for younger consumers. It has been commercially successful to the extent that TOMS Shoes has now given away 35 million pairs of shoes. The organization's programme works to ensure shoes are provided to needy individuals on a lifetime basis.

However, even a corporation with an ethical basis for its foundation still can come under criticism for its ethical conduct. For example, TOMS Shoes are made in China and development commentators have questioned why the corporation has not looked to manufacture their shoes in more needy countries. Jobs and the direct improvements to quality of life being as, if not more valuable than shoes. The company has been responsive to this criticism and recently opened a factory in Haiti.

SOURCE: See TOMS Shoes in recommended reading

The 'modes of managing morality' (MMM) model

As noted earlier the 'modes of managing morality' (MMM) model looks to how the organization actually handles ethical dilemmas and was considered by the authors of the model to be a more satisfactory way of assessing and researching ethical behaviour. Key to understanding this approach is the focus on management's 'preferred' way of resolving ethical dilemmas to determine which mode is predominant. Five modes have been identified. These are:

Immoral mode

Managers in this mode see ethics and business as mutually exclusive. A company cannot be in business and be ethical. Like the 'amoral' company cited earlier, profit is the object. Unethical conduct is a necessary condition of doing business and is rationalized with a Darwinian approach; only the strong survive. Importantly these ideas are not merely excuses but seen as core business philosophies. There is no scope for employees to make or even discuss making a decision on an ethical basis.

Reactive mode

Management in this mode give a pretence that they apply an ethical code but this is mere window dressing to avoid consequences such as strikes, consumer backlash, or government intervention. Their codes of conduct are superficial and simply ignored within the organization. Focus is on the appearance of the code rather than its meaningful introduction into the culture. The code must 'look good'. There is no depth in management to engage with the ethical issues and instil positive values in their workforce.

Compliance mode

These organizations create codes to apply as a standard to be adhered to. Employees are trained, their conduct monitored, breaches are punished and those who model the expectations are rewarded. Management is motivated to avoid the negative consequences of unethical behaviour such as litigation, damage to brand, or scandals. Management may also desire to create a positive image in the market place in order to attract clients and high-quality recruits.

Integrity mode

The key difference between this and the compliance mode is that management does not seek to impose its values but aims to have employees share the values. The aim is to embed the ethical code in the culture. There is less compulsion required because the values are organically applied. This strategy is more complex and to implement it requires a more sophisticated and knowledgeable management team. Commonly, there will still be some compliance element to the organization's code and practice as a risk management exercise to mitigate its exposure to serious consequences.

Totally Aligned Organization mode

In this mode, ethical behaviour is fully integrated into the corporation and not a separate element that needs to be managed. The value system is such that it forms part of the definition of the organization and part of its reason for being. Both the internal and external stakeholders have a clear understanding of expected behaviour. Trust is a given and is central to interactions and relationships. Unethical conduct is not only seen as unacceptable but a risk to the future.

Exercise

Using the examples noted in the previous section (Snow Brand milk, Tylenol, Ford Pinto, TOMS Shoes), under which mode of managing morality would you place each one?

Demonstrated ethics of the leadership

Ethics theorists and researchers understandably have turned their minds to the role of leaders in organizational decision making. Intuitively, it is recognized that the values of senior management are a major influence as to whether a corporation is ethical or not. This is supported by empirical evidence. In one study over 75 per cent of managers felt their personal standards conflicted with what was expected of them from their superiors. Another study found that a majority of young managers would follow the lead of their superiors (Ferrell and Gresham, 1985).

Large corporate collapses that attract the most public attention are those perpetrated by the senior leadership. However, despite the importance and high-profile nature of these cases, they are not the norm. The majority of CEOs and senior executives are not committing criminal acts of fraud but their values and influence on the culture of the organization are still critical. As noted earlier, leaders play a significant role in creating and maintaining a workplace culture. Their own values are often reflected in the conduct of the company. It is equally important that a leader be engaged with the organization to drive the desired values and ensure an ethical workplace.

Qualities of ethical leadership

A study to identify the qualities of ethical leaders interviewed 20 ethics officers and 20 top executives from the Fortune 500 list (Trevino *et al*, 2003). The majority of these corporations employed tens of thousands of people and in some instances over 100,000. Ethics officers were included because they have a day-to-day involvement with the whole of the organization regarding ethical issues, and could provide an opinion outside of the executive team. It is interesting to note that more than 50 per cent of these large corporations employed a senior-level officer dedicated to ethics, such were the concerns about the conduct of their organization.

The interviewers asked the participants to choose an executive, not necessarily from their own organization, for their focus in answering the questions. The identity of this 'executive' was not revealed so that the interviewees could speak candidly. The other feature of this survey was the use of a contrast; participants were also asked about the qualities of an 'ethically neutral leader'. This leader may either not be aware of an ethical dimension or may not see a place for ethics in business. This category was used as a contrast in preference to the 'unethical manager' because in the initial test interviews the subjects did not consider that there were 'unethical managers'. The ethically neutral manager as a category was more reflective of their reality.

The results of the survey showed that rather than a focus on personal values, ethical leaders were predominantly perceived as having a 'people orientation'. They cared about and respected their employees; they were focused on developing the individual and ensuring good treatment for the workforce. The ethically neutral manager was 'self-centred' and 'less caring about people'. Ethical leaders were also visible 'role models' for the organization, they acted appropriately, and were approachable as well as having personal integrity.

The ethical leaders not only helped create the standards but they were also active in implementation. Leaders ensured sanctions for breaches and rewards for compliance. While being committed to the profitability of their organization, they also had a broad understanding of the moral dimension and acted for the common good. The ethically neutral manager is only concerned about the bottom line. Lastly, the executives in the survey emphasized fairness in the decision-making process and usually had a quick test like 'how would this look on the front page of tomorrow's newspaper?'

Qualities of an ethical leader:

- people oriented (cares about people);
- visible role model (this is less about their values and more about what is seen);
- have processes to ensure values are applied (rewards and punishments);
- concerned for profit but understand the wider social responsibility;
- ensure fairness in decision making (have quick tests to assess decisions).

Qualities of an ethically neutral leader:

- not people oriented, focused on self;
- overriding priority is the bottom line;
- largely unaware or uninterested in wider social responsibility.

Being ethical and the importance of being seen to be ethical

One particularly interesting result of the survey mentioned in the previous section was the point of difference between the ethics officers and the senior executives (Trevino *et al*, 2003). The majority of senior executives refused to accept the concept of an ethically neutral leader while the ethics officers had no difficulty with this concept. The authors of the survey concluded that the senior executives saw ethics as an inherent part of decision making. Decision making at the senior level nearly always has a moral issue embedded; the executives' argument was that a CEO could not be ethically neutral.

The ethics officers looking from the outside in, like the majority of workforces in large corporations, do not see the decision-making process. The workforce sees other manifestations of the executives' values such as engaging staff with core values, and how the values apply in their day-to-day operations. It is not necessarily apparent to staff what the CEO's commitment is to the corporate values. Senior management must also overcome the image the community has of business leaders.

The scandals and the depictions of executives in fact and in fiction paint a negative picture. Combine this with anything that could be perceived as questionable behaviour for profitability, and it is not difficult to understand the all–too-common cynicism of employees towards their leaders. This is the reason that those outside the executive team can relate to the ethically neutral leader.

The lesson here is that leaders should not presume that just because they are making the right decisions, the rest of the organization will appreciate that: it is the visible behaviour that counts. This idea of misalignment between management and employee perceptions was also reflected in a study using Hartman's axiology (see 'language' in Index). This study examined the gaps between management and staff perceptions of what was expected and what was actually occurring (Connor, 2006).

The study showed that there was a considerable disconnect. For example, while both groups saw a heavy emphasis on rules, the workforce considered that to be management's total focus. The employees felt overwhelmed by the administration that accompanied complying with the corporations' standards. Yet the management itself had a much greater belief in the importance of individual values as part of the process. The study drew out three major issues:

1 lack of clarity about what values the corporation had and where they expected these values to take them;

2 management presumed that the organization's values automatically translated into reality, when often they didn't; and

3 what people say are their values are different from what is actually valued.

Given the importance that the models cited above (in the moral development of a company) have placed on the integration of personal and organization values, this is a concerning result for any corporation. While caution has to be used when extrapolating from this set of results, it is still instructive and likely applicable to a large number of organizations.

The importance of action to reputation

Ralph Lauren bribery

Ralph Lauren corporation has been a luxury clothing and goods manufacturer with a worldwide market for over 45 years. Between 2005 and 2009 the corporation's Argentinean subsidiary had been bribing customs and other government officials to expedite the import of their product. These actions were a breach of the US Foreign Corrupt Practices Act. This was discovered by the company's own internal audit area and was reported to the Securities Exchange Commission and the US Federal Justice department within two weeks of discovery.

The swift action by the corporation along with its full co-operation with authorities was a major factor in substantially reduced penalties as well as possible harm to the exclusive brand.

SOURCE: See Ralph Lauren bribery case in recommended reading

A comparative of Japanese and United States leadership styles

Japan's miraculous economic recovery, starting after World War II and culminating in the 1980s and 1990s, created enormous interest, particularly as to how they had been able to develop products of exceptional quality which were competitively priced. Considerable attention went into the examination of manufacturing and production methods, but there was less interest in looking at the underlying values of the Japanese community. There is a strong argument to suggest that the explanation lies in the ethics of their culture rather than anywhere else.

The role of ethics within the Japanese leadership style was comprehensively covered by Taka and Folgia (1994). To those unfamiliar with Japanese leadership style it is very alien, particularly when there is awareness that balancing morality and profitability is not an issue for Japanese corporations. It is not a priority for a Japanese corporation, when working through ethical issues, to be thinking about workers abusing the organization by careless work or theft. Probably most confronting is that employees are the priority for a Japanese leader, not shareholders. From a Western perspective it is a rather remarkable explanation for their success.

The embedded ethos of Japanese leaders is that everything is linked to a higher purpose: transcendentalism. This is a given within Japan, cutting across religious and other cultural differentials. Within that concept there is a commitment to an individual on a journey of ongoing development. Given that work constitutes a large portion of a person's life, work is seen as an important vehicle for achieving that development. For this reason no work is valued as more or less important. This belief applies not only to individuals but also to groups. In this context, groups are businesses and units of businesses and each has a path and a development to pursue.

Japanese leaders are expected to follow three ideals:

1 to focus primarily on self-realization, not only of themselves but of employees and sometimes other stakeholders such as suppliers;

2 to accept diversity; and

3 to trust other people.

Note that these are ideals and not always followed or achievable. This is well recognized in Japanese culture. It is interesting to note that a common theme in Kabuki theatre is that of the Samurai who has somehow failed in his sacred obligations. These ideals do, however, play an important role in the operation of business. Japanese managers generally work towards the ideals that, in turn, support and align with long-term growth rather than short-term profit. A longer-term focus is intrinsically a more moral approach.

Inequality in the sense that there are higher- and lower-paid workers is acceptable provided that the actions of leaders are for the good of the whole, improving the conditions of the lesser paid. Maintaining the workforce is about maintaining the relationship with that workforce. The closing of factories and the sacking of staff is a desperate last resort and everything is done to mitigate the harm to the individuals if it has to occur.

There are multiple pay-offs from the Japanese approach. The loyalty and honesty of their staff is a given. The self-realization underpinning this ethos is important. To workers a job is not just a job, it is part of their purpose in life, so there is an aspiration to do well and to achieve good outcomes for the business. Also, as all work has equal value the opinion of the worker, as the specialist of that discrete function, is valued.

Their opinions about improvements are given serious consideration and their decisions are respected. In turn this leads to better practices and products. For example, the practice of production line workers having the authority to stop the line if there is an issue with quality originated in Japan and is now common practice in manufacturing worldwide. This is why Japanese leaders do not think in terms of balancing ethics with profitability. For them, profitability comes from being ethical.

As noted, and as any quick scan of corporate scandals in Japan will confirm, theirs is not a perfect system. Their ethical code is narrow, for example, and women in the workforce do not rate the same treatment. The loyalty of workers to the corporation can lead to acceptance of business practices that are unethical. However, there are still important lessons to learn, especially when compared to the US system.

In this study, researchers saw in the US system that shareholders were sacrosanct, focus was on short-term profitability and employees were subordinate to that. If employee numbers must be cut to achieve profitability then it is expected. Types of work are seen as more or less important. Employees are regulated rather than trusted. There is not an obligation on executives to align their remuneration to a duty to improve the lives of their workers. The question is compelling – what is the better way of conducting business from moral and profitability perspectives?

TABLE 4.2   Comparison of Japanese and US leadership styles

Country	Japan	United States
Priority	Employees	Shareholders
Features	Commitment to self-realization. Sackings are a last resort. Executive committed to improving the whole. All work considered of equal value. All opinions respected and listened to. Acceptance of diversity. Trust in employees. Long-term focus.	Commitment to profitability. Sackings if in the interest of profitability. No commitment from executive to improving good of the whole. Some jobs seen as more important than others. Short-term focus.
Ethical consequence	Underlying assumption that ethical conduct is profitable.	Constant tension between ethical behaviour and profitability.

What behaviour is rewarded?

The models of conditioning and learning developed by psychologists Pavlov, Watson and Skinner are very relevant for the corporate environment. Individuals are powerfully influenced by rewards. Simply put, if a middle manager is meeting or exceeding their financial objectives, then they are likely to be rewarded, paid more, promoted, and given awards or kudos. If this involves a compromising of ethics, then these rewards also reinforce the unethical behaviour.

Such a cause and effect scenario impacts not only on the surface but at a very deep level of the psyche. It is a lesson that to be 'pragmatic', to skirt the rules to obtain company profit, is to succeed. This success and the recognition it brings satisfies a core need in people. People are social animals and they are hardwired to want acceptance from the group. In such a situation it is very understandable when the next time the 'pragmatic' manager is confronted with the profit/ethics dilemma, they will choose profit.

Worse still a pragmatic manager breeds a pragmatic culture. As the pragmatic manager moves up the hierarchy they select other pragmatic people to manage behind and below them. The other employees watching this happen learn that success equals pragmatism. The business becomes 'pragmatic'. The extent of the pragmatism also expands. It starts with minor breaches but in the face of 'paid more, promoted, given awards and kudos' the breaches become more serious.

Of course, for this simple model to work it needs to be presumed that this pragmatic manager cannot breach the rules so much that it creates a bigger problem elsewhere. The pragmatic manager therefore is the one who can achieve the organization's outcomes even if this includes breaches of ethics up to an indeterminate point where the cost of the breach is too great, be that financial or union conflict or damage to the brand. The 'pragmatic' manager is therefore a combination of leader and tightrope walker, guessing how far their risks can be taken.

There can be few people working for Western organizations who have not experienced or been exposed to this environment. Studies confirm that the majority of Western organizations rewarded 'pragmatic' managers (Wines and Napier 1992, Ferrell and Gresham 1985, Hegarty and Sims, 1978, Trevino and Youngblood, 1990, Trevino, 1986). There is a study involving 86 MBA students that contradicts this result, suggesting that more weight will be given to the ethical decision over the objectives of the organization (Kohut and Corrigher, 1994).

Did executive remuneration play a role in the GFC?

Lehman Brothers

There has been an ongoing debate about whether or not remuneration of executive bankers was a significant contributor to the Global Financial Crisis (GFC). It is significant to note that the top 50 executives of Lehman Brothers, one of the major banks bankrupted as a result of the GFC, stood to be paid a total of nearly US$700 million in bonuses if the crisis had not occurred.

Regardless of the 'unproved' relationship between reward and behaviour, in the GFC, a number of governments internationally have enacted legislation to limit salaries and bonuses to executives in order to limit risk-taking behaviour.

SOURCE: See Lehman Brothers in recommended reading

Presence and enforcement of ethical codes

Throughout this chapter the role of ethical codes including their drafting, implementation and application has been prominent. Codes have been important in determining levels of moral development in a corporation or determining what is the preferred mode of ethical problem solving. Any examination of a company's culture needs to ask the question 'is this code a beautifully crafted sham or is it something that is meaningful to the corporation?'

This chapter has also discussed how a leader's engagement with a code has been an important factor in the success or failure of creating an ethical organization. However, even without that background it is intuitive that the written guidelines or rules and the steps an organization takes to embed the values in its workforce are central to building an ethical business culture.

Despite the high-profile cases of misconduct it is important to remember that the majority of corporations do not commit serious fraud and that 'codes of conduct 'are a necessary starting point to understanding the organization's values. The presence of a code should be taken as *prima facie* evidence that the organization has a set of behaviours that it wants its workforce to reflect. In the alternative, where a company has no ethical code, whether this is intentional or not, it is inherently ethically inferior. The members of the organization have no reference point and there can be wide discrepancies about what constitutes ethical behaviour. Codes generally cure ambiguities and make clear expectations.

It is easy to be cynical in the face of all the unethical conduct that is reported in the media and we frequently see this as a part of our everyday lives. Ethics should not only be viewed through the negative lens – working for the 'amoral company' or the company that chooses the immoral mode of resolving ethical dilemmas or working for the 'ethically neutral leader'. The sections below outline positive examples and opportunities to implement ethical behaviour.

Just communities

This chapter has already discussed how Japanese culture inspires better behaviour and there is research that confirms that ethical behaviour improves when individuals are involved with school, tertiary or business programmes that teach and live ethical behaviour (McCabe *et al*, 1996). A number of schools in the United States established what they referred to as 'just communities', programmes focused on instilling moral codes of behaviour in students.

The programmes were democratic with all stakeholders participating in the development of the 'rules of the community'. Once in place conformance was rewarded and breaches punished. Research confirmed that ethical behaviour and improved levels of responsibility were greater in schools with 'just communities' than in schools without the programme.

Similarly a number of US colleges have long-standing 'honour codes' where students promise to act ethically and report those who don't. Like the 'just communities', following the code is rewarded, particularly the giving and receiving of trust, and breaches are punished. The students have the opportunity to live in an environment based on mutual trust. Again, this has been shown to reduce unethical conduct in colleges.

The interesting part of the research, however, showed that this behaviour continues into the working environment particularly if there is 'a code of conduct' that is lived and enforced. The implication is that the more exposure an individual has to 'ethical environments' the better their conduct. Even without the prior experience with 'honour codes', the researchers found that there was a reduction in unethical behaviour where there was a functional code of conduct in an organization. They found a direct relationship between the quality of the ethics code and unethical behaviour.

The researchers attributed this phenomenon to the concepts of 'scripts'. 'Scripts' are programmes that individuals use to make sense of the world; they help people assemble the information and provide a direction to resolve issues. Progressively people build up these scripts, and the more a person has to examine and resolve issues from an ethical perspective, the greater the number and quality of scripts that the person carries around with them.

Cultural differences between codes

Studies looking at ethical codes across cultures have seen differences (Stajkovic and Luthens, 1997). Codes in the United States are mainly a defence against criminal behaviour (such as breaching a government regulation) or the threat of litigation. These codes tend towards being prescriptive about employee behaviour, spelling out conduct that is inappropriate, such as bribery, consumer offences or insider trading. They may also include what is unacceptable socially; for example, what is unlawful in the United States might not be unlawful in other particularly less-sophisticated countries. But as discussed earlier, mistreatment in a developing economy can have a consumer backlash.

Japanese codes reflect their cultural standards in regards to job security, promotions based on seniority, collectivism and stability of prices. They also tend to be more philosophical. Japanese corporations also write two codes; one for local use and one for international use. The international code is focused on the values of the local cultures.

Opportunity to act unethically

Understanding of why people behave in unethical ways has produced a number of significant studies. This line of research gained particular emphasis after World War II because of the atrocities that were committed. Some key experiments had their genesis in trying to understand how both Germany and Japan, which had been thought of as civilized countries, had been capable of such wide-scale barbarism. In considering ethics in modern business this may seem to be disproportionate, but the reality is that the difference between someone cheating in a business sense and someone participating in officially sanctioned torture is a question of scale. The same underlying psychological principles apply.

The debate as to how ordinary people (German soldiers) committed these crimes against humanity was between the 'individualist' and the 'situational' views. The individualist view held that the German soldiers were not ordinary but must have been fundamentally psychologically disturbed to engage in these acts. The 'situation' view held they were ordinary people but it was the circumstances that caused the behaviour.

Overwhelmingly experimenters found that the situational variables were the greatest contributors. This was borne out by Milgram's experiments where the subjects of the experiment were set up to believe that they were to deliver electric shocks to another person as part of a learning experiment. No shock was delivered: the 'learner' was in fact an actor who had to fake being electrocuted (Milgram, 1977).

Against all predictions 67 per cent of the research subjects took the voltage to the top level of 450 volts after the time when the fake learner had simulated passing out from the treatment. The point was that when an individual considers that they are authorized (they were directed by official-looking university people in white coats) and that the cause was justified (assisting learning) then they will behave inconsistently with their values (Zimbardo, 2006).

In another experiment conducted by the psychologist Phillip Zimbardo, subjects were assigned as 'prisoners' or 'guards' in a prison created in the basement of Stanford University. Zimbardo was careful to screen his subjects to ensure he used psychologically sound individuals. The experiment was a landmark: when 'institu-tionalized', the subjects quickly took to their roles. The guards became brutal to the point of sadism in subjugating their prisoners. Zimbardo stopped the experiment six days into the 14-day time period set because of the harm it was causing the subjects.

The important point is that 'ordinary individuals' who wouldn't under other circumstances cheat or steal or defraud in the tens of millions of dollars, will do so when the situation allows it, ie when superiors and other staff are endorsing and justifying the behaviour (Zimbardo, 2006).

Access to technology

The exponential changes in technology are becoming a greater factor in the degree to which unethical decisions are taken by business. This is particularly true in the area of industrial information gathering. Most organizations sensibly gather information about their competitors and their clients and there is *prima facie* nothing illegal or unethical about that activity. However, modern technology creates a temptation to obtain information that previously would have required significant risk.

This can now be performed with minimal exposure. Hacking into systems, and data-mining the vast quantities of information that are available are functions that can be undertaken from a desk with the right skills and equipment. This impersonal factor makes it easier psychologically as well. From a personal perspective it is much easier to crack a network than to bribe an employee for information (Rittenburg *et al*, 2007).

Other organizational issues

Organizations and ethics

A few decades ago the modern corporation was likened to the medieval church. The church has its hierarchy (bishops and laity/CEOs and workers), rites (services/company songs), ecumenism (mergers), sackings (excommunication), and catechism (belief in the company ethos). Whyte (1960) argued that the modern corporation now minds its believers in a manner that emulates the medieval church – those who remain within the fold are minded from induction to death (from first employment to retirement).

Anthony Jay writing in 1987 has applied the principles of Niccolò Machiavelli to this area. He argued that Machiavelli's frankness, and non-moral stance make an ideal guide. Parallels are drawn between instances of regal and baronial behaviour and those of modern corporations. Conquered principalities correspond to taken-over firms. Religious faith equates to belief in the company philosophy and products. The reason that faith must be asserted and enforced is that, to use Jay's words, '... in corporation religions, as in others, the heretic must be cast out not because of the probability that he is wrong but because of the possibility that he is right.' Jay's analysis ranges over issues as divergent as the Danish conquest, naval policy, and the British Royal Court (Jay, 1987). The comparisons are both persuasive and useful.

Industrial relations

Industrial relations are a significant feature of employee issues. Such issues include:

- the less tangible quality of working life (including status);
- scope for self-development and self-fulfilment;
- comradeship;
- pride in skill;
- a sense of belonging; and
- value to others of the work done.

As well as these intangibles there are specific material issues such as fair wages, personal security, and occupational health and safety. Of critical importance are the right to give and to withhold labour, the right to strike on vital issues of employee concern, and the right not to suffer discrimination. Throughout this text there are a number of examples which at their core relate to the relationship between corporations and their employees. This has even been extended to the labour that a corporate subcontractor might use. It should be noted that labour associations are seen by the United Nations, the Organisation for Economic Co-operation and Development, and the International Labour Organization as a basic human right.

Other than the strict legal dimension, recognizing that most countries have legislation protecting workers' rights, corporations should turn their mind to the importance of trust in the employment setting. At the core of business is the relationship between management and workers. It is an important consideration for business ethics, whether looking at strategy or developing a code, to consider the kind of relationship that the corporation wants to have with its employees. For example, a corporation may require drastic changes as a result of changes to the market, and it may be vital for the co-operation of the union. That is more likely to occur in an atmosphere of trust where staff have a sense of partnership in the enterprise (see the Harley-Davidson example later in the book).

Emergent ethics

The notion that corporate entities evolve, as do living organisms, is appealing. Few entities stay in their original form, or are incapable of modification. Theory in science, in ethics, in art, and in biological organisms, is in a state of constant flux; this is no less true of business. The idea that business ethics is emergent has been canvassed by Lloyd (1990). He argued that we have, so far, encountered two alien forms of life; one is the company or corporation, the other is that of artificial intelligence (the computer). Noting that intelligence does not have to be advanced or broad in its application, an intelligence can be very narrow and specific, such as Google's self-driving car.

The comparatively recent development of the concept of the corporation parallels that of the evolution of living organisms. Corporations are subject to modification, and benefit in the same way from competition and co-operation. The basic thrust of Lloyd's argument is that it is now appropriate to be concerned with business ethics; he also argues that this is in the best long-term interests of an organization. He noted that, at least by human standards, the organization has 'feral energy', and went on to say that '... the company unfettered and rampant, is a familiar villain in the dystopian visions of the future depicted in our literature'. Lloyd described the company as a non-moral entity '... motivated by greed... companies are monsters created by decent human Frankensteins, which monsters we need to control.' This is why we need such infrastructure as company law, various governmental agencies, and regulatory bodies.

The three basic propositions of Lloyd's book are:

1 Companies collectively constitute a conscious, intelligent, non-human species at a relatively early stage in their evolution.

2 The theory of evolution represents a powerful, ready-made model for a dynamic theory of business economics.

3 Recent changes in the chemistry of the corporate medium favour the emergence of strategies, internal as well as external, that are 'nicer' than traditional strategies.

Corporations have done much that is positive, and much that makes our lives better, than almost any other human enterprise. The corporation has '... created order out of chaos, wealth out of rubble and work out of idleness'. Despite it having been predatory it has never been 'cowardly or indolent'. As Lloyd put it, 'the admirable qualities of boldness and vigour that have inspired great achievements. Corporate activity has "tamed the elements" and has had a significant influence in moulding our environment' (Lloyd, 1990: p xiii).

One of the difficulties of using the evolutionary metaphor is that no metaphor is an exact fit. It is possible that the inheritance of acquired characteristics is a more appropriate explanation of the development of corporate behaviour than the Darwinian one. Lloyd recognizes that in biological evolution the gene is the basic unit of inheritance. That cannot be true of the corporation. In its place he proposed that strategic themes are the building blocks of corporate evolution. Corporate life evolves by the natural selection of those who engage in the differential use of strategic themes. Just as genes propagate themselves in the gene pool via sperm and eggs, so 'stremes' (strategic themes) are propagated in the streme pool by the propensity to emulate winning strategies (Lloyd, 1990, p142).

An example of an advantageous streme is that competitive advantage is a matter of producing new products quickly rather than existing products cheaply (Lloyd, 1990, p147). Those corporations able to adapt are the ones most likely to prosper. An example of a streme is that of using a 'hollow corporation'. Such a corporation is entrepreneurial in that it has the business idea but contracts out the work. This allows for speed of response, reduces its need for infrastructure and capital, and makes it easier to contract with suppliers of goods and services who have an ethical standpoint. Among recent changes in corporate functioning are the ways in which information is being substituted for capital equipment and money, and the recurrent theme that people are the prime consideration.

Conclusion

The purpose of this chapter was to examine and discuss the importance of culture in the organizational setting and continue to build on the picture started in Chapter 3, which covered national, culture and environmental issues in cross-cultural ethical decision making.

The research and analysis in this chapter provides a comprehensive insight into the organizational context. This chapter also provides a lead-in to Chapter 5, with its focus on individual decision making. Again it is important to note the interactive and dynamic nature of these components. This chapter, like Chapter 3, underpins ways of analysing and improving corporate culture and ethical decision making, as will be discussed in Chapters 8 and 9.

The following chapter is focused on factors affecting individual decision making and is intended to complete the review of major themes in research into cross-cultural ethical decision making.

Focus questions

Organizations and ethics

1 What are the two different ways of categorizing a corporation in terms of its ethical development? What is the fundamental difference? Describe each in detail.

2 What is the role of leadership in ethical decision making?

3 What is a just community?

4 Do ethical codes assist companies to make ethical decisions? Is the presence of a code the only factor? If not what additional factors are there?

5 How important is opportunity to ethical decision making?

6 Has the increase in technology changed ethical decision making in business?

7 Other organizational issues.

8 What is the significance of Anthony Jay's work?

9 Why is trust important in employee–corporate relations?

10 Do corporations evolve like living organisms?

CASE STUDY   Being asked to lie

Kate is a senior software engineer for a major international consulting firm. She is invited by her manager to lunch to discuss an upcoming and important contract negotiation. Kate is surprised as she has never been 'treated' in this way previously and during the first part of the conversation she notes that her manager is according her with an unprecedented level of personal interest.

Halfway through the meal Kate's manager explains that the client is concerned that the product will not deliver a particular functionality that is required. Kate knows this to be correct. The manager then explains that the client has stated that if Kate gives an assurance that the functionality is available they will proceed with the contract. Kate is surprised; she thought she had built a good relationship with the client, but not to this extent.

Her manager instantly agrees that the functionality is not there but explains that the functionality is minor in the operation of the system and that they are vigorously working to resolve it. The contract is critical to the firm; without it they would not have sufficient work for their current staff numbers. Her manager tells Kate it would be a big favour to him and the firm if she could give that assurance.

What should Kate decide?

Would the answer be different if Kate knew that to integrate the product before the start of the project was impossible?

Factors to consider

Kate's position is not at all uncommon in a modern working environment; managers do ask their staff to lie. Sometimes it is direct, as in the above scenario, and sometimes it is implicit in the outputs and timeframes that are expected. The expectation to lie goes unspoken but it is nevertheless very real: 'the blind eye' is turned to the cheating because the financial outcome is usually the focus. As has been noted in this chapter most managers feel they have had to compromise their own values to meet workplace expectations.

Kate could take a strict approach, as she is clearly a person of integrity, given the client's opinion of her. She could see lying is against his values and refuse.

In the alternative Kate could take some time to consider all the stakeholders, the likelihood of the possible outcomes and the net benefits or gains. Such issues as:

1 the likelihood that the firm can remedy the shortfall;

2 the minimal importance of the functionality;

3 Kate's reputation with the client if the software fails to deliver;

4 the importance of the contract to the company;

5 her relationship with her manager;

6 her job and reputation in the software industry, internally and externally; or

7 her financial position (is she single with no debt or a single wage earner with a mortgage and children?).

She may conclude that 'on balance' it is a small lie and the risk of discovery minimal, and comply with her manager's request. This scenario also raises the issue of how often in business unethical conduct begins in a relatively small way but then expands into more serious conduct. Enron did not occur overnight; the first 'adjustment' to the accounts was likely very minor and seen as necessary to not draw attention to some small lapse that they intended to quickly rectify.

There is a phenomenon in psychology called the 'boiling frog'. The temperature detectors of frogs are much less refined than humans; there must be a faster degree of temperature change before it is recognized. Therefore if you drop a frog in a pot of hot water it jumps out, but if you put the frog in tepid water and you turn the temperature up slowly, beneath the level its senses detect, it will remain in the water until boiled. Psychologists use this as a shorthand to describe a person whose life changes so incrementally that, before they realize it, they find themselves in vastly changed and unpleasant situations they would not have accepted if the change had occurred quickly. Many serious frauds most likely begin with the smallest of breaches which grew progressively until they were major. Many managers have been 'boiling frogged', making minor unethical decisions easily rationalized until they are engaged in more serious unethical practice.

Recommended reading

Ford Pinto

Bazerman, M and Tenbrunsel, A (2011, April) Ethical breakdowns, *Harvard Business Review* [online] https://hbr.org/2011/04/ethical-breakdowns

Dowie, M (1977, September/October) Pinto madness, *Mother Jones* [online] http://www.motherjones.com/politics/1977/09/pinto-madness

Lee, M (1978) The Ford Pinto case and the development of auto safety regulations, 1893–1978, BHC [online] http://www.thebhc.org/sites/default/files/beh/BEHprint/v027n2/p0390-p0401.pdf

Longhine, L (2005, November/December) Display cases: Ralph Nader's museum of tort law will include relics from famous lawsuits – if it ever gets built, Legal Affairs [online] http://www.legalaffairs.org/issues/November-December-2005/scene_longhine_novdec05.msp

This day in history: Fatal Ford Pinto crash in Indiana [online] http://www.history.com/this-day-in-history/fatal-ford-pinto-crash-in-indiana

Turley, J (2014, April) Has GM pulled a Pinto? Los Angeles Times [online]
http://articles.latimes.com/2014/apr/14/opinion/la-oe-turley-ford-pinto-gm-cobalt-20140414

Lehman Brothers

Davis, K (2011) Regulatory reform post the Global Financial Crisis: an overview, *APEC*
[online] www.apec.org.au/docs/11_CON_GFC/Regulatory%20Reform%20Post%20
GFC-%20Overview%20Paper.pdf

Kirpatrick, G (2009) The corporate governance lessons from the financial crisis, *OECD*
[online] http://www.oecd.org/corporate/ca/corporategovernanceprinciples/42229620.pdf

Marques, L B *et al* (2014, October) Global Financial Stability Report (GFSR): Risk taking,
liquidity, and shadow banking: curbing excess while promoting growth, *International
Monetary Fund* [online] http://www.imf.org/external/pubs/ft/gfsr/2014/02/

Tangel, A and Pfeifer, S (2012, April) Lehman Bros: elite stood to get $700 million,
Los Angeles Times [online] http://articles.latimes.com/2012/apr/27/business/
la-fi-compensation-20120427

Nike

Nissen, M (2013, May) Why the Bangladesh factory collapse would never have happened
to Nike, *Business Insider Australia* [online] http://www.businessinsider.com.au/
how-nike-solved-its-sweatshop-problem-2013-5

Ralph Lauren bribery case

Gallu, J (2013, April) Ralph Lauren Agrees to pay $1.6 Million in US bribe cases, Bloomberg
Business [online] http://www.bloomberg.com/news/2013-04-22/ralph-lauren-agrees-
to-pay-1-6-million-in-u-s-bribery-cases.html

Snow Brand milk

Snow lied after milk poisoning case (2000, July) *Japan Times* [online]
http://www.japantimes.co.jp/news/2000/07/05/news/snow-lied-after-milk-poisoning-
case/#.VMatdPmSxqU

Snow brand faces criminal probe over tainted milk (2000, July) *Japan Times* [online]
http://www.japantimes.co.jp/news/2000/07/13/news/snow-brand-faces-criminal-probe-
over-tainted-milk/#.VMauAvmSxqU

Snow brand to dispute link to death (2001, December) *Japan Times* [online] http://
www.japantimes.co.jp/news/2001/12/13/news/snow-brand-to-dispute-link-to-death/
#.VMauZvmSxqU

TOMS Shoes

Favin, J (2013, April) Some bad news about TOMS Shoes, *WhyDev* [online]
    http://www.whydev.org/some-bad-news-about-toms-shoes/
Timmerman, K (2013) The problem of TOMS Shoes and its critics, *Where am I Wearing?*
    [online] http://whereamiwearing.com/2011/04/toms-shoes/
TOMS Shoes (undated) Principles, policies and charitable activities worldwide, *Tom's Shoes*
    [online] http://www.toms.com/one-for-one-en

Tylenol

Fletcher, D (2009, February) A brief history of the Tylenol poisonings, *Time Magazine*
    [online] http://content.time.com/time/nation/article/0,8599,1878063,00.html
Kesling, B (2013, October) Tylenol killings remain unsolved and unforgotten after 30 years,
    Wall Street Journal [online] http://www.wsj.com/articles/SB100014240527023034925045
    79115573613137300
Markel, H (2014, September) How the Tylenol murders of 1982 changed the way we
    consume medication, *PBS Newshour* [online] http://www.pbs.org/newshour/updates/
    tylenol-murders-1982/

Individual factors in business ethics

05

Introduction

In Chapters 3 and 4 it was established that the core to understanding ethical decision making in global business is an appreciation of national and organizational cultural influences. This chapter complements the previous two by completing the discussion of these influencing factors. It specifically examines the research into individual decision making. As noted earlier, ethical or unethical decision making is a function of multiple interrelated and interactive influences, but ultimately it is the individual who is the decision maker, not the culture. Therefore there is a body of research centred on the individual.

It is important to be aware that there is some overlap between the influencing factors: for example, religion is a cultural factor but it also operates directly on the individual. The different lenses of examination provide different pictures that collectively build our general understanding of how business decisions are made with regard to ethical issues. In conjunction with the previous two chapters, this chapter will also provide some of the groundwork for addressing ethical problems to be discussed and worked through in Chapters 8 and 9.

Key learning points

This chapter will address research undertaken from the perspective of the individual's ethical decision making. These influences are:

- Education, language and religion.

- Cross-cultural ethical intelligence.

- Personal experience and background.

- Field dependence, ego strength and locus of control.

It will then look at psychological theory about the deprivation of benefits, motivation and ethics, and address other relevant social factors such as:

- Formal versus informal relationships.

- The benefits of co-operation.

- Business and the professions.

Finally, we will look at physical factors that impact on decision making, specifically considering:

- Brain evolution.

- Environmental factors.

- Diet.

The individual and ethics

Understanding the moral development of individuals commences with Kohlberg's (1976) theory of the 'moral developmental stages'. This section will first outline Kohlberg's theories and then explore the main themes identified by researchers in this category, noting that, given the necessary overlap of the framework, some of the themes and research have been touched upon earlier, such as the role of religion and 'significant others' (Strubler *et al*, 2012).

Moral developmental stages in humans (Kohlberg)

Kohlberg (1976) has argued that the development of a moral sense in a child goes through phases. At the earliest phase the child defers to physical superiority, and does not understand that others have consciousness and desires. The second phase has proper actions serving to satisfy the person's own needs; deference to the needs of others leads to personal satisfaction. Subsequent phases progress through loyalty and affection within the sphere of immediate family and friends: motivation to be a 'right person' in the eyes of others; determining right and wrong by loyalty to his or her own nation. At the highest level there is a quantum lift in moral understanding that has the person trying to develop impartial points of view, using self-justified moral principles.

This develops the notion of conflicting opinions and views, and sees moral values as relative and needing to be tolerated. The final stage is that of seeing moral principles as being universal and consistent. Actions are completed according to abstract principles, and the behaviour of others is seen as fitting or not fitting such moral criteria. The general thrust of Kohlberg's work helps us to understand how moral sense develops, and how its development is hierarchical. Clearly, a code of business ethics should attempt to achieve the highest of the nominated categories.

Among the criticisms levelled at Kohlberg's approach are its ethnocentricity, its failure to properly address sex differences in moral development or considerations of family devotion, and in its lack of attention to community feelings. Further, the Kohlberg theories focus on a cognitive style approach. In fairness to Kohlberg it is noted that cognition is one of the shared attributes of all humanity, and so to criticize this common base may be going too far (Kohlberg *et al*, 1990).

A more generous approach would be to regard Kohlberg's work as an initial benchmark, and a point of departure for future work on ethical developmental theories. The general thrust of his work helps us to understand how moral sense develops, and how its development is hierarchical. Again, a code of business ethics should try to achieve the highest of Kohlberg's categories.

More recently than Kohlberg, there have been analyses of approaches to moral development that have been adopted by a variety of theorists (all psychologists). The analysis is supported by some empirical work, which includes subjects from different cultural backgrounds. This shift of the Kohlberg view from the Kantian emphasis on reason to a revived interest in the cultural issues involved is timely (Matsumoto, 2001). The theme expressed there was that culture has a significant influence on behaviour, and that morality is part of that very process.

Importantly Kohlberg's theory sees the development of morality as a cognitive rather than an emotive function; the greater the cognitive ability the greater the ability to process dilemmas of increasing complexity. Consistent with this there is evidence to support a correlation between IQ scales and stages of development. Kohlberg's stages of development can serve as one basis for predicting a manager's ethical behaviour and there is some empirical support for this (Trevino, 1986).

Personal experience and background

Hunt and Vitell (1986) proposed that a key element in understanding ethical decision making, along with the cultural, industry and organizational environments, was personal experience. Once recognizing an ethical scenario, an individual will apply one or both of the following approaches:

1 An assessment of the right or wrongness of the choices, by comparing to a personal internal set of criteria such as 'is it fair', 'is it stealing', 'is it cheating', 'is it a breach of confidentiality'. This personal set of norms would likely have accumulated through their life experience.

2 An assessment of the consequences of each action: 'what is the likely impact on each of the stakeholders', 'what is the likelihood of the consequences occurring', 'what is the appeal of each consequence', 'what is the relative importance of each stakeholder (such as their immediate manager)'.

It is unlikely a manager would ignore possible consequences of a decision; the model is therefore likely a combination although perhaps more oriented towards one or the other method. Managers' intentions and judgements have been strong predictors of behaviour (Trevino, 1986). That is not to say managers make decisions consistent with their own moral processing system. As cited earlier many managers consider that the expectations of the workplace, specifically their superiors, compel them to take a different standard in many decisions. They may take a decision different to their ethical standpoint because they perceive that there is a preferred outcome, such as a significant benefit to themselves (Hunt and Vitell, 1986).

How important are personal values?

Konosuke Matsushita

Konosuke Matsushita is not particularly well known in the West but is a legend in Japan. He is the founder of Panasonic. After his birth in 1894 his family had a financial crisis that reduced them to poverty and compelled him to seek work in the city. After a few years of work and with almost nothing he started a small firm making electrical fittings of his own design in 1918. An innovative person, he branched into new products such as bicycle lights, electric irons and radios. His business became substantial. Mr Matsushita saw business, particularly supplying an abundance of inexpensive goods, as a means to relieve poverty in the community.

Mr Matsushita also believed that his workers should be treated as family, guaranteeing lifetime employment. He is considered by many as the person that started this industrial culture in Japan. During the Great Depression in the 1930s he did not sack staff nor lower their wages; he reduced production and redeployed staff to sales positions. In 1965 he reduced the working week to five days, unprecedented in Japan at the time.

Mr Matsushita believed that companies had a greater social responsibility. He stated in 1929:

Our business is something entrusted to us by society. Therefore, we are duty bound to manage and develop the company in an upstanding manner, contributing to the development of society and the improvement of people's lives.

SOURCE: See Konosuke Matsushita in recommended reading

Field dependence, ego strength and locus of control

Psychologists see that some individuals, when making decisions in ambiguous situations such as ethical dilemmas, look to others to assist in removing the ambiguity. If this occurs to a high degree the individual is referred to as having high 'field dependence'. A typical scenario would be that of a junior manager confronted with a situation giving significant weight to his superior. High field dependence will be a factor that will influence an individual to make a decision away from his own internal judgement schema. A person with low field dependence will act more independently, will be less likely to make a decision inconsistent with their own values and will act more consistently (McDevitt *et al*, 2007; Trevino, 1986).

Similarly, psychologists have identified persons who view their world as something they exert little influence over. These 'externals' see that life happens to them whereas 'internals' see that they exert more control over their life and destiny. Therefore, we can expect an 'internal' to take greater responsibility and act more ethically than an 'external' (McDevitt *et al*, 2007; Trevino, 1986).

A third variant of research in this area is 'ego strength'. 'Ego strength' is the extent to which a person holds to their own beliefs and their capacity for self-regulation. Research has shown that these individuals will more often act on their own beliefs than not. A study that coupled Kohlberg's stages of development with ego strength showed that individuals with high ego strength cheated less than those with low ego strength at the same 'stage of development' (McDevitt *et al*, 2007; Trevino, 1986).

Education and gender

Socialization of an individual and its effect on moral behaviour is a theme that commenced in an earlier chapter, and recurs throughout the discussion of organizational culture. It has already been noted that there has been some uncertainty about religion influencing decisions inside the United States whereas it appears to be a factor in other countries (Wines and Napier, 1992).

Noting that the 'stages of moral development' are a cognitive function it would be expected that education would advance an individual's stage of moral development. This is reflected in increased ethical behaviour of students who experienced the 'just communities' programme discussed. There is also direct evidence that shows a correlation between the stages of development and the extent of an individual's education. There has also been evidence that ethical training increases a person's stages of development (Trevino, 1986).

In a study, a group of MBA students, taking into account factors of managerial experience, position, age, gender and the presence of a written ethics code, were tested using a series of vignettes on a seven-point Likert scale (1 being 'strongly agree' and 7 being 'strongly disagree'). The results only found a statistically significant difference in regards to gender. Females tended to have more ethical responses (Kohut and Corrigher, 1994).

Cross-cultural ethical intelligence

A relatively new development in assessing an individual's ability to manage cross-cultural situations has emerged. Referred to as Cross-Cultural Social Intelligence (CCSI) the concept refers to an individual's ability to work across cultures (Ascalon and Schleicher, 2008). CCSI was developed to assist in the management of ever-increasing exchanges of business people internationally. The researchers extracted to two dimensions that were critical:

1 Ethnocentrism; and

2 Empathy.

Ethnocentricity refers to an individual's degree of unwillingness to accept the ways of another culture; the major impediment to resolving intercultural situations. Individuals with high ethnocentric ratings view other nationalities as stereotypes and make little effort to adjust their communication style. Empathy is the level at which an individual can identify with another's situation and a fundamental of successful social intelligence. The individuals most effective in dealing with cross-cultural situations rate low in ethnocentricity and high in empathy. The researchers have developed tests to facilitate selection and training. Testing in selection assists in ensuring the correct candidates are placed. Pretesting assists in better targeting programmes to develop staff working in international roles.

Strubler *et al* (2012) also examined the cross-cultural dimension but more from a communications viewpoint. The researchers' observations were that cross-cultural problems are the result of miscommunication resulting from the fact the participants do not share the same language, background and culture. Central to their model is that values are culture based and that individuals and organizations need to work towards building a greater understanding of each other's culture; what they refer to as sharing a 'field of experience'.

Following the standard communications model (see Figure 5.1 below) the more overlap between the sender and the receiver the greater the ability to decode the message to avoid misunderstanding.

Both at an individual and organizational level improving cross-cultural interaction is not a quick process. Individuals and organizations must have a commitment to building up their understanding over time, widening the field of experience. The process includes greater focus on 'intercultural competency', reducing ethnocentricity, improving empathy, developing trust across cultural borders and knowing when to

FIGURE 5.1   Communication model

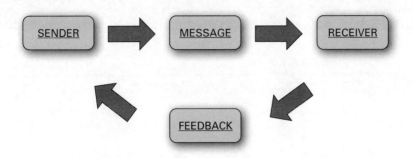

challenge a proposed solution. Importantly it means a greater engagement with not only the foreign ethical framework but with that of the company or the individual. This will allow the setting of ground rules and process between the participants. The authors of the study propose a phased approach:

Phase 1 – entering the new cultural environment, making initial engagement focusing on processes including rules to build trust and understanding between members of the group.

Phase 2 – continuing to learn about the other culture, using the ground rules established in the first stage to reconcile any differences. There is still a focus on building trust.

Phase 3 – a set of norms and objectives is established.

Phase 4 – creating a common identity and undertaking the project or work required.

This four-step process repeats itself with each new project or task, continuously building the field of experience. Success in each venture reinforces the process.

Strubler *et al* (2012) used a 'stages of development'-type approach to propose a 'Cross-Cultural Ethics Maturity' model to assess how advanced a company is in its cross-cultural ethical capability. As with the 'stages of development' models, this model sees a cumulative and hierarchical progression for companies as they move into and adapt to new cultural environments. At the first level, the company has essentially no cross-cultural ethical awareness, is ethnocentric, doesn't consider cross-cultural issues in its decisions and responds only when compelled.

Progressively moving through the levels, the company develops greater awareness, building definitions, integrating understanding across the organization, and becoming more proactive until cross-cultural considerations are part of business as usual. In a global economy a corporation that fails to recognize and learn about the values of their international employees, partners and customers is failing to realize their potential.

TABLE 5.1   Corporate cross-cultural ethical development model

Level	Stage	Features
5	Cross-cultural ethics embedded.	Cross-cultural ethics is part of organization culture.
		Business processes are aligned to account for cross-cultural ethical issues.
		The organization is forward looking, assessing foreign environments before engaging.
4	Cross-cultural ethical systems oriented.	Greater incorporation of cross-cultural ethics across the organization.
		There is a programme and mechanisms to assess progress.
		An alignment between decisions and cross-cultural ethical issues.
3	Decision-making process oriented.	Some cross-cultural ethical issue processing is specified.
		The relationship between the specialized area and other areas is specified.
		Skills and knowledge of managing cross-cultural ethical issues are maintained.
2	Capabilities oriented.	A component of organization has a specified role to be responsible for cross-cultural ethical issues.
		Knowledge is not transferred or understood across the organization.
		No leadership support.
1	Passive.	Little to no cross-cultural knowledge.
		Ethnocentric.
		Cross-cultural ethics not part of business considerations.
		Reactive only in crisis such as legal compulsion.

SOURCE: Strubler *et al* (2012)

Are there limits on the size of a cross-cultural project?

Millennium Bug

There were concerns heading into the year 2000 that the computer convention that recorded dates using the last two digits of a year (01/01/15) instead of the full four digits (01/01/2015) would cause serious issues. There was a risk that computers would consider the year 2000 to be the year 1900 and create havoc. Among the anticipated consequences was the possibility of machine failures, potentially life-threatening in aircraft. Mainly the concerns were around more pedestrian matters but nevertheless crucial to the vast worldwide computing systems such as booking, invoicing, cash transfers, accounting and other electronic data storage.

Government and private organizations across 180 countries had to work collaboratively to solve a common problem. Gigantic networks of people across borders formed to share information, ideas and solve the myriad of problems. Interestingly the dilemma did not challenge any country or company separately or differently. The Millennium Bug did not distinguish. The event was unprecedented in human history.

Two important features arose. First, the worldwide efforts to resolve the bug were so effective that there was a widespread belief that the impact had been exaggerated. Second, those involved considered that it not only resolved the problem but was a major learning in regards to working across cultures.

SOURCE: See Millennium Bug in recommended reading

Psychological theories and ethics

At the psychological level there is another theory that has strong implications for ethics. The deprivation of former benefits can lead to strong reactions. It is an important and interesting observation that people seem to dislike losing money more than they like gaining it. It explains why investors hold losing stocks, and why losing a $50 note evokes more emotion than does finding one. It also helps to explain the increase in suicide during the 1929 stock market crash.

The theory is called 'psychological reactance', and outlines '... a set of motivational consequences that can be expected to occur whenever freedoms are threatened or lost' (Brehm and Brehm, 1981). It is, in other words, a theory of motivation and behavioural control. The theory holds that people are motivated to restore their freedoms when those freedoms are threatened. The question here is, to what extent does a deprivation provoke a reaction that might transgress ethical principles?

Individuals display an astonishing variety of response to ill fortune. In any disaster – fire, flood, volcano, war, disease – there are inevitably those who risk their lives to save others and to protect property, while at the same time, and in the same population, there are those who loot and rape and destroy. There was a term, now fallen into disuse, known as 'moral insanity'. Just as there are people whose rationality is so minimal as to cause us to make the judgement of insanity, so too there are people whose moral notions are so primitive as to suggest the notion of a lack of moral intelligence.

Social

Sociobiology

There is a field of inquiry called 'sociobiology'. It may be defined as the study of the biological nature and foundations of social behaviour. This important development is still in a state of controversy, although a synthesis has been proposed (Wilson, 2000). Human sociobiology covers a diverse array of topics, such as aggression, optimal social group sizes, sex, parenting, and kin selection. Among the features sociobiology tries to explain is that of altruism.

The Darwinian emphasis on competition should be complemented by a consideration of the virtues of co-operation. There may be a biological basis for complementary altruism, just as there is a basis for biological symbiosis. Our origins as tribal entities may find expression in the way that we structure our social institutions. The small tribe had functional significance.

The optimum size of a tribe depends on whether the group is hunter-gatherer or agricultural. Notwithstanding, the group size is considerably less than that of most modern corporations. That human beings band together in groups of about 10 has its origins in optimal size for survival. Perhaps for this reason the structure of organizations reflects our social origins. It can be seen in the use of work teams in Volvo in Sweden, the departmentalizing of organizations, or the parallel but independent functioning of the various entities under the US multinational 3M banner.

One of the original expositions of sociobiology held that ethics is derived from biology. As a consequence the notion of handing over ethics to scientists was advocated. A refutation of that idea has been published by Singer (1981), who asserted sociobiology '... enables us to see ethics as a mode of human reasoning, which develops in a group context, building on more limited biologically based forms of altruism.' While sociobiology does aid our understanding of ethics it is not a sufficient explanation of them.

Formal versus informal relationships

Relationships within organizations may be formal or personal. Where they are personal there may be a conflict of interest in that personal interests may be at variance with those that benefit the organization. Office politics may cut across both of those issues. The imperative of boosting a career through administrative strategies may not be in the best interests of the organization, but is nonetheless a powerful motive. Parkinson's Law of the constant expansion of bureaucracies (with an in-group of controllers) might be an expression of our sociobiological origins (we might note that Parkinson's original law was that work expands to fill the time available).

It might be argued that relationships between individuals are the basis of all relationships; but that is to ignore the independent identity and temporal continuity of organizations. Large unions, nation states, traditional associations, and religious institutions all have an identity that is greater than any of the individuals of which they are comprised. Some organizations have a corporate culture so strong that it resists changes by individuals who wish to subvert it (old universities, for example): other organizations have so fickle a culture as to be readily subverted (such as new organizations with weak leadership).

The benefits of co-operation

Our general understanding leads us to believe in the benefits of co-operation. That intuition has been buttressed by the experimental work of Axelrod (1990). His project began with a simple question: 'When should a person co-operate, and when should a person be selfish, in an ongoing interaction with another person?' In the Axelrod studies a number of strategies were used from a variety of disciplines. The clear winner was the 'tit-for-tat' strategy (TFT).

The 'tournament' played was the 'prisoner's dilemma', which involves two players (masquerading as prisoners), each of whom has two choices (co-operate or defect). Neither player knows what the other will do. Two individuals are detained by the police and charged with a bank robbery, which carries a hefty jail sentence. There is no solid evidence, so if neither says an incriminating word, the charges will have to be reduced to that of carrying firearms, attracting a much lighter penalty. However, each is offered the chance to plea bargain – to go free by turning in the other.

Two alternatives are available to each prisoner: to co-operate, with the motive of increasing benefit to both players jointly, or to compete, so as to increase individual benefit at the expense of the other. The best individual outcome is to go free and keep the money: the worst is to be betrayed and languish in jail in the unpleasant knowledge that the other is disloyal, free and rich.

The best joint outcome (where both prisoners remain silent) is to receive a light sentence for carrying arms, but that is unstable since either individual can do better for himself by deviating (securing the best individual outcome for himself – but producing the worst individual outcome for the other). The worst joint outcome (where each betrays the other) lands them both in jail, though with a lighter sentence than a solitary burglar would receive. If both betray, then both lose – hence the dilemma. Such dilemmas clearly implicate ethical values. Thus the seeming, and real, advantage of the TFT strategy is that it is basically 'nice'. While defection receives a reaction, it is a forgiving and clear strategy. Defection yields a better immediate payoff but co-operation yields a better long-term gain.

It would seem on first reading that Axelrod has made the definitive statement, but recent work on games theory has yielded more sophisticated analysis. It is not so much that Axelrod's analysis has been proved wrong but, like so many scientific discoveries, it has now been seen to have a more circumscribed application. The 'prisoner's dilemma' is a strategy appropriate for a two-person relationship, and appropriate for many professional relationships. For this strategy to work best, a stable repetitive relationship is required.

When individuals are compelled to make decisions about people they don't know the risk is greater. Where the individuals have known each other for some time they are in a better position to take risks because they can presume the other's likely response. More complex social structures require further analysis. Those interested in more recent developments in games theory relevant to this discussion are recommended to read Ridley (1996) and the article by Majolo (2007).

The prisoner's dilemma in action

Court settlements

When a civil dispute escalates to court the participants find themselves in the 'prisoner's dilemma'. Whether the dispute is about contracts or about negligence the underlying factors are common, with each party weighing serious risks. Hiring lawyers and running matters is expensive and frequently the final cost to this might be unknown: customarily the longer a matter lasts the larger the costs grow. Importantly too, if the person or entity loses, they must pay the costs of the other side. (It should be noted that lawyers who work on a 'no win no fee' basis are only referring to their own costs, not those of the other side.)

There are a number of other factors similar to this in the system to encourage parties to come to a negotiated settlement. Litigation, especially lengthy trials, is an expense on the State so there is significant incentive for the Courts to push parties to resolve quickly. Each factor ratchets up the pressure on the individuals – big benefits if you win, huge costs if you lose.

One of the major blockers has been the culture of the legal profession in many countries (Common Law countries such as UK, United States, Canada, Australia, New Zealand) where the central underpinning is an adversarial process. The process in its purest form is about having a confrontation. It is now recognized that this is not conducive to resolving matters quickly and efficiently. Legal educators, legal societies, governments and the courts have all been looking to change the culture to first try to find a common resolution. This includes lawyers and adjudicators building relationships over time consistent with the research cited earlier.

SOURCE: See Court settlements in recommended reading

Business and the professions

The groups who may exercise, or misuse, power are the professions, the unions, social control agencies, and quasi-governmental bodies that control business. The professions have commonly operated according to their various ethical codes. Perhaps the oldest known is that in medicine (the Hippocratic Oath) discussed in detail later. Its first precept, do no harm, is a good starting point. Business is not governed by any such general code, but as noted, legislation in a number of countries has been progressively requiring greater ethical standards from large corporations.

Given that professions are governed by their respective codes, it might be believed that the professions behave more properly, but that proposition may be more apparent than real. Professions have long operated on a few rules that may not be in the public interest, such as limiting the number of members so as to ensure demand remains sufficiently high so that better remuneration can be claimed.

There is concern at present that complaints about professionals are directed towards boards consisting largely of members of the profession about which the complaint is made. Justice may be done, but may not always be seen to be done. Medical practitioners in many places may charge what they like rather than be contained by law as a means of protecting the financially vulnerable.

Some boards have required the participation of a lay member who will represent the interests of consumers. Clearly there are similarities and differences between professional codes and business codes. Both, however, require such features as safety, honesty, the preservation of human dignity, loyalty and honour.

Physical factors

Brain evolution and ethics

One of the curiosities of biology is that of the human brain. Where most structures are modified into new structures (as the eye evolved from a light-sensitive area of skin to the focusing colour-sensitive organ it is now), the brain has evolved in a different way.

MacLean (1990) has pointed out that the 'old' (reptilian) brain remains and has an added 'mid-brain' (primitive mammal). In turn the 'mid-brain' remains and has an added higher order 'fore-brain'. Each of these structures retains its original function, but the function of one part is sometimes at odds with that of another. The warring impulses emanating from these different neural structures become what we perceive as conflicts, inconsistencies, and the difficulties of ethical judgements.

That the three brains retain much of their original function may, according to Koestler, be the origin of human aggression and inconsistency. To use his graphic illustration, a psychotherapist talking to a client is simultaneously addressing a crocodile, a horse and a human being (Koestler, 1967).

Environmental factors

Aspects of the environment worthy of comment include noise, air pollution, crime rates and a feeling of safety: studies on subjects such as these form a useful counterpoint to sociological, psychological and legal approaches. One issue of common knowledge is the effect that temperature has on mood. Other environmental factors include noise, barometric pressure, wind, rain, humidity, ozone, the quality of the light, and hours of sunlight per day. At the Dead Sea the air contains bromide leached into it by evaporation. The resultant combination of warmth and a calming agent may have something to do with its popularity as a holiday resort.

The climatic variable that seems to have received much attention is the wind. In many parts of the world it is given a special name – the 'sirocco', the 'mistral', the 'hamsin', the 'chinook', the 'monsoon'. Folklore notes a relationship between wind and mood; it may be remembered from schooldays how a windy day will bring about a corresponding boisterous reaction in children, and those who have dealt with horses will know how disturbing a wind is to their mood.

Diet

Dietary factors are also known to affect mood. These factors include vitamin deficiency, allergies, aberrant metabolism, and the psychologically destabilizing effects of some food additives (such as dyes and flavour enhancers). The damaging effect of monosodium glutamate (MSG) on certain individuals is well known. Yet other dietary preferences appear implicated in behaviour. Behavioural disorders can stem from mercury, carbon disulphide and thallium poisoning. These chemicals are also known to aggravate epilepsy.

Deviant behaviour may also stem from abnormal mineral levels; high levels of lead and cadmium, and low levels of potassium and sodium also tend to be associated with undesirable behaviour. One of the best-researched areas of food intake and behaviour disorders is that of the control of hyperactive children. This work originated with Feingold (1976), who showed that many children who were diagnosed as hyperactive were suffering from a reaction to damaging food additives. He showed that many troubled children could be helped by the elimination of certain additives from their diet. Conversely, behaviour and intellectual capacity – and health problems – may be affected by the absence of some substances. The disinhibiting effects of alcohol are well known. One of the best-known effects of intake (or lack of intake) is that of iodine deficiency, which may produce mental retardation.

In a review of nutrition and IQ, a psychologist reached the general conclusion that both mood changes and performance may be affected by nutrition (Wright, 1992).

Summary of physical factors

This array of evidence is sufficiently persuasive for us to be alert to the effects of physical factors on mood state. We know that certain psychotropic medications are prescribed to change mood state. Among the effects they can produce are changed dispositions to others and to events. Since mood and attitude are so closely related, and assuming that the disposition to ethical stances is mood related, the physical factors discussed may affect ethical judgement.

Conclusion

This chapter closes the examination of three major topic groups of research and analysis into global ethical decision making: national culture and environment issues, organizational culture issues, and factors impacting the individual. The research and analysis in this chapter provides a comprehensive insight into the forces working on the individual's decision making in the organizational context. Again it is important to note the interactive and dynamic nature of these components. This chapter, like Chapters 3 and 4, underpins the discussion of ways of improving corporate culture and ethical decision making in Chapters 8 and 9.

This chapter also looked at additional social factors such as strength of the organization's identity, the benefits of co-operation, physical factors and professional ethical codes. This chapter concludes Part One: The necessity, justification and research into cross-cultural business ethics. The following part looks at the theoretical issues in business ethics.

Focus questions

Individual factors in business ethics

1 What are Kohlberg's stages of moral development?

2 In making ethical decisions, what role does personal experience play? What processes have been identified?

3 What role does education play?

4 What does the term 'field of experience' mean and why is it important to companies operating in another country?

5 What does 'ethnocentricity' mean and why is it important for companies to be aware of it?

6 What are the psychological factors important to ethics?

7 Does a company have an identity? If yes, what types are there and why does it matter?

8 What is the prisoner's dilemma? What does it tell us about co-operation?

9 Do professional codes have something to add to ethical codes for businesses?

10 What are the physical factors that impact behaviour and why?

CASE STUDY   Bending the rules

Debbie is chairing a selection committee. At the end of the process there are two candidates who are closely rated. An internal candidate well referred by his manager, who is also Debbie's manager, and an external candidate with a disability that involves a stuttering speech impediment. The candidate with the disability is marginally better in Debbie's opinion. Significantly Debbie has a very strong personal belief that not enough is done to level the playing field for disabilities. The impediment is not something that staff could not work with but it would require some effort. Debbie's company specifically advertises itself as an Equal Opportunity employer. The other members of the committee are split on the decision and it is effectively Debbie's to make.

What should Debbie decide?

Would Debbie's answer be different if the disabled candidate was clearly superior?

Would Debbie's answer be different if her manager informally expressed serious reservations?

What if the disability was depression (a non-visible condition) – would her answer be different?

Factors to consider

Equal Opportunity laws speak in absolutes but the reality of the global workplace is that there is an infinity of grey where the law cannot resolve matters. Similarly there are internal codes that speak to how staff should behave, but like the laws they do not always provide answers, however much their authors might think they do. Worse, a strictly followed process may produce a disastrous answer.

The informal networks within organizations provide rumour and innuendo but they can also provide critical information. Would, for example, you select a person you knew to be a troublemaker simply because there was no evidence on paper that would allow you to formalize that? Or would you find another way? Corporate officers are frequently in this position and often stretch formal rules.

Debbie could look to her own value system and make the decision in favour of the disabled candidate. Everyone comes to the workplace with beliefs, as has been noted in this chapter; is it invalid to not apply those values? Equity is an important value to have in the business world today but is her belief a 'conflict of interest' in its own right, skewing her assessment? Is it fair to impose your own values on work colleagues? What if Debbie found that instead of a disability she was interviewing a fundamentalist whose religious beliefs, in Debbie's opinion, were oppressive of women? Would that change the decision-making process? What weight should she give her own values? Is there something she could do to be more neutral in the situation?

Many companies have clearly defined job selection processes that are designed to ensure that company officers do not breach certain standards. Importantly these processes limit what is to be considered. However, if a strict adherence to these principles produces a bad outcome, should Debbie override the rules? If so what would the new considerations be?

1   Should she look to the welfare of the disabled candidate? What if she could see that the work environment would be toxic for them? Or the equipment was insufficient?

(Many companies 'talk the talk' on disability but don't provide the necessary equipment.)

2   Should she look to the impact on other stakeholders, the people that the candidate would have to work with? Is that right? If inconvenience to colleagues was a factor then there would be very little reform or progress in the workplace.

3   Should she speak to her manager?

Recommended reading

Court settlements

Chaffey, C (2011, June) Tough guy lawyers impeding ADR, *Lawyers Weekly* [online] http://www.lawyersweekly.com.au/news/8580-Tough-guy-lawyers-impeding-ADR

Rau, A S (2012) The Culture of American arbitration and the lessons of ADR, *Texas International Law Journal*, **40**, pp 449–535 [online] http://www.tilj.org/content/journal/40/num3/Rau449.pdf?origin=publication_detail

Konosuke Matsushita

The Founder Konosuke Matsushita (nd) *Panasonic* [online] http://panasonic.net/history/founder/

Economist (2009, July) Guru: Konosuke Matsushita, *TheEconomist* [online] http://www.economist.com/node/14117858

Millennium Bug

Anbari, F T, Khilkhanova, E V, Romanova, M V and Umpleby, S A (2003) Cross-cultural differences and their implications for managing international projects, *George Washington University* [online] http://www.gwu.edu/~umpleby/recent_papers/2003_cross_cultural_differences_managin_international_projects_anbari_khilkhanova_romanova_umpleby.htm

Y2K (2014, January) *Encyclopaedia Britannica* [online] http://www.britannica.com/EBchecked/topic/382740/Y2K-bug

PART TWO
Theoretical issues in business ethics

Theoretical approaches

06

Introduction

This chapter commences Part Two: Theoretical issues in business ethics, and will cover an overview of the main philosophical concepts that underpin ethics and major issues with their application. This chapter will also discuss the importance of excellence and its role within an ethical framework. Understanding these elements will equip persons to analyse ethical problems, and understand and apply ethical codes in the international environment, themes that will be developed throughout Part Three.

Key learning points

This chapter will discuss the nature of ethics and the key principles. It will then specifically examine theories of morality:

- Deontology.

- Utilitarianism and Act Utilitarianism.

- Confucianism.

- Virtue ethics.

- God's ordinances.

- Kant.

This chapter then discusses the naturalistic fallacy.
    Finally we will address excellence and its role in ethics. Specifically these are:

- Excellence in Western values.

- Ethics as part of the judgement of excellence.

- Excellence is positive and profitable.

The nature of ethics

Ethics may be regarded as knowing what is right, doing what is right, and feeling what is right; morals and ethics share these features. The terms ethics and morals are sometimes used interchangeably, although there are distinctions. 'Morals' refers to the standards held by the community, often in a form not explicitly articulated. 'Ethics', on the other hand, concerns explicit codes of conduct as well as value systems. Further, ethics has restricted application (as in legal ethics, medical ethics, etc). Not being a member of a profession exempts a person from being bound by that particular code.

A useful definition in this context is that ethics is a highly explicit codified form of behaviour designed to produce particular ends and act in accordance with particular values. There are values that are not directly matters of ethics (such as wealth or success); there are other values that are of direct concern (such as honesty or fairness).

How ethics relates to life's values has been a debated subject from Plato to existentialism. An examination of this search for meaning and value finds expression in every age. Living ethically may consist either of following a set of rules, or the precepts of an organization; or it may consist in reflecting on how to live, and then acting in accordance with the conclusions that are reached. This latter view is not about ethical absolutes, but rather about acting reflectively and with consideration.

There is, of course, an extensive theoretical background to speculation about ethical rules, the best-known principle being that of the 'golden rule' (do to others as you would have them do unto you). In order for such a principle to be acceptable it should be of universal application across every conceivable situation. This is more difficult than it sounds. For example, if a masochist were to act according to this principle, that person would consider it a duty to inflict harm on others in the expectation that everyone would receive pleasure from it.

The 'Darwinian' justification, the 'survival of the fittest', given frequently by business people for their questionable actions is a corporate equivalent. The phrase implies that they hand out the treatment that they themselves expect to receive.

Those who derive pleasure and benefit from adhering to fundamentalist religious doctrines might wish to coerce others to believe the same. To invite is one thing; to coerce is another. In a pluralist society coercion is unacceptable because the accepted freedoms include those of being free from duress to accept ideas that they find disagreeable. The issue is one of personal utility rather than one of concern for universal value. In essence it is a preventive rather than punitive approach. A variation of the philosopher Rousseau's doctrine might be regarded as an improvement: 'Do what is good for you with the least possible harm to others.'

TABLE 6.1   Ethics and morals

Ethics	Morals
An explicit code of conduct (incorporating a value system) with application to a particular group or to special circumstances	The standards of the community often implied

Ethical principles and exceptions

One of the key conceptual divisions in ethical analysis is between Deontology and Consequentialism. Deontology is a philosophy that specifies that the rightness of behaviour is in the act itself; for example 'a person should never lie'. Thus we might say that Deontology concerns duties. The outcome is less of an issue. Consequentialism is the reverse; the rightness of the act is not the important issue but rather the result, for example 'a lie is acceptable even desirable if it produces the right outcome'.

Philosophical theories can be said to fall under each of these categories. It is extremely difficult to formulate an ethical principle for which there isn't an exception. It can be debated whether or not ethical principles ought to be judged by their consequences and ignore the motivation. Similarly normative ethics attempts to set ethical standards (or norms) for conduct but this ignores intent. Ethical codes are designed to produce particular ends but, just as importantly, they are also designed to tell us how to behave.

TABLE 6.2   Deontology and consequentialism

Deontology	Consequentialism
Behaviour is assessed by the act itself; eg it is wrong to lie, steal or kill	Behaviour is assessed by the consequences; a lie may be justifiable

Theories of morality

The essence of an ideological view is that all 'facts' are interpreted in a manner consistent with the underlying world view, for example fundamentalist religious views or rigid adherence to laissez-faire economic principles. This kind of approach to ethics is unlikely to lead to a commonly accepted frame of reference. For that same reason the notion of professional ethics having the perspective of Kant, Mill or G E Moore is unlikely. What is more likely is that we take from such theories those elements that would add to our understanding.

Deontology

Deontology, as noted above, is essentially concerned with duties. It requires a commitment by the individual to the ethical act. Duties are not in the abstract but, rather, towards some person, group or idea. In hierarchical form they range from duty to self, to family, to local community, to the nation and to humanity; they also range from the intensely personal to conforming to an ideal.

It is also to be noted that Deontology does not specify which moral principles are to be adopted. The derivation of the word is 'deon' (duty) and logos (a discourse upon). In essence its view is that there are not specific moral principles that must be followed, rather it obliges individuals to 'do their duty'.

A problem with deontology is that it is not possible to specify what exactly a person's duties and moral obligations are, only that actions are to be judged by the intention.

Utilitarianism and Act Utilitarianism

One doctrine could be that pleasure or happiness should be the goal ('hedonism'); however, what if an action were to produce happiness in some and unhappiness in others? Is the happiness of the greatest number a better criterion? This form (greatest happiness of the greatest number) is known as Utilitarianism.

Utilitarianism is the most recognized form of consequentialism and derives from John Stuart Mill. Mill was a 19th-century thinker who was both philosopher and social reformer and who wrote two influential classic books, which covered four areas: logic, political economy, liberalism and ethics. His books, *On Liberty* and *Utilitarianism*, are still widely cited in political and ethical debates. The central thesis in *On Liberty* is that the only justifiable reason for interfering with the liberty of action of any mature person is to prevent harm to other people. The central theses of *Utilitarianism* are that happiness is the highest good, that there are lower and higher types of happiness, and that there are individual people as well as groups of people such as associations and societies. States should aim to maximize the best happiness of the greatest number of people.

Among the supposed weaknesses of Mill's political and ethical accounts is the difficulty his two theories have in avoiding collision. It is not hard to imagine cases where reducing the freedom of some individuals would increase the happiness of a much larger number of people. This difficulty of failing to give due recognition to the rights of minorities might be regarded as a significant weakness in ethical theory. The lesser numerically is not the lesser morally.

Act Utilitarianism involves a commitment to impartial universal benevolence. It is an account of ethics that holds that an action is morally right if it produces at least as much happiness as any other act that a person could perform. It will be seen that it goes only part way to satisfy the concerns justifiably levelled at conventional Utilitarianism.

TABLE 6.3 Utilitarianism and Act Utilitarianism

Utilitarianism	Act Utilitarianism
The act should do the greatest good for the greatest number	The act should produce at least as much good as any other choice

Confucianism

One of the earliest bases of ethics was that of Confucianism. Confucian ethics is not one of prudence, but rather of behaviour appropriate to relationships. The essence of Confucianism is the respect for tradition and the preservation of traditional relationships. According to one article the best translation is that of 'sincerity' (Windt *et al*, 1989). Individual behaviour must be appropriate to the specific relationship, and thus optimize the benefit to both parties.

Chan (2008) addressed the parallels and differences between Confucian ethics and contemporary (largely Western) business ethics. Despite the parallels between Western ethics and Confucian ethics we should note the latter's 'emphasis upon hierarchy, Guanxi (see text box following), social traditions, and harmony' and 'focus upon the concrete individual moral actor rather than the metaphysical self'.

Understanding Chinese business

Guanxi

Any business person dealing with China or Chinese communities should be aware of the term 'Guanxi'. It is Confucian in origin and its *prima facie* meaning is the relationships a person has. It has, however, a much greater cultural meaning than that. Guanxi is the cultivation of a personal network who mutually support one another. It may not even be spoken but understood that the people in your relationship network will take your interests into account when making decisions.

At its core is an exchange of favours; if a person needs something done he can call upon another who is part of his network to expedite it, whether access to materials, money needed on short notice, or better treatment at an hotel. Like a bank account, the more favours you perform for someone the more they are indebted to you. It is considered the height of social impropriety to refuse a request if you are a person within Guanxi.

While it is not difficult to see how this principle would have advantages, it is also not difficult to see how Guanxi can collide with Western principles. How would a Western company react if a Chinese partner purchased a product of lesser quality and greater expense to satisfy Guanxi?

Similarly, it is not difficult to see how a 'boiling frog' scenario (as noted in an earlier case study) could evolve in the Guanxi scenario. Minor favours build to major favours then minor improprieties into major criminal acts. The indebted person might find themselves too deeply committed to withdraw from the situation.

SOURCE: See Guanxi in recommended reading

Virtue ethics

Originally expressed in Aristotle's *Nicomachean Ethics*, 'virtue ethics' denotes that human nature is characterized by aim. The most important one of those is to aim at 'the good'. It is thus that virtue ethics may be seen as being governed by ends to be achieved. According to Aristotle a person's 'soul' is divided into two parts – the rational and the irrational.

The rational part is characterized by the intellectual virtues such as logic, evaluation and mathematics whereas the irrational part is characterized by desires and wants. Rather than trying to reduce morals to rights and wrongs the Aristotelean view prefers to cultivate the virtuous individual. Important here is that seeking 'the good' is for character training, for others, and for the body civic.

For Aristotle a person without high moral values was not to be admired. There are ample examples to draw from in our own time – dictators, corrupt politicians and cheating business people. On the other hand there are those who have lives dedicated to the loving service of others. The psychopathy exhibited by some in the community is a counterpoint to the altruism displayed by others. It may be relatively common to distinguish one from the other. Saints, both religious and secular, act as an inspiration, and are accorded acclaim and cited as role models.

This may seem to be an obvious point but it was not so in Ancient Greece. Aristotle was the outlier trying to persuade the population to take a different view of the world. The mass of Ancient Greeks were focused on appearance rather than substance. It was believed that to be attractive was a blessing from the gods and conferred on you great wisdom. Therefore the good looking of the community held a belief that not only were they attractive but clever and chosen to be so by the heavens (Hughes, 2015).

It might be considered that people use virtue, morality, and ethics as though they formed a hierarchy, with virtue being at the top of the pyramid. That notion is akin to Maslow's Hierarchy of Needs (see text box following), and has the same problem. It could be noted of the Maslow analysis that a person does not need to satisfy basic needs before moving to higher needs. People will sacrifice their lives for an ideal, without any lower need being gratified. In a similar vein a person might be virtuous even though it is significantly detrimental to their own interests.

The term 'virtue' does not have sufficient meaning in itself. The dictionary definition of 'moral excellence or goodness' tells us little. A more analytical appraisal would include:

- moral virtues (such as honesty and decency);
- intellectual virtues (such as intelligence and curiosity);
- communal virtues (such as charity and respect for others); and
- political virtues (such as a respect for law and a belief in the common good).

This is analysed in much the same way as the Maslow Hierarchy of Needs, where lower order needs are satisfied before higher order needs are considered. In assessing political morality the electorate first judges the legislature by considering the provision of basic services (such as civil service or social welfare). When those needs are perceived to be satisfied then the electorate considers other issues such as social direction.

What motivates people?

Maslow's Hierarchy of Needs

Maslow was interested in motivation, what drives people to do the things they do. He conceptualized that there was an order to human need and that each had to be satisfied before moving up to the next level. At the bottom we find our biological needs: food, water, sleep, warmth. Once these basic needs are met human beings turn their minds to safety which includes shelter, a community of stability and so forth up the ladder. Although as noted in the text above the model is limited.

The hierarchy has been modified a number of times over the years but the underlying principle is the same: meet the need, move up to the next level.

Maslow's original Hierarchy of Needs is set out below:

1   Biological needs.

2   Safety.

3   Love and belonging (friends, relationships, intimacy).

4   Esteem (having a sense that you are valued in the community).

5   Self-actualization (deep self-fulfilment, looking for development).

Unsurprisingly Maslow's hierarchy has had significant traction in human resources and management circles. Businesses are keen to attract and retain quality staff as well as get the most from them. In most professional organizations the fundamentals like a living wage and safe working environment are presumed (but should always be remembered). Most of these organizations are looking to motivate their staff by appealing to those higher levels, giving staff a sense of worth and opportunity to develop.

Importantly though, it must be remembered that Maslow is not always completely correct. Persons can enter in and out of the hierarchy at different levels, not being dependent on satisfying the level below. For example, starving individuals sacrificing themselves for others.

SOURCE: See Maslow's Hierarchy of Needs in recommended reading

God's ordinances

There are some poor bases for ethical systems; one basis is that the rules should be founded on God's ordinances. The difficulty here is that God's ordinances are interpreted differently by different people. Because of such inconsistencies the perceived ordinance may be no guide at all. Here the problem is whether or not good and evil lie within our nature. In the 4th century a moral debate was entered between Bishop Augustine and a Romano-British monk, Pelagius. The former held that the inclination to evil is inherent in human nature; the latter that evil was self and situationally determined. By and large the former view prevailed. While the argument for the perfectibility of human nature (as by Rousseau, and by the Fabians) is difficult to demonstrate, it is a doctrine of hope.

Kant

By way of contrast it is noted that, according to Kant, morality consists not in the result but rather in the intention (whatever the result). Kant is therefore taking a Deontological approach. Specifically his principle is known as the 'categorical imperative', and may be called the imperative of morality. Right action, so Kant argued, is not based on intuition or inclination but rather is based on law determined by reason. The human conceptual apparatus may know its form and limits; knower and known are interdependent. In essence his view is that an action involving morality should be treated as though the instigator would like it to be a universal principle (Kant, 1971; 1998).

Bases of ethical theories

There are seemingly different principles from which we may derive morality. One of these is the intention that lies behind our ethical decisions; another is concern with the rules of conduct, ways of behaving and methods of procedure. The results we desire may come from ethical intention, or from following specific processes. An ideal system would have both of these criteria acting in harmony.

The naturalistic fallacy

The naturalistic fallacy is the supposed error of proceeding from factual statements – assertions about what is – to value statements about what ought to be. Thus a description of what Members of Parliament do is quite different from statements about what they ought to do; what drug dealers do is by no means the same as what they ought to do. To emphasize, it cannot be known what should be done from looking at what is done. An additional framework is needed.

Some moral philosophers have tried to bridge that gap by appealing to intuitions about what they take to be moral reality, while others have argued that the distinction is often bogus since many important terms such as 'enjoys', 'needs', and 'suffers', may be both factually true and morally significant. What is important here is to be cautious about moving readily from an 'is' to an 'ought'. Political correctness, often the enemy of ethics and of democracy, frequently confounds these prescriptive and descriptive modes in setting restrictions to what is and what ought to be.

Excellence

A characteristic of excellent professionals is that they feel they live in an imperfect world; things are rarely as good as they should be. Given the frailties of human nature, the demands of time and of competing values, the solutions to almost all problems are less than perfect. Modern professionals of quality frequently experience a phenomenon labelled 'imposter syndrome'. It is the idea that somehow the individual has achieved a position that they are not entitled to, that they are a fraud. There is an ever-present sense that they will be found out. Their self-perceived inadequacies will become evident to the external critic.

This is not an issue for those that are less skilled; they commonly have a strong belief that they hold abilities not reflected in their skills or outcomes, much to the frustration of those around them. An essential precondition of intellectual or artistic excellence is the vision to see how things might be – to have an insight into ways of doing things better, of perceiving failings, and the power to persuade others.

This power to persuade may need to be exercised in the face of determined resistance – the will to go ahead despite powerful opposition. With such a view goes what seems a paradoxical humility. Knowing how things ought to be induces in first-rate professionals the idea that they must cope in a flawed world. This imperfection may be seen as something that invites adverse judgement. Exactly who is to bring judgement, or why such a judgement might be brought, is not fully explained. It is the sense of imperfection that lies at the heart of the concern.

Lesser operators do not seem to be troubled by the notion of imperfection, and that may be the core of the issue. As was noted earlier in the text, pragmatic managers are preferred by workplaces; it is not difficult to understand why corporations prefer people who can get things done. This should not presuppose that most managers are unethical, it is that their values are strained and tested. It is a constant struggle for individuals in leadership positions who must compromise to keep the wheels of their particular industry turning.

There are a few who, mainly through circumstance, find themselves acting in an extremely unethical way. However, the majority recognize a sense of scale, know what fights are worth having and maintain an equilibrium between what they believe and what they must do. In the imperfect world good managers do what they can, take strategic approaches and move their organizations towards desired behaviours. Poor managers accept or can't see what is inappropriate conduct and take no or wrong action.

The search for perfection is evident in many cultures, and exists within our framework of dreams and aspirations. It has found expression in that near-formless yearning for the 'golden age'. The commitment to total quality management (TQM) and best international practice is an expression of that idea, transferred to the business context. There is no doubt that quality sells goods and services, and benefits an organization in the longer term.

This interest in corporate performance has predominately been driven by commercial imperatives. As competition increases so too does the need to strive for excellence. It is curious that we expect, and get, total quality management in symphony orchestras (no sour notes, excellent performance, prompt starting, etc). Why can we not get the same from car repair garages, computer technicians, and airlines? Perhaps it is the 'luxury' nature of the product that demands such quality; people would not otherwise pay such money for a non-necessity.

The importance of excellence

Harley-Davidson

The Harley-Davidson Motorcycle Corporation had been a market leader but, after a dysfunctional takeover, quality fell; new bikes were known to leak oil on showroom floors. In the face of this poor quality and the growing competition from Japanese manufacturers, by the early 1980s it appeared that the company was heading towards liquidation. A group of executives who were committed to the product and its loyal customer base bought the company out and negotiated a five-year import duty with the US government to buy time.

Taking their lead from the Japanese manufacturers they then focused the corporate culture on excellence. They introduced several new strategies such as 'Just-in-Time' stock; by keeping only what was needed a defect in a part could be spotted before it was installed in hundreds or thousands of units. Employee involvement was also a key. Blue collar workers were empowered and had an equal say in how changes to the production line would be introduced and the right to stop the line if a fault was detected.

So successful was their rehabilitation of the company that they requested that the government lift the tariff restriction a full one year before it was due to expire.

SOURCE: See Harley-Davidson in recommended reading

Excellence and Western values

We might ask the pertinent question as to whether or not Western values are consistent with the search for excellence. Cormack (1991) concluded that there is such a set of values, and identifies them as inherently valuing humanity, both in what it is and in its potential. Completing something worthwhile entails fulfilment. As Cormack put it:

> The importance of service. This is not only service to customers, it is service to all: customers, neighbours, subordinates, etc. It is better to give than to receive; performance is judged by the stewardship of assets.

It might seem that these values are more philanthropic than commercial. Cormack argued that it is only by the adoption of these wider community values that we can become excellent.

Ethics as part of the judgement of excellence

In most professional work excellence is judged, in part, by the ethical codes. However, excellence is more easily recognized than codified. It is seen as a journey as well as a destination; a process as well as an achievement. As Peters and Austin so aptly put it, 'excellence happens when high purpose and pragmatism meet' (Peters and Austin, 1985). Judgements are not made on single issues, but on overall evaluation. The difference between legendary businessmen like Mr Matsushita and others is that the former have a broader vision, substantial confidence in their own insight, a constructive approach, and a moral tone to their views and behaviour.

The judgement of how well such criteria have been satisfied must be left to those fitted to judge. Exactly who such judges are is a matter for debate. It may be that outsiders are best equipped: pilots may not be the best judges of aircraft design; vignerons not the best judges of wine; nor surgeons the best judges of the desirability of surgery. There are some forms of professionalism in which sheer competence and artistry are sufficient; musicianship, for example. In most forms of professionalism, however, values become significant.

We do not accord to dictators the notion of excellence, despite their efficiency, dedication and list of accomplishments. Those to whom we accord excellence have acted according to commonly accepted ethical standards. Over recent decades various theories of management have as one of their unstated, perhaps even unrecognized tenets, the search for more ethical ways of doing things. Team work theories, theory X and theory Y, primary social motives, and the application of Swedish and Japanese methods have a common motivation.

Excellence is positive and profitable

Excellence is construed in the positive rather than the negative sense. It is worth noting that the corporations on the Peters and Waterman criteria of excellence were also market leaders in their respective and diverse fields. Excellence, including ethical excellence, is clearly profitable. In order to achieve potential, some values need to be emphasized and these include:

- personal worth and self-esteem based on the uniqueness, significance and importance of the individual;

- loving our neighbours, esteeming them and promoting their growth and well-being rather than pursuing our own interests at the expense of those around us;

- community and the responsibility of businesses to take the social and human dimension into their areas of shareholder accountability;

- personal and corporate vision and the importance of our personal and corporate responsibility for tomorrow as well as for today (Peters and Waterman, 1982).

The conclusion drawn here is that the presence of excellence can be recognized, but often there is a doubt as to whether a quantified judgement can be made. Excellence is both an achievement and a form of dedication, perhaps of passion.

Although it is not possible to pronounce upon all of its attributes, it might best be captured by the notion that excellence is a process as well as an achievement; ethics is one of the travel documents, as well as the destination. Various levels of explanation might be offered to account for ethical stances. These range from the physical, through the psychological and social, to the anthropological. Further, the explanations may be of practical or of religious account. What follows is essentially of a practical and empirical nature.

Conclusion

This chapter has provided an overview of the main philosophical theories that form the basis of understanding ethical frameworks. In particular it looked at the major Western and Eastern theories of morality that have been developed over the last three millennia. We then discussed how these theories relate to ethics and some of the main issues that need to be taken into account. Finally we looked at the notion of excellence and its importance to ethical theory. This chapter continues the process of building the picture so that people can better resolve ethical problems as well as developing and embedding ethical codes and culture in the global economy.

Focus questions

Ethical theory

1   What is the difference between morality and ethics?

2   What is Deontology? How would you distinguish it from Consequentialism?

3   What is Utilitarianism? How would you distinguish it from Act Utilitarianism?

4   What is Guanxi? How does it relate to Confucianism?

5   What are virtue ethics?

6   What are the limitations of using 'ordinances of God'?

7   Is Kant's theory consequentialist? If not, why not?

8   What is the naturalistic fallacy?

9   How would you describe excellence? Why is it important to ethics?

10   Why is excellence important to business?

CASE STUDY   Which values take precedence?

Brian is an expatriate manager working in Shanghai and is in the process of approving the contract for a new recruit. On reviewing the paperwork he notes that the recommended candidate is not the most qualified. He calls the local assistant manager who is a Chinese national to ask for further information. The assistant manager uncharacteristically provides vague and unsatisfying answers to Brian's questions. Frustrated, Brian says that he is unwilling to sign the contract and asks the recommendation be changed to another candidate.

The assistant manager is clearly agitated and suggests that it is likely to have negative consequences for the company. He explains that the recommended candidate is the son of an important business partner of the company, and that by not selecting this candidate it would likely be difficult to do business, not only with the candidate's father's company but with a number of other companies. Brian, and therefore his company, would be seen to be disrespectful of the locals and their business culture.

What action should Brian take?

Factors to consider

Brian's own cultural beliefs would suggest that what is being proposed is improper. At his head office the selection process is strictly merit based; however, he is now confronted with the prospect of seriously damaging his company in an important market if he ignores local custom.

Brian could take a Deontological approach, look to his own values, supported by his own company's policies and overturn the assistant manager's decision. He could request guidance from his head office about what action to take. Brian may have shifted the risk but then the situation is no longer in his control. There is an attendant risk with asking the question formally or even informally when the answer is uncertain because he will be bound by the answer.

In the alternative he could take a Utilitarian approach and ask what will give the best outcome. The factors he might consider are:

- the interests of the candidate who is the best qualified and whether it is unfair to deny them the opportunity;

- his company's reputation in this market place and the harm that might occur to their local reputation;

- the reputation of the assistant manager; refusing the recommendation could mean a significant 'loss of face';

- his own 'loss of face' in the local business community;

- the immediate commercial harm that may occur to the company;

- if he were to approve the assistant manager's recommendation what harm might come if it were discovered and reported to head office;

- giving way this time to allow himself the opportunity to develop a strategy;

- the damage to his career if a successful overseas operation is significantly damaged;

- the action of refusing the recommendation might send a message that he (and the company) were operating to a merit system and that this might ultimately in the long term be a better business strategy (the message going to both the local staff and the rest of the business community).

The important point to make is that this is a significant failing of a corporation to have put Brian in this situation. An ethically cross-culturally aware organization should have ensured that there was a process in place. A code of conduct and supporting rules should have been mutually developed so that there was not a clash between the corporate values and Guanxi. This, however, does not help Brian; like many executives, he is caught between the proverbial 'rock and the hard place' and his career most likely rides on the decision.

Recommended reading

Guanxi

Hope, K (2014, October) Doing business the Chinese way, *BBC News (Business)* [online] http://www.bbc.com/news/business-29524701

Los Angeles Chinese Learning Center (nd) Chinese business culture: Guanxi, an important Chinese business element, Los Angeles Chinese Learning Centre [online] http://chinese-school.netfirms.com/guanxi.html

World Learner Chinese (nd) What is Guanxi? World Learner Chinese [online] http://www.worldlearnerchinese.com/content/what-guanxi

Harley-Davidson

Bieber, S (1988) Harley is 'a classic turnaround story' Executive Interview Vaughn Beals, Harley-Davidson Inc, *The Morning Call* [online] http://articles.mcall.com/1988-04-18/business/2634587_1_harley-dealers-american-motorcycle-manufacturer-big-motorcycles

Gross, D *et al* (nd) The turnaround at Harley-Davidson, from Forbes Greatest Business Stories of All Time [online] http://www.uic.edu.hk/~kentsang/powerst/forbes-The%20Turnaround%20at%20Harley-Davidson.pdf

Imposter syndrome

Burkeman, O (2013, November) This column will change your life: do you feel like a fraud? *Guardian* [online] http://www.theguardian.com/lifeandstyle/2013/nov/09/impostor-syndrome-oliver-burkeman

Maslow's Hierarchy of Needs

Cherry, K (nd) Maslow's Hierarchy of Needs, *About Education* [online]
    http://psychology.about.com/od/theoriesofpersonality/ss/maslows-needs-hierarchy.htm
Maslow's Hierarchy of Needs (nd) *NetMBA Business Knowledge Centre* [online]
    http://www.netmba.com/mgmt/ob/motivation/maslow/
Maslow's Hierarchy of Needs (undated) *Businessballs* [online] http://www.businessballs.com/
    maslow.htm

Legal aspects of ethics

07

Introduction

Throughout the text there has been frequent discussion about the law and ethics, most notably the idea that many business people and commentators have a belief that morals are not the concern of business. They see it as the responsibility of the civil authorities to make laws to regulate the community. Throughout the text, the argument that this is unreasonable and unsustainable has been a principal theme, which will be further developed in this chapter. It will look more closely at the relationship between the law and ethics. They are closely related yet serve different purposes. They inform each other on content; for example, when there is a view that something should be formally regulated, any codes of conduct might be used as a starting point. As noted in Chapter 1, codes and ethical behaviour have been progressively given greater legal weight in recent years.

In the global economy we see the law and ethics wrestling with similar issues; laws from different jurisdictions and ethical codes from different cultures may clash or not connect. How can these parallel systems be reconciled? Persons reviewing ethical scenarios often take note of legal principles, such as 'natural justice' in determining a matter. Lawyers often have cause to look to ethical codes to assess whether conduct is reasonable or not, for example when looking at the duty of care owed in negligence matters.

This chapter also provides foundations for developing codes and resolving ethical issues as discussed in Chapters 8 and 9.

Key learning points

This chapter will discuss the relationship between morals and the law. Specifically, it will address:

- Is there a role for morality in business or does the sole responsibility rest with lawmakers?
- The relationship between informal and formal codes.
- The Hart-Devlin debate.
- The difference between complying with the law and complying with an ethical code.
- Natural justice.

This chapter then looks at commonalities between law and ethics, addressing:

- The difference between hard and soft law.
- Legal pluralism.

Finally this chapter will address the relationship between ethical codes and the law, specifically:

- The legal weight of codes.
- Ethics as contract.
- Self-regulation.

Legal or moral?

Is there a role for morality in business or is it the responsibility of the law alone to regulate business behaviour? In earlier discussions it has been noted that businesses quite frequently resorted to the argument that they were acting within the law. As has also been noted previously the well-known economist Milton Friedman argued that there is no role for morality in business, which is another way of saying that the only obligation that a company has is to operate within the law. Any line of reasoning that delegates the responsibility for morality to civil authority is problematic.

First, this notion presumes that the law is comprehensive. The law does not and cannot be expected to keep up with every nuance and change in human activity, particularly in an age of rapidly accelerating technology. The practice of using 'precedent', the decision of an earlier judge being applied to a different case with a similar fact situation, is recognition by the system that knowing and accounting for every situation in advance is not feasible. This is not to say that the law doesn't develop principles that can assist in the development of rules to help govern the society. It is to say that human interaction and commerce is complex and dynamic. Legislators and judges, even using the precedent system, cannot be expected to know it all.

Second, the notion presumes that the law is current. Even where a problem is recognized the response may be complex. It might take from months to years to never to implement. This timeliness question is demonstrated by the difficulty that the world authorities are having in coming to an agreement about the way to regulate the financial markets in the wake of the GFC. Discussions have been progressing for years but there still continues to be significant disagreement. Even outside such a large forum different solutions to problems often need to account for many stakeholders with competing interests. There are very few instances where governments are in a position that they have the political capital to act decisively on a contentious issue. The enactment of laws usually takes considerable time.

Third, it presumes that everyone has equal access to the law. Wealthy individuals and corporations can harness legal resources on a large scale. With this power loopholes can be found and tactical delays deployed against opponents with fair claims.

Fourth, this position presumes that the law is uncontaminated, that it is fair and just. This does not take into account the reality that laws are not always fair and just. The making of laws is influenced by interest groups. Business is not the only interest group but it is a significant one and the subject of this text. Many companies have economies bigger than some countries. Companies provide large amounts of money essential for political campaigning to candidates who will think of their interests while holding political powers. So governments as a whole and the individuals within governments are influenced by business.

One of the most significant problems faced in the world today is dealing with 'profit shifting' by multinational companies to minimize tax. Examples such as Amazon, Starbucks and Google have been cited earlier. Their actions are lawful but are they socially responsible? What harm does it cause to the general population when this money is not available?

Forgetting welfare for a moment, even security is compromised when defence budgets have less buying power. The situation becomes more complex when the interconnectivity of global governments is considered. Necessarily governments have different laws and sometimes a different basis for those laws; this can and does impede the interconnectivity of trade and also of countries generally. This issue is discussed in 'Legal pluralism' below.

To address this, countries enter into treaties that as much as possible harmonize the operation of each other's laws. Therefore, where one treaty partner has tax laws that permit a form of profit shifting then other countries who have signed treaties are often compelled to allow that practice as well. This is at the core of the current global tax debate on profit shifting. Senior political and tax administrators have been meeting to work together to formulate a solution.

Despite this being a recognized problem for years, there still has not been any real movement towards a solution. Certainly this is not an easy matter to resolve in its own right: governments have to be cautious of looking to be anti-business and discouraging investment. Governments benefiting from these arrangements are unlikely to be anxious to see changes. However, the question that should be asked is, 'what is business's involvement in the delay?' It is very likely that there are business forces looking to resist this kind of change, as it is detrimental to their profitability.

This is not to say there isn't a backlash against profit shifting. As the examples cited have mentioned, there is significant popular resentment to this behaviour. There have been recent developments (see 'Luxembourg leaks' in text box) that have prompted European leaders to call for reform and President Obama to call corporations who profit shift 'unpatriotic'.

However, an observer would still be forced to conclude that this outrage is insufficient to significantly shift the conduct of the offending businesses or the governments trying to regulate the behaviour. Should everything then be left to the law? It would appear that this is a race to the bottom: unethical practices that are lawful, profitable and without much consequence become self-perpetuating. As noted earlier in reference to India, many business people considered that it was not feasible for them to be in business otherwise. What are the long-term consequences for a country where its largest taxpayers don't pay tax? Does ethics have a role to play?

Question

Is the role of ethical corporations merely to be ethical themselves? Or is their role to lobby both unethical companies and government for laws that change unethical practices?

In Chapter 1 the sale of poison gas to be used in the Nazi extermination chambers was cited as an example of an action that was lawful but morally reprehensible. Admittedly, the example is old and extreme; however, corporations acting lawfully but immorally are not just a matter of history. As cited above, the non-payment of tax is socially irresponsible. The effect of non-payment of taxation is washed out to a large extent by the system. The community at large who are the victims of this behaviour are so diffuse and the harm so general that the action is more easily justified and rationalized. The same could be said for the conduct of financial organizations, like Lehman Brothers, leading up to the Global Financial Crisis. It is, however, no less wrong.

Acting unethically, though lawfully, may have a more readily identified group of victims. Again, there have been several examples throughout the text: Apple and the Foxconn employees in China, Amazon warehouse workers, persons killed or injured in Pinto automobiles, Hershey and the child slaves in West Africa. In each of those cases the companies have faced often massive community backlash. Again, the argument that a corporation's judgement is merely governed by what is lawful, seems feeble.

A turning point?

Luxembourg leaks

A recent investigation (December 2014) by the International Consortium of Investigative Journalism (ICIJ) lead to the leaking of documents relating to favourable tax treatment to over 300 companies by the Duchy of Luxembourg.

The enquiry, which covered the period 2002 to 2010, disclosed that Luxembourg authorities provided favourable rulings organized by accounting firm PricewaterhouseCoopers (PwC) based on complex structures that allowed these companies to significantly reduce their taxation liabilities. It is estimated that hundreds of billions of dollars of tax revenue has been forfeited.

The release of this information has unleashed worldwide anger at the companies and at the Duchy. Leaders across the world have committed to action. The UK has announced new measures to be revealed shortly. Somewhat disturbingly, there has been little change to the share price of the companies implicated, suggesting that the market is not expecting significant harm to be caused (and by implication, little change to the international tax regime).

SOURCE: See Luxembourg Leaks in recommended reading

Formal and informal codes

The difficulty of distinguishing formal from informal codes is well illustrated by Williams (1971) who referred to the unpublished work of McNaughton-Smith, who suggested that society operates with parallel codes: Code One equates to the formal laws, statutes and regulations whereas Code Two equates to our informal but general social understanding. When someone breaks our informal rules (Code Two) we think of legal sanctions that might be applied (Code One).

A common threat of unions is that their members will 'work to rule'; that is to say that they will only do exactly what they are required to do. It would typically involve every person working exactly to their hours, taking exactly their required breaks at the specified times, not performing relatively trivial tasks without authorization, performing only to their exact job description.

Anyone who has been subject to or participated in a 'work to rule' campaign will know how harmful to operations this can be. An organization can come to a halt if the campaign is vigorous enough. It is simultaneously a demonstration of how business operations are dependent on agreed conventions (informal codes) and how important those agreed conventions are for operations.

Hart-Devlin debate

In the early 1960s there was a debate about the application of law to the enforcement of morality. Lord Devlin, then Lord Justice of the Appeal Court in the UK, argued in 1959 that the community's morality was an important guide to the law (Devlin, 1961). That there were acts that were inherently wrong because they breached an underlying natural law. That if community values were offended by a particular behaviour then it was appropriate to legislate against this conduct.

Devlin concluded that the judges of England may not be highly original, but have been craftsmen rather than creators. That the law was in effect already there and it was the judges who needed to discover it. As he put it, they needed the stuff of morals so that they could fashion the law.

This general argument about the enforcement of a common morality and the use of the criminal law was contested by Professor Hart of Oxford (Hart, 1963). In rebuttal he noted, among other issues, that it is not possible for a community as large and diverse as the United Kingdom to have a firm and unambiguous moral position. The common stock of ideas on right and wrong probably does not exist. Further, although there is an obligation to obey the law, not all would hold that position without question. There is a corresponding need to consider laws that are patently unjust.

He opposed Devlin's view that any society may take any steps needed to preserve its own existence. The two points here are: (i) it depends on what sort of society we want, and (ii) what steps are necessary to achieve that society. In other words, Hart raises the question of the social ends we wish to achieve, and what means of achieving those ends are permissible. An attendant fundamental question here is that of society having the right to enforce morality. The essence of the tension posed by these competing points of view is between the preservation of the state as such, and the preservation of ideals.

There is an account of the scope and limits of the moral argument as a basis of law (Raz, 2009). It was noted that the issue of instrumentalism – which acts are instrumental in producing certain ends – is critical to our understanding. Among the other issues raised are that certain axioms lead to certain principles of behaviour that may be unattractive; that often morality as a basis is without proof; that many of the concepts that invest this argument are blurred and indistinct; that we must at least consider the logical adequacy of the espoused propositions; and that we might be in favour of a course of action but deplore the consequences (in favour of war but do not want to be conscripted and sent out to kill).

In the introduction to his book on jurisprudence it was noted by Waks (2012) that the bases of law are variously listed as the wish for social control, the serving of sectional interests, local customs, the environment, and derivative and prescriptive morals. The contrast of the Devlin and Hart positions is that, on the one hand, the suppression of vice is as much the law's business as is the suppression of subversive activities; this is contrasted, on the other hand, with the view that the realm of morality is not the law's business. The perspective on the issue of obedience to the law, and related to that debate, may be read in an earlier excellent summary by Campbell (1965). It is clear that this debate is one of enduring quality.

The difference between complying with the law and complying with an ethical code

The law has one function; a code of ethics has another although there are many overlaps and similarities. Primarily the text has noted that a strict application of the law will not on its own be adequate to protect and support the community. Ethics is expected to fill the breach where the law cannot reach. Ethics is therefore timely and looks to the principles that underlie a functional society rather than the complex and specialist web of legal administration. Ethics is therefore approached differently to the law.

The best guiding principle here is that whatever ethical solution is adopted it should improve the ethical position. It is recognized that in a somewhat contentious and difficult world whatever solution is adopted should leave the ethical position improved (see also the section on preventing and dealing with ethical problems). In addition to the substantive issues of the law there is also the ethical issue of how basic legal processes are used.

It is not the function of a code of ethics to be an alternative to the law. If the law is seen to be inadequate or mistaken or outdated or ambiguous then the proper legally permitted procedures should be followed to have the law amended. Ethical arguments may inform the law, be an aid to the law, but never supplant it. Ethical codes also fill some gaps in the law. The sweep of ethical codes allows conduct to be considered in broad terms rather than the narrow specifications required of legal machinery. The Hippocratic declaration of 'do no harm' can capture what a complex set of rules cannot (see text box).

Sometimes codes, such as in professional associations, express the aspirational mode, and set standards in a manner that is a guide to both training and practice – in this sense they have an ethical as well as a legal compass. The distinction may not be a line but, rather, a grey area. For example, various National Health and Medical Research Council rules on research are at once both regulations and ethical guidelines.

Writing ethical codes in the spirit of the law is helpful. One of the difficulties is to ensure that strict formal codification does not lead to 'creative' opportunities to subvert the intentions of the code. It is sadly common for the prescriptions of law to be so precisely worded that the precision is used as a means of subverting the intention of the legislation, proving one of the major problems with the law (see 'Luxembourg leaks' above).

The reasons why people comply with the law are complex. What is clear is that internally dictated reasons for being law-abiding are more effective and cheaper than forced compliance. Such internal imperatives are also readily modified by experiences with the legal system. Being treated with courtesy and dignity by the legal system, and perceiving it to be fair, are among the significant determiners of subsequent attitude to legal compliance. Readers may be interested in a US study that examined the reasons why people comply with the law. Although from only one particular country, the study has some instructive points to make (Jackson *et al*, 2012).

How old are codes of conduct?

The Hippocratic Oath

The Hippocratic Oath is considered by most people as the first example of an ethical code. The oath is said to have originated in Ancient Greece and was the creation of Hippocrates, the person considered the father of modern medicine. The oath was a promise that physicians made to care for their patients. It is widely known that a key precept of the oath was 'to do no harm'. However, what is less well known is that the oath also committed doctors to use their judgement and skills to the best of their ability. They also swore to be honest and to not use their position for advantage, particularly sexual advantage. The idea was that the responsibility of the physician put them in a special position, relative to the rest of the community.

Hippocrates' work, including the oath, was lost during the dark ages and then rediscovered during the Renaissance. It has been reworded and redrafted many times since, but its basic premise of social responsibility is still a feature of many medical schools today.

SOURCE: See The Hippocratic Oath in recommended reading

Natural justice

There is a concept called 'natural justice' which, in essence, asserts rules and procedures to be followed in adjudicating disputes. This concept is an interesting one in that it is a legal concept, but is based on an ethical standard. The main principles are to act fairly and without bias. Each party should have the opportunity of stating and defending his or her case, and of challenging the evidence of the other side. It is clear that the right to be heard, the right to confront accusers, not to be a judge in one's own cause, precise notice of accusations, and so on are all essential elements.

Natural justice is an invented concept, a human device, and the reason why we have departments of justice. If there were natural justice we would not need to invent a judicial system. Similarly, there are no natural ethics, and that is why we invent them. To paraphrase Malcolm Muggeridge, no one who has examined his own nature for half an hour can seriously believe in human perfection.

Accountability and responsibility lie at the heart of ethics. To place the accounting where it rightly belongs, and to make persons responsible, is crucial to our notions of justice and to ethical fairness. As a former British Lord of Appeal (Lord Moulton) held, there are actions constrained by law and the domain of free personal choice. Between these lie that which is neither free nor legally fettered; this is the area that he regarded as 'obedience to the unenforceable'. It is also this area that is probably the largest domain, and the one in which our conscience is most active.

Commonality between law and ethics

Hard and soft law

This notion of the legally persuasive argument of having a code might be termed soft law; soft law being one that provides options of ways to comply. Voluntary schemes, with government involvement, are often useful. However, this line between ethics and the law is progressively contracting as governments increasingly compel corporations to adopt ethical practices as noted in Chapter 1. Subscription to a code of ethics may be seen as a contract. Although ethics is not law, the fact of subscribing to a code may have some of the attributes of a legal contract.

Corporations, particularly when under scrutiny for some perceived inappropriate conduct, often try to deflect the prospect of legislative control with promises to improve their ethical behaviour. As the vast majority of corporations have established codes (many are into a fourth generation of ethical code) this will usually involve some serious revision and recommitment to what already existed. Even in these circumstances it is advantageous to have the flexibility of a self-governing system rather than the prospect of external control or scrutiny.

It is not the purpose of a business code to be an alternative to the law; neither is a code meant to be a means of challenging the law, even though this runs counter to the principle of resisting unjust laws. Ethics should lead, inform, and persuade rather than be a passive follower. It is not intended here that ethical codes should be used to ignore issues (such as safety), but a code may be useful to raise unusual issues that require resolution.

In a cross-cultural challenge this rather abstract point may be illustrated by the use of a factory example. If an employee from a culture in which all of the men wear turbans – and therefore cannot wear safety helmets – were to work in an environment requiring helmets, should such an employee be absolved from wearing a safety helmet? Further, if the wearing of a turban prevents helmet use, and the turban wearer is responsible for others not of the same faith, does occupational health and safety override cultural ways?

Legal pluralism

The relationship between statutes and codes of conduct is complicated by issues of legal pluralism. Legal pluralism is where a specific community is subject to multiple legal codes. Primarily this arises in the global environment as commercial enterprise moves across borders. Although there are other forms of legal pluralism, such as where there may be rules pertaining to some members of the population and not others, there may be indigenous rules competing with that of a nation. The attempt to cope with legal pluralism is just as difficult as trying to cope with cultural pluralism. 'Private international law' (or 'conflict of laws') is the name given to our attempts to cope with legal pluralism in the global forum, the objects of which are to:

- prescribe the conditions under which the court is competent to entertain any given matter;
- determine for each class of case the particular internal system of law that will be applied; and
- specify the circumstances in which a foreign judgement resolves the conflict.

One example of legal pluralism is that of law in French colonies in Africa where people who were subject to customary law were distinguished from those subject to civil law. The French colonial legislation was special to a colony, but legislative authority for colonies was vested in the central government in France. The laws of metropolitan France did not extend to the colonies unless this was specifically stated. In legal pluralism not only can the precepts of law be explicitly different, but so may be the assumptions underlying them (see Berman, 2009).

There are 'families' of law among which are 'Romano-Germanic', 'common law', 'socialist law', and the 'law of philosophy and religion'. It is the impact of colonial expansion, of the export of other forms of law, and the need to deal internationally that has generated this issue. These 'families' of law sometimes act in a complementary way. Thus the civil codes of Egypt require judges to fill in gaps in those codes by reference to Sharīʿah law.

Countries that have an indigenous population face the question of how to reconcile tribal law with that of majority law. That problem is compounded by the formalization of only one of the systems of law. Such 'frozen' law may be used inappropriately instead of being used and transmitted in an adaptive fashion.

One form of law that illustrates the adaptive oral tradition is that of the Bedouin. Although formally predominantly Moslem, their religious practices do not conform entirely to Sharīʿah law. Indeed, in some instances they predate it. The aspects of Islam that do not find full expression in Bedouin life are those more appropriate to sedentary or settled lifestyles. Desert survival depends on being nomadic, so as not to deplete the minimal grazing available. The economic and social principles developed by the Bedouin are designed to foster tribally appropriate ends.

Notions of restitution and revenge play an important part in Bedouin law. There is no notion of 'policing' in the Western sense: issues are either personal or familial. Although they operate by their own orally transmitted system of justice, they are subject to the sovereign state in which they live. In such cases the sovereign state may seek to leave the greater part of legal governance to the tribal tradition.

There is a good illustration of the difference between Sharīʿah law and the international commercial contract principles (UPICC). Sharīʿah law bans usury (see below) whereas it is allowed in the international commercial contract principles. However, there have been a number of financial instruments developed that satisfy both Sharīʿah law and Western-style finance.

How a bank can operate without interest

Sharīʿah law

The rise of the Islamic world has brought greater interaction with the West. Islamic people, as well as people in the West, are looking to do business with one another. Both sides can see advantages to this exchange. An important factor for Western companies to be aware of is Sharīʿah law. Sharīʿah law specifically prohibits entering into or financing activities that are prohibited by Islam: gambling, pork and alcohol production. Sharīʿah law also prohibits 'usury' which many interpret as interest but is in effect 'uncertainty'.

The principle behind this very ancient rule was to stop persons in the stronger business position taking advantage of the weak. A scenario that Sharīʿah law is attempting to prevent could be where a person is loaned money for a year but at the end of the year they are unable to repay so the debt is double. If the same thing happens again in another 12 months the debt is quadrupled. Therefore it is prohibited, as interest is uncertain. So, proceeds and costs must be certain and clear at the beginning of the transaction. Islamic finance is arranged so as to be very specific about the profit to be made.

Below are specific examples of Islamic financial arrangements:

Murābahah – items are sold where the profits are known to buyer and seller.

Mudārabah – funds are held on trust by a third party who completes the task then returns the principle and profit that was specified at the start of the contract.

ījārah – plant or machinery purchased by the financial institution but lent to the customer who may eventually take ownership.

Muqaradah – promissory notes issued by a financial institution to fund a specified venture.

Bai'mu'ajjal – buying and then reselling property on a programme of payments over time.

Bāi'salam – payment is made at the time of agreement but the physical transfer occurs in the future.

SOURCE: See Sharī'ah law in recommended reading

Ethnic differences and the law

The problem of ethnic differences and the law is compounded by those who come from cultures accustomed to a different form of law. For those not of the dominant culture there is the dual difficulty of not finding the law relevant, and of not understanding what is different about it compared with the law in their countries of origin. In most societies the dominant culture determines both the content of statutes and the forms of legal process. Where there is a tendency to draw a distinction between countries, that distinction must be seen as arbitrary. In an increasingly borderless world it is easy to forget the commonalities (see Hansen and Papademetriou, 2013).

Codes of conduct as law

The legal weight of codes

Although a code of business conduct is not legislation, the adoption of, and adherence to, a code carries legal weight in certain circumstances. As noted before, global companies are likely to have a legal obligation to have a values code about expected behaviour in the organization. This takes a number of shapes and varies from jurisdiction to jurisdiction, but the main mechanism is mainly through the various stock markets.

Both the NASDAQ and the New York Stock Exchange compel any corporation listed to have, report on and make available codes of conduct. Similarly in the UK publicly listed companies are expected to conform to the regulations of the Financial Reporting Council which includes expectations in regards to ethical standards. Serious misconduct (including bribing foreign government officials) or poor ethical behaviour over the long term can see companies delisted. Importantly for global companies poor ethical behaviour in one country can create obstacles for activities in another country.

In the United States, the Sarbanes-Oxley Act (2002) stipulated that there must be a code of conduct for the executives of public companies or an explanation as to why they didn't have a code. The Federal Sentencing Guideline for Organizations (FSGO) provides for reduced penalties for companies that have ethical codes and mechanisms for compliance and has done since 1991. They were revised in 2004, requiring companies to create ethical culture within their organizations. Other developed nations around the world have similar stipulations. Ethical behaviour and the law have, in some respects, never been as tightly meshed or as difficult to tease apart. It is important to note that having an ethical code and processes to support it does not convert a principle in a company's ethical code into a law, although as noted previously serious unethical behaviour can have far-reaching consequences for a global operation.

One of the major issues for global corporations and governments is the variations between jurisdictions. Harmony here is difficult to achieve. Even within the European Union, where the Transparency Directive and the International Financial Reporting Standards (IFRS) had been agreed to by member states, it was found that there were improvements, but still national differences (Williams and Seguí-Mas, 2010).

An organization may be able to use its code as a persuasive defence or a factor to mitigate penalty when faced with allegations of impropriety. A company could propose to the court that while their employees (the agents of the company) had committed some wrongdoing, the organization itself had taken meaningful steps to create an ethical culture. Specifically it had a code to which they were genuinely committed (refer to the following chapter for factors demonstrating ethical culture).

Further, the commitment of the organization to the cause of ethics could be presented to the court by way of mitigation, arguing that the breach was outside the norm, that the organization acted in good faith, and that the breach was an anomaly.

Codes of conduct and industry codes can provide evidence in legal matters, such as negligence cases, as to what is a reasonable standard of care. If, for example, advice had been given which resulted in significant financial loss to another party, a code might be indicative as to whether the giver of the advice had done so appropriately or not. Similarly, codes might help to mitigate culpability in a matter. For example, where the court perceives outrageously bad behaviour it can award punitive penalties (extra amounts to punish that behaviour).

In the Ford Pinto matter referred to earlier, the damages awarded were US $125 million, a significant amount in the 1970s. This was a punitive award going beyond a normal damages claim that seeks to put the injured party back in the position they ought to have been as far as is possible. A code might assist in reducing the risk of punitive damages and help demonstrate to the court that the behaviour was of an acceptable standard. Codes are double edged though: if used well they are a defence, but if not properly adopted they are a weapon in the hands of the opposition.

How corporate breaches in one jurisdiction can have implications globally

News of the World

The newspaper *News of the World,* part of the News Corp conglomerate, was shut down after 168 years in response to the 'phone-hacking' scandal. In brief, journalists paid for illegal phone tapping of celebrities and other newsworthy individuals. After it was alleged that the phone of a murdered schoolgirl, Milly Dowler, had been accessed and messages deleted (giving Milly's parents the impression she was still alive) the matter escalated to a massive investigation. This investigation revealed a corporate culture that encouraged this behaviour, with thousands of phones being tapped. The case had serious ramifications for News Corp and many related parties.

To list some of the major consequences:

- massive damages have been paid in dozens of cases;

- government MPs branded News Corp Chairman Rupert Murdoch as 'not a fit person';

- his son James Murdoch stood down as chairman of satellite broadcaster BSkyB; and

- there was the potential for a US investigation under the Foreign Corrupt Practices Act.

Given that ethical conduct is a criterion for being listed on the stock exchange, the improper behaviour presented a threat to extensive operations in the United States, as well as the UK.

SOURCE: See News Corp in recommended reading

Self-regulation

Self-regulation does, however, monitor the performance of a significant number of the larger entities, and often serves as a means of developing rules that may eventually be given legal force. One of the most significant changes in recent times has been the institution of a number of legal safeguards. These include such governmental institutions as the ombudsman, administrative appeals tribunals, and privacy commissioners, as well as industrial complaints councils. On balance there is much to be said for self-regulatory codes: they have all the mentioned merits of ethical systems, with the backstop of the law to support them.

The government has within its power the capacity to give legislative status to codes. It could decide, for example, that professional or business codes that are properly monitored or prepared should be accepted as the legal standard. Here the public availability of codes, ministerial control, proper supervision, and legal consequences are matters that might be improved by legislation.

Conclusion

In this chapter the focus has been on the various relationships and interactions between the law and ethics. It has examined the idea that 'morals are not the issue of business' and why this is an untenable and unsustainable model. It has also looked at the difference between formal and informal codes and some of the background to the conceptual links between ethics and the law. This chapter considered ethics as soft law, and the idea of where multiple systems, both ethical and legal, overlap. Finally it has explored where ethics can be part of the legal system. As with the previous chapters this continues to build up an understanding in resolving ethical dilemmas, building ethical culture and developing ethical codes as discussed in Chapters 9 and 10.

The next chapter will look at ethical gradualism, creating an ethical culture and the importance of codes.

Focus questions

Legal aspects of ethics

1 Is it feasible that business concerns itself solely with remaining within the law? If not, why not?

2 How would you describe the difference between informal and formal codes?

3 What are the major differences between the positions of Lord Devlin and Professor Hart?

4 Is there a difference between complying with an ethical code and the law?

5 What features would a process need to satisfy 'natural justice'?

6 Why is ethics sometimes considered as soft law?

7 What is legal pluralism? Give an example.

8 Are ethical codes for global companies relevant to the law?

CASE STUDY

Amhed is a manager currently working in India. His multinational company sells small agricultural equipment. He is approached by his marketing manager, who informs him that he is quite concerned about a new product a small competitor is about to release. The product is very close to something Amhed's company is seeking to release in a couple of months. From what the marketing manager has heard, the product is well perceived and likely to be very popular as it is made locally. His anxiety is that they will lose enough of the market share that it will hurt expected results and everyone's bonuses. Worse still it will give the other company a foothold in the market place and will inevitably erode their own profitability in the future.

The marketing manager proposes a solution – litigation. Launch proceedings against the competitor over patent infringements and get a court injunction to halt the sale of the new product. Given the Indian court system they won't be able to get the order lifted for years and they will go broke fighting it long before then. Amhed asks if there is any foundation for the claim. The marketing manager smiles and replies there might be as they did hire a couple of workers who had been employed with Amhed's company. He can't be sure but then adds 'and, if not, who cares?'

Should Amhed adopt the marketing manager's strategy?

Factors to consider

Nothing that the marketing manager has suggested is illegal. The agenda, though, is not about correcting the theft of an idea but of using the legal process to get a market advantage. Larger companies that have greater resources can often bludgeon their opponents into liquidation or into simply giving up. This practice is common and occurs across the world but it is often easier to do in places where the judicial system is overwhelmed and inefficient.

Does Amhed take an approach of looking to his values and simply say no because this is a malicious practice (a Deontological approach)? Or does he assess the consequences of the possible actions (a Utilitarianist view), in which case he might consider:

1 His action is likely to put an innovative young firm and its employees out of work.

2 His company should compete fairly in the marketplace and their own products should stand or fall on their own merits.

3 What if this action is seen as the blatant ploy that it is? Could there be a local backlash? Could their brand be damaged?

4 His own company's position (as well as that of his fellow employees) – what if his competitors seriously damage their own local position as the marketing manager is alluding.

5 What if there has been a theft of ideas, however slight, and he hasn't acted? (What impression might that make when it is discovered by head office?)

6 The system as a whole, if innovation is stifled like this. What might it mean for the country in the future? Will it be the poorer for it?

Recommended reading

The Hippocratic Oath

Baker, R (1999) Codes of ethics: some history perspectives on the professions, Centre for the Study of Ethics in the Professions (CSEP), 19 (1) [online] http://ethics.iit.edu/perspective/v19n1%20perspective.pdf

Copland, J (1825) The Hippocratic Oath, *The London Medical Repository Monthly Journal and Review*, Thomas & George Underwood, London [online] http://books.google.ie/books?id=Oe0EAAAAQAAJ&pg=PA258#v=onepage&q&f=false [accessed 08 February 2015]

Crawshaw, R (1994) The Hippocratic Oath is alive and well in North America, *British Medical Journal*, 309, p 952 [online] http://www.ncbi.nlm.nih.gov/pmc/articles/PMC2541124/

Luxembourg Leaks

Boland-Rudder, H (2014, November) Pressure on Juncker at G20 summit over 'LuxLeaks' revelations, *ICJI* [online] http://www.icij.org/project/luxembourg-leaks/pressure-juncker-g20-summit-over-lux-leaks-revelations

Bowers, S and Guardian readers (2014, November) What do you want to know about Luxembourg's multi-billion dollar tax secrets? *Guardian* [online] http://www.theguardian.com/business/2014/nov/05/what-do-you-want-to-know-about-luxembourgs-multi-billion-dollar-tax-secrets

IJIC (nd) Luxembourg leaks: global companies' secrets exposed, *ICIJ* [online] http://www.icij.org/project/luxembourg-leaks

Luxleaks tax source should not be charged ~ petition (2014, December) *Guardian* [online] http://www.theguardian.com/world/2014/dec/23/luxleaks-tax-source-should-not-be-charged

News Corp

BBC (nd) Phone-hacking scandal: timeline, *BBC* [online] http://www.bbc.com/news/uk-14124020 [accessed 12 February 2015]

CNN (2014, October) UK phone hacking scandal fast facts, *CNN* [online] http://www.cnn.com/2013/10/24/world/europe/uk-phone-hacking-scandal-fast-facts/

Neate, R and Swaine, J (2015, February) Newscorp won't be prosecuted in US in relation to phone hacking, *Guardian* [online] http://www.theguardian.com/media/2015/feb/02/news-corp-phone-hacking-us

Sharī'ah Law

Economist (2014, September) Big interest, no interest, *Economist* [online] http://www.economist.com/news/finance-and-economics/21617014-market-islamic-financial-products-growing-fast-big-interest-no-interest

Warren, C S (nd) Commercial Law, *Oxford Islamic Studies Online* [online] http://www.oxfordislamicstudies.com/article/opr/t236/e0156 [accessed 8 February 2015]

Zaman, M R (2008) Usury (Riba) and the place of bank interest in Islamic Banking and Finance, International Journal of Banking and Finance, **6** (1) [online] http://epublications.bond.edu.au/cgi/viewcontent.cgi?article=1009&context=ijbf

PART THREE
Solving problems

Ethical gradualism, culture, quantification and codes

08

Introduction

This chapter discusses issues with, and the practical application of, ethics. It commences with ethical gradualism as a workable path for corporations to develop their ethical culture. It then explores issues and methodologies around defining corporate cultures and how ethics can be measured. This chapter then looks at how to foster an ethical culture with an emphasis on learning strategies. Importantly it summarizes and ties together the important features of an ethical corporate culture that have been discussed earlier. Finally this chapter examines the nature, feature and importance of ethical codes.

Key learning points

This chapter will discuss ethical gradualism, then progress to matters of ethical corporate culture. Specifically these are:

- Defining the corporate climate.

- Corporate climate audits.

- Ethics consultants.

- Quantification of ethics.

- Social and environmental accounting.

- Urgency versus importance.

- Sequence of questions.

- Essential elements of an ethical corporate culture.

This chapter will discuss then examine how to foster an ethical culture and sensitizing to ethical issues with particular emphasis on learning strategies, including:

- Online training.

- Lectures.

- The use of case studies.

- Simulations.

- Mentoring.

We will also discuss the importance and critical considerations in ethical codes.

At the beginning of the text the reasons business should be ethical were provided. The evidence supports the idea that businesses should be socially responsible. It is, however, important not to lose sight of the fact that business is a messy environment and that reality has a way of interfering with good intentions. An important question is whether or not ethical principles should be bound by time or circumstance. To say that a scenario is particular or exceptional obliges us to examine the scope of the ethical principle.

Ethical principles need to be considered in the time context: they are principles that are for the long term rather than the short term. In the long term, ethical behaviour is better for business, but that is of no help to the hard-pressed executive who needs to make a profit or meet an objective now in order to survive in his role. Occupation of the high moral ground makes us feel good, but we need to ask the question, 'does it enhance the prospect of corporate survival?' For example, the issue of genetically modified organisms has come to the attention of the law. This seemingly ethical and practical problem has, inevitably, invited legislation: the law must be seen to be within reach of this problem.

Among the issues that arise are those of the genetic modifications that might be brought about by the over-use of pesticides and industrial waste; the legal status of new genetic entities; the consequences of the human genome project; the moral issues of cloning; and the way in which profit and danger in these genetic enterprises might relate not only to the commission of ethical breaches, but also become a significant issue in risk management.

It is noted that a number of jurisdictions have legislated control of genetically modified organisms. For example, the legislation in force covers such jurisdictions as the United States, England and Wales, and Australia. The European Union has a view on the subject, which is to be found on the relevant website (see Genetically modified organisms in References).

Ethical gradualism

To be effective in shifting individuals and organizational culture it is important to be pragmatic about ethics in recognizing real-life complexities. An unbending attitude also makes teaching ethics difficult and hinders the evolution and improvement of ethical codes. Such pragmatism is not synonymous with compromising basic principles, nor is it synonymous with gradualism, which will be discussed shortly. Ethics does not exist in a social vacuum, and in that sense we are all ethical consequentialists. Whatever code we operate will have real-life consequences (see Francis, Gius and Coin (2004) for a further discussion).

This section sets out the explicit principle of gradualism in ethics, and provides both a justification and illustrations. While it may be tacitly acknowledged that we approach learning of most subjects by a series of approximations, this section argues that we might make gradualism an explicit policy in ethics. While a philosophical approach to ethics has demonstrable virtues, in modern professional practice we need to move to a more action-based approach.

Like any other professional skill or insight, ethics may be taught. In Plato's *Cratylus* and *Protagoras* there is a discussion as to whether or not virtue may be taught. In *Cratylus* Plato has Socrates say that all things are knowledge, including wisdom, understanding and judgement, and are thus teachable. If we did not believe that Socratic precept then we would live in a Hobbesian world (the war of all against all, where life is poor, solitary, nasty, brutish and short), and likely to adopt a doctrine of despair, and not believe in the improvability of the human condition.

In contemporary professional and business ethics we are, rightly or wrongly, less troubled by definitions than was so in the Socratic dialogues, but we still need to be clear about our subject matter and our definitions: less reflective, but more practical in our professional commitment to the keeping of confidences, to professionalism, to openness, to goodwill, and to collegiality.

If we need a practical justification for being ethical it lies in such arguments as that an ethical code affords a reference point to help the inexperienced, is a distinct aid for those hard pressed by time-pressured problems, helps busy professionals make sensible judgements, is a means of fostering a good ethical culture, and is a promoter of the collegial enterprise. It is just such reasons that are appealing to those doubtful about the value of ethics.

In the practical implementation of ethics, the notion of a guided approximations approach has many precedents. It is strongly noted that traditional training as well as informal education relies almost totally upon gradual approaches towards insight and skill development. Mastery does not emerge fully formed but, rather, proceeds by way of sub-skills, partial insights, unfolding understanding, and of encouraging change. As has been noted by theorists as diverse as Pestalozzi and Skinner, such understanding and behaviour are 'shaped' over time.

Most who teach ethics use some form of approximation. The introduction of dilemmas of lesser import, and the use of creative resolutions lend themselves to a gradual approach to ethical training. While we remain attentive to unbreakable principles, there is still scope for flexibility, and for approaching ethical dilemmas in a manner that approximates ideal solutions. Just as we teach by way of approximations in languages, mathematics and history, so too might we use such an approach in ethics, as will be shown in instances given below.

Aspiring professionals first encountering business dilemmas are in a most receptive position for insights into ethical problems, potential solutions, and the importance of business ethics. The training function and effectiveness of the gradual approach may be formalized into certain propositions:

- No compromise should be at variance with the law, or with any basic principles of any code: there are issues of such import that one does not compromise.

- Each solution to an ethical dilemma probably has a creative component that should be captured for future reference when the code is being updated.

- Not to be unduly distressed if not perfect: practitioners should, however, constantly try to improve, noting that accumulations for successive cases will amount to a substantial improvement in the medium to long term.

- The gradualist approach is seen to be a way of improving the ethical situation without compromising basic standards and by making ethics more accessible and less daunting.

- The accretion of a series of small successes may be done creatively and amicably, and should give a reputational advantage that will build up credits upon which practitioners may draw in future occasions.

Gradualism in action

Wegmans

We are all familiar with gradualism. We may not know the term but it exists around us all the time. Success stories are rarely 'overnight'.

The supermarket chain Wegmans is a good example. They are a US company who, unlike many of their competitors, put their employees first. (The search for US success stories usually involves 'slash and burn' strategies.) Wegmans don't fire people; they ensure employees are well trained to the extent that some are sent around the world to gain a better understanding of the products that they are selling. This is particularly impressive as they have over 40,000 employees. The company is exceptionally profitable and successful. Importantly, despite their success, they do not rapidly expand. They limit themselves to opening a small number of stores each year so that they can ensure these new stores are opened using their best people. Needless to say this gradualist approach has worked well for them.

SOURCE: See Wegmans in recommended reading

It is desirable that those who teach ethics are the ones who help resolve real-life dilemmas: the one skill complementing the other. The cross feed between resolving sundry ethical dilemmas gives the experience that makes useful improvements to the code, and helps teach ethical behaviour.

We have to recognize that there is a problem with the extreme of the ethical-gradualist approach. In order to use the gradualist approach we must compromise – yet some issues are not for compromise. Thus a country health practice might use nurses as the first point of contact, handing only those cases in need of more expert attention to a doctor. It is less desirable than using registered medical practitioners on prime call but at least it provides a service that is far better than no service. The use of gradualism therefore needs to be tempered with the knowledge that the compromises do not imply acceptance of breaches of major principle.

A major problem may occur in professional training. There are students in professional courses who master the formal syllabus yet seem to be less committed, or even partially blind, to ethical concerns and by whom ethics is perceived as largely irrelevant. The dilemma here is what one does with candidates who have passed formal examinations but whose trainers and examiners entertain serious concerns about their suitability for hands-on business experience. Unless formal assessment in ethics is set in the regulations, the training personnel and organizations may well lay themselves open to charges of adverse discrimination, and even of lawsuits.

There is no one best way of inculcating ethics – but there are several ways of which the explicit principle of gradualism could be one. Ethics is one of the most important issues that professionals address, often informally rather than formally. Its importance is paramount in that it also contains our human obligations and duties, brings repute to ourselves and our organizations, preserves careers, and improves the quality of life for the community. While professionals cannot compromise on some issues (public revelation of professional confidences, for example) there are many cases in ethics where an improving and creative solution is possible.

It is concluded that to set a counsel of perfection may be both intimidating and non-achievable. Rather, whatever ethical action is taken should result in an ethical improvement. If every ethical decision were to result in an improvement, the multiplier effect would be enormous. The only caveat for this position is that it should not be taken as counsel to effect lesser ethical changes.

Creating an ethical corporate culture

Defining the corporate climate

A corporate climate, for the purposes of this work, refers to the prevailing ethical ethos of the organization. To attempt to be precise about the corporate climate is to try to define the indefinable. We all know about concepts such as love and hate, happiness and depression, poverty and wealth. Such concepts seem to evaporate under close scrutiny, but their seeming disappearance makes them no less real in our everyday lives. The corporate climate is another such idea. It cannot be formalized, but we recognize it when we experience it. Perhaps the nearest we can come to explaining it is to say that it is the values, ideals and assumptions (VIAs) that permeate the organization.

These VIAs are not made explicit, nor are they necessarily part of any selection or induction process. Rather, they are an implicitly understood frame of reference for operating within the organization. Airline pilots are not selected on the basis of being asked to subscribe to a policy of no crashes; academics are not required to formalize the principle of acting with academic honesty; presumably no one asks an archbishop elect whether or not he is a devout believer.

This understood frame of reference is not illustrated with expressions in rhetorical style; more, it is illustrated by myth and legend. That point is well illustrated in Peters and Waterman's *In Search of Excellence* (1982). 'All companies we interviewed, from Boeing to McDonald's, were quite simply rich tapestries of anecdote, myth, and fairy tale.' One of the illustrations given is; '... two HP engineers in their mid-twenties recently regaled us with an hour's worth of "Bill and Dave" (Hewlett and Packard) stories. We were subsequently astonished to find that neither had seen, let alone talked to, the founders.' Behind this mythologizing and implicit subscription to values is the notion of meaning.

It is difficult to imagine being a happy and successful employee of an organization that provides meaningless goods or services. It is equally difficult to imagine being a happy and successful worker in an organization for which the product or service is regarded as either alien or destructive.

Corporate climate audits

There are several ways in which corporate climate functioning might be measured. Among the more obvious measures are those of staff turnover, absenteeism, customer/

client complaints, sales (or clients seen), amount of service provided, quantity and quality of products, increases in receivables, and decreases in orders or referrals. Organizations, like countries, have a prevailing social climate.

The corporate climate is also an essentially human attribute. It is the corporate philosophy, the prevailing attitudes within the organization, the quality of the leadership, the efficiency of the organization and the emphasis placed on the team. The purpose of the corporate climate audit is to do the corporate equivalent of a medical check-up. Just as a medical check-up examines particular functions in detail, so too would the corporate audit.

Such an audit would examine both the organizational processes themselves, and the individual's role within the organization. What is being proposed here is that accounting might also include issues such as employee matters, the production of goods, the provision of services, community involvement, the environment, intellectual property, organizational plans, as well as financial accounting.

The main advantages of the kind of audits proposed here are twofold. The first would be to understand the general climate in which an organization operates; the second, to develop some concrete proposals for the improvement of company functioning. By using external experts to do the audit there is the advantage of bringing a fresh perspective to the corporate philosophy and to corporate effectiveness. Among the issues that might be canvassed in the audit are:

- staff morale and job satisfaction;
- occupational health and safety;
- staff selection and promotion;
- compliance with legislation;
- relationships with customers and suppliers; and
- dealings with other organizations.

Prominent in such an audit is the matter of ethical dealings and principles (perhaps combined with a report on the ethical status of the organization). To be ethically effective, corporate social accounting should not be simply a public relations exercise.

It is because of the evanescent nature of a corporate climate that it needs expert examination. There are parts of a corporate climate audit that could be carried out by different consultants with various backgrounds, and some aspects that require particular skills. The preferred outcome of the climate audit would be a written report to management, to be supplemented by an oral presentation to the staff on the findings of the study.

In addition, evaluations of particular staff members could be commissioned. This would involve, with the staff members' co-operation, the preparation of a report based on the job description, the staff members' perception of their jobs, their superiors' views, psychological testing and background information. One could imagine that a set of practices would be developed, rather like the Statements of Standard Accounting Practice (SSAPs) – a point made by many nations, and exemplified by accountants in Britain (see Statements of Standard Accounting Practice in References).

Ethics consultants

It is curious that where we have consultants for just about everything there are so few ethics consultants. Such experts are in a position to help to arbitrate disputes and carry out independent audits of codes and procedures. They would be in a position to assess the ethical status of organizations, and to advise how to comply. They would also be able to assist courts in their deliberations. In this latter role their function is similar to that of other expert witnesses (under current rules of evidence). Ethics experts would be well placed to conclude whether or not an organization was sincerely committed to an ethics policy, and had a properly set up ethics infrastructure rather than just public relations window dressing. Thus ethics is a defence against imputations of impropriety.

The ethical audit

One particularly useful function in order to assess ethical performance would be to perform an ethical audit, canvassing such questions as perceptions of the value of an ethical code, degree of commitment to its implementation, what ethical issues are perceived to be important, and how an organization is rated ethically.

There are various ways of doing this. Among these is the salient distinction of whether one looks at statements, or at behaviour. A manufacturing organization might have a policy on waste recycling, an instruction to employees, and even provide waste recycling bins. Although the bins may have been filled appropriately they then might be taken to the ordinary rubbish tip.

An ideal situation is one where there is appropriate instruction and logistics, backed by actual behaviour that reflects the intent of the instruction and infrastructure. A guard of such probity would be the commission of an independent consultant to verify the actual situation, and to report to the CEO with a view to inclusion in the Annual Report. (See also previous section on corporate climate audits.)

Quantification and ethics

One of the common criticisms of ethics is that it is imprecise. As Lord Kelvin once remarked – if something exists it exists to some amount, and is therefore potentially measurable. The quantification of ethics fulfils that aspiration in that it makes it more precise, allows for operational definitions, and permits us to compare and contrast the different ways of considering ethical issues. The provision of quantitative techniques encourages us to consider such simple techniques as asking, 'How much would I need to pay you to do X?' to the more sophisticated techniques such as paired comparisons. By considering such issues we come to a better understanding of what constitutes the nature of judging according to value systems. One may make decisions according to various principles. Some examples are:

- Fine balance of probabilities (I would rather play golf than chess).
- Minimizing tragedy (I assign the only dialysis machine to patient X rather than patient Y on the basis of Z).
- Forbidden considerations (I would sacrifice my only son rather than lose my faith in God).
- Prudence (do not over-drink).
- An absolute moral value (I would not betray my child for anyone, anything, or any amount of money).
- A moral precept (My moral action will always be in accord with the principle of preserving and fostering equality).

There are so many things in the world that we admire, but seem unable to measure. Take the example of shiny coachwork on cars. We admire the glossy finish, but cannot ordinarily assess how glossy and perfect it is. There is a story that Rolls Royce wanted to set a benchmark for good paintwork, and came up with a ready measure. They decided that the standard of good paint finish would be met if someone with good eyesight could read *The Times*' ordinary print by the reflection in the paint when the newspaper was held 15 inches away from the coachwork.

Human judgement about values is a bit more problematical. However, there are ways of doing this. One technique is to use money as the reference point. Using money as a common denominator, a colleague comes up with the idea that it might be used as a means of quantification. He proposes, for example, to ask how much you would charge a bank to make all women staff wear purdah (or at least some form of modest veil). How much would a citizen take to dispense with periodic elections? How much to betray your country to a foreign power?

A second technique is called the 'Delphi technique' (a variant of the nominal group technique). This is a method of getting answers to difficult and ambiguous questions. It is used as an analytical tool to make forecasts of issues characterized by complexity and uncertainty. It utilizes the principle that several heads are better than one, and that a sequence of attempts to solve the problem is superior to a one-shot approach. It is, in other words, a reiterative technique.

The main aims of the Delphi technique are to set out the goals and objectives; to consider a wide array of possible choices; to order those choices for importance; identify group values; gather whatever facts might be available; and use all of these to come to a conclusion. This technique is also invaluable where a pooled judgement is considered appropriate. It also makes better use of those with special expertise. This technique commonly uses the sequence of:

- identifying the issues;
- identifying the options; and
- determining an initial position.

The first phase gives rise to a consolidation of what is known and held. From this first phase disagreements are likely to become apparent. The next phase is, therefore:

- exploring the disagreements, and the reason for them; and
- evaluating the underlying reasons for such disagreements.

This evaluation leads to a restructuring of both the evidence, and what such evidence might mean. It will be seen that the Delphi technique requires several 'rounds' in order to make proper use of its potential, but that is not to say that it cannot be used in one session. There are practitioners now that use computerized systems to record responses and rapidly (almost simultaneously) identify the issues and the priority of importance of those issues to the group. The technique should properly be called the 'nominal group technique'. Those wishing to learn more of this technique are recommended to read books on group techniques. One good example contains several instances of the kind of problem for which the use of the Delphi technique is readily applicable (Furnham, 2005).

To work this technique a reference group is chosen to select (say) the important ethical principles that should appear in the company code. The group is asked to write down, without reference to each other, the principles they consider to be most important; they are then asked to rank them in order of importance – one being the most important. The group mediator then asks for the principles and enters them on a board, visible to the group, ending up with a list of ethical principles.

With this comprehensive list the mediator then asks, for each principle, how many ranked it first, then how many ranked it second, then how many ranked it third. The results are entered in a tabular form (see Table 8.1). For the sake of simplicity suppose that there are 10 people in the group, and five principles. Overall there are 30 judgements (10 people, each with their three listed choices). Each principle is considered for all 10 people in the group, and so there are 10 rankings of 1st, 10 rankings of 2nd, and 10 rankings of 3rd.

TABLE 8.1 Ranking of importance of principle

	Principle 1	Value	Principle 2	Value	Principle 3	Value	Principle 4	Value	Principle 5	Value
Person 1	1		4		2		5		3	
Person 2	3		4		2		1		5	
Person 3	2		4		3		1		5	
Person 4	2		1		4		3		5	
Person 5	1		2		4		5		3	
Person 6	1		2		4		3		5	
Person 7	1		3		5		2		4	
Person 8	1		2		4		3		5	
Person 9	2		1		3		4		5	
Person 10	2		1		3		4		5	

Continues overleaf

TABLE 8.1 *continued*

	Principle 1	Value	Principle 2	Value	Principle 3	Value	Principle 4	Value	Principle 5	Value
No. times ranked 1	5	25	3	15	0	0	2	10	0	0
No. times ranked 2	4	16	3	12	2	8	1	4	0	0
No. times ranked 3	1	3	1	3	3	9	3	9	2	6
No. times ranked 4	0	0	3	6	4	8	2	4	1	2
No. times ranked 5	0	0	0	0	1	1	2	2	7	7
Sums	10	44	10	36	10	26	10	29	10	15

Giving a value of 5 to first rank, a value of 4 to second rank etc., allows us to derive a value for each Principle

The values are given to the immediate right of the Principle rankings

From the table it is clear that Principle 1 ranked highest, with Principle 2 second, and Principle 5 least important

The presumption is that the first ranking is worth more than a second ranking and so we weight the ranks. A first ranking gets a weighting of 5, a second ranking a weighting of 4, third gets 3, and so on. This is rather like the way in which punters and tipsters on horse races have places weighted. If we add the weighted scores (bolded) we arrive at a weighting of that principle for that group. We may well find that financial probity scores highest and honesty second. Openness and conflict of interest rank third equal. If need be, these numbers can be manipulated statistically.

A second phase follows in which the group looks at results and may now discuss them. After that discussion they are asked to repeat the ranking process, and perhaps add, delete or combine principles. The quantifying process is then repeated. After about three or four reiterations the conclusions will become stabilized. A significant bonus for this technique is not only that it allows us to quantify the seemingly unmeasurable, but also that it engages the attention of the participants so that they become 'owners' of the conclusions, and more committed to their implementation.

Quantification may sometimes act as a guide to the importance of an issue. For example, in recently past times the amount of money spent on foreign wars could be far more than is spent on medical matters and unemployment benefits combined. The criteria of financial success in business might be expressed as hourly return per employee, or capital value increase, or gross profit, or market share, or turnover.

One of the questions to ask is, does the size of misdemeanour matter? Is cocaine dealing less moral than selling tobacco? Are arms manufacturers ethical by delivering quality goods at a reasonable price and on time? Is selling a lot of alcohol worse than selling a bit of heroin? The answers to such questions should enlarge our understanding of what we regard as important.

Another quantification insight to us is the potential for crimes committed within the corporation. One might compare the numbers of crimes to cities of the same size. Within a giant corporation there will be a proportion of murders, rapes, assaults, thefts and embezzlement. While it is true that the populations at risk may be different, and offenders differentially detectable, the force of comparison is still there. It would be impossible to believe that any corporation hires only the saintly, and has employment practices so perfect that HR only employs those who will not lie, cheat, steal or assault.

Professional and business mobility works against developing a loyalty to one organization. How does one promote loyalty in a shifting set of commercial and industrial alliances? If national espionage is permissible, why not industrial espionage? Are company mergers for personal profit to be ethically permitted? Should ethical statements be cast in culturally appropriate terms? Under what conditions is it ethical to accept gifts in a business context? For a comparative account of teaching business ethics in several countries see White and Taft (2004). More recently there is a paper that considers the importance of the impact of religious beliefs on the teaching of business ethics (Ruhe and Lee, 2008).

Social and environmental accounting

Accounting is traditionally concerned with the financial description of economic events in a specific organization to specified users, typically reporting to investors and management via various securities and commissions. Corporate social reporting retains the focus on the organization but examines the other constraints, the determinants of traditional accounting. Thus corporate social reporting, social accounting, has three dimensions:

- To whom should one account? In addition to the investor and manager, can rights to formal and systematic information be claimed by, for example, employees, trade unions, consumers, local communities and society in general?

- How should one account? What are the limitations of financial description? Are there times when it might be best to account in non-financial quantitative terms, or in qualitative terms?

- For what should one account? What are the restrictions that the description of economic events places on the picture presented by accounting? Should one also be accounting for employees, for the consumers, for the effect on local communities, for the effect on society, for the effect on the environment?

This topic, like so many others, has inherent difficulties. Among such difficulties are the absence of universally accepted regulations; the absence of wider benchmarks; the scarcity of annual disclosure on these issues; and an explication of stakeholder relationships. Even if these issues were less problematical there would need to be a balance between financial, social and environmental outcomes. An account of the impact of such competing on the bottom line can be found in Elkington (1999). Further review of this area is to be found in several places, most notably in Lindgreen and Swaen (2010). In a more recent account Savitz (2014) made the point that the triple bottom line can be significantly associated with profitability, which is true also of long-term sustainability (a point already asserted by Willard (2012)). Both have a similar view on the advantages of triple bottom line and sustainability concern.

These broad themes have led to many theoretical and practical developments. The most important of the theoretical developments is the recognition that traditional accounting is a tightly restrictive subset of wider potential social and environmental accounting. This restriction is especially difficult to justify on theoretical grounds, and is important in considering the current 'green' debate.

Corporate social reporting

The Body Shop

The Body Shop is a well-known brand of personal care and cosmetic products. They have a very long history of acting in a socially responsible way, from stopping animal testing on cosmetics to arguing with Shell over its land use in Africa. This socially responsible attitude was initiated by their founder, Anita Roddick, whose overriding objective was 'to dedicate our business to the pursuit of social and environmental change'.

An important feature of the company's reporting is a 'social and environmental' report that seeks to make visible their corporate behaviour. It is produced every two to three years and is currently up to its seventh cycle. The report has received awards from the United Nations Environmental Programme and has been referred to as 'trailblazing'.

SOURCE: See The Body Shop in recommended reading

The way in which business presents ideas should conform to agreed principles of accepted behaviour. One major difficulty is that of distinguishing between agreed principles and ideology. Those 'explanations' that derive from a particular view of the world might take an ideological form (such as a particular religion, psychoanalysis, Marxism, moral re-armament, economic rationalism, etc).

The essence of an ideological view is that all 'facts' are interpreted in a manner consistent with the underlying world view, and courses of action are guided by those same views. Some of what passes for economic theory is really special pleading for an ideological position. For example, Marxists tend to 'reduce' activities to economic ones, leaving out cultural and idealistic dimensions. Although there are economic aspects to education, public broadcasting, health, policing, museums and religion, such services cannot be expressed in purely economic terms.

The collapse of European communism might lead to the idealization of capitalism with perhaps a diminishing concern with the provision of services for the public at large, and to the economically and socially disadvantaged in particular. The point here is that the kind of reporting being discussed needs to be in terms of the general norms, and not as a case of special pleading. The extent that an ethical code has been adopted by the corporation's culture may also be measured in a number of ways which include:

- translation into behaviour (actually do ethical things in ethically ambiguous situations);

- provision of precise ethical learning goals to staff (master the company code by a certain date);

- showing how the achievement of ethical goals contributes to self-worth and company profile;

- creation of new ways of judging ethical performance, and the provision of appropriate non-tangible rewards (such as honourable mention).

This translation may be made concrete in some specific questions such as the following:

- How many insider trade deals were done?

- How many technical breaches occurred?

- How many customer complaints suggesting unethical behaviour were received?

- How many union principles were breached?

(List is a modified version of that appearing in Drummond (1991).)

Urgency versus importance

All managers, whether assessing an ethical issue or generally conducting their day, need to prioritize. Some days need to be approached from a strategic perspective and time allocated to those matters that need attention in the correct order. First, time can be divided into fixed (scheduled events) and flexible (time that is not scheduled). With the flexible time a manager must then consider whether a task is urgent or important; often these ideas are merged and tasks are addressed in a sequence that is not optimal. A task can be important but not urgent (the finalizing of a crucial contract not due for six months). In the alternative, a task can be urgent but not important (routine work reports due at 4pm). Both need to be addressed but the question is when. Many managers make the mistake of working on the important (crucial contract) at the cost of the urgent (their work report).

TABLE 8.2 Urgency and importance

	URGENT	NOT URGENT
IMPORTANT	Crises Deadlines Pressing problems	Planning Relationship building Recreation
NOT IMPORTANT	Phone interruptions Some mail Some meetings and reports	Trivia Time wasters Some phone calls

SOURCE: Adapted from Kasperczyk and Francis, 2002

Readers will be able to make their own list. The important point here is to be aware of the distinction.

Fostering an ethical culture

The purpose of business is to make money; if it does not, it will have failed in its primary aim. If it does make money, but does so in an unethical fashion, it will be in breach of our social system, which permits and fosters its commercial activity. It is the aim of any learning strategy for ethics to constantly make the point that the purpose of business is to make money, and to be socially responsible in doing so.

Ethical infrastructure is that combination of processes and organizational structures that together constitute the minimum requirement for genuine ethical commitment. The four main constituents are a code, persons that are responsible (staff, local managers, ethics officers, ethics committees and the leadership team), reporting and training.

Ethical codes may be fostered by a number of devices. These include using outcome measures (discussed previously), providing specific learning for which due recognition is given and devising outcome measures that may be used in promotional material. The actions that might be taken to foster a code include:

- a clear code of business ethics set up, printed and widely disseminated;
- roles and responsibilities for managing ethical issues established and communicated (as noted earlier);
- open, fair and transparent processes for dealing with breaches (discussed in Chapter 9);
- clear conditions of reporting on particular ethical cases;
- a comprehensive training programme that commences at induction and continues throughout the person's working life in the company (include seminars that would engage and instruct employees).

Ensuring that the corporation's ethical code is known

The first point of ensuring that employees are ethical is to ensure that they are familiar with the corporation's ethical code. Codes of ethics may be disseminated through company booklets, annual reports and induction and training programmes. The primary advantages of ethics codes are to:

- clarify management's thoughts on what constitutes unethical behaviour;
- help employees to think about ethical issues before they are confronted with the reality of a situation;

- provide employees with the opportunity for refusing compliance with unethical action;
- define the limits of what constitutes acceptable or unacceptable behaviour; and
- provide a mechanism for communicating managerial policy.

A code of ethics is the most visible sign of a company's philosophy in the realm of ethical behaviour. In order to be meaningful it must assist in the induction and upskilling of employees, truly state its basic principles and expectations, and realistically focus on potential ethical dilemmas.

The aim of any learning strategy for ethics is, among other things, to sensitize students, employees, front-line managers and executives to the scope of ethical issues, and the way in which they permeate all business activity. Bennett *et al* (1994) state that commitment to a code requires the development of the following seven aspects:

- knowing the code;
- knowing the applicability of state and federal laws and regulations;
- knowing the rules and regulations of the corporation where the employee works;
- engaging in continuing education in ethics;
- identifying when there is a potential ethical problem;
- learning a method of analysing ethical obligations in often complex situations; and
- consulting professionals knowledgeable about ethics.

Learning strategies

There are a number of learning strategies available, ideally in combination, but they are only likely to work well if the employees are committed to the notion of ethics. To have them involved in the development of an ethical programme is vital; the demonstrable commitment by management to an ethical code, and its encouragement, is necessary.

As mentioned, among the justifications for learning strategies for ethics is that of skilling employees to discriminate urgency from importance. To be exposed to decisions in a non-threatening environment is valuable practice for later decision making under adverse conditions.

Listed below are the learning methodologies that can be applied.

Online training

One of the major methods deployed by corporations is the use of online training courses. They have numerous benefits, including:

- they are relatively inexpensive (compared with the cost of providing trainers, training rooms and travel time for the participants);
- generic training (like principles of ethics) can be purchased off the shelf (or obtained from the OECD, or from this book);
- training can be readily tailored to an organization;
- training can reach a mass audience very quickly (important when you are considering organizations with thousands of employees);
- a form of assessment can be built into the course (important for organizations to be able to provide assurances that particular values have been read and understood);
- they are useful for reporting as participation and assessment can be recorded automatically.

They are not necessarily ideal, as they really do not allow for a conversation to clarify issues or have the ability to develop issues beyond the scope of the course but they are efficient and expedient.

Lectures

Lecturing is very effective in getting across an overview of information, of providing a structured approach to the subject, and of exposing the audience to the enthusiasm of the practitioner. However, lectures can sometimes be abstract and call for more concentration; they may be intellectually demanding and can, if not done well, seem remote from real life. The quality of lectures is mainly a reflection of the quality of the lecturer as a subject matter expert and a communicator.

With the rise of online training and information available through the internet and social media in particular, the traditional model of the lecture is under threat even within the university system. Many students find the lecture a cumbersome way of learning. A majority of universities are finding students are staying away from lectures and finding other ways to access the learning. Some university professionals are considering different approaches to connect with students in ways that adjust for new social norms and the opportunities that the technology presents.

The obvious observation to make is that it is feasible now for 'the best lecturer' in the country or the world to deliver the subject material to as many people as need to learn. Other strategies involve combinations such as short, targeted videos with high production value supported by links to powerpoint slides and useful websites. Some lecturers are providing interactive technology (such as phone apps) to encourage broader participation in the lecture process.

In keeping with this development an increasing number of courses (referred to as Massive Open Online Courses – MOOCs) are becoming available on the internet. This was initially focused at people wanting to learn but unable to physically attend, but it is now a growing strategy to connect with all of the student body. MOOCs overcome the limitations of using purely online learning by providing online forums to allow discussion of topics. It is not unusual to see students undertaking a mixture of MOOCs and traditional courses. These are useful strategies for business to consider either in creating their own content or sourcing content already available.

The use of case studies

Case studies fit into a number of delivery mediums (for example online, lectures, tutorials, seminars). They are useful surrogates for experiencing ethical dilemmas, particularly for those new to business or new to management positions and their issues. This can be done by giving factual illustrations of potential and actual conflicts of values, or of competing principles (eg loyalty and truthfulness). Among the most efficient methods of embedding ethical behaviour are training programmes using three specific goals, to:

- enable managers to recognize the ethical component of a business decision;
- decide what to do about it once it is recognized; and
- learn how to anticipate emerging ethical issues (Drummond, 1991).

Case studies, on the other hand, may seem too particular, or irrelevant to the form of industry or commerce in which the participants are engaged. Like lectures case studies are only as useful as the authors make them. They need to be tailored for relevance to the audience.

Simulations

There are a number of strategies that use simulations, which include:

Convening an ethics committee – This involves taking an ethics case and convening the learning group as though it were an ethics committee. Role playing is usually an important component. Sometimes the technique is used of giving roles to those who find the views they are meant to represent opposite to their own. This is a useful way of getting someone locked into an ethical position to appreciate the countervailing views.

Using the 'hypotheticals' – Everyone is given a copy of the case to read. The panel, run by a chairperson, asks each member in sequence what has contributed to the problem. When the views have been gathered, new information that could have an impact on the conclusion likely to be drawn, is added.

Using videos on ethical issues – An ethical story is shown from some appropriate source (eg videos made by professional associations and government agencies). The participants view the video, decide and discuss what the issue is, what relevant code or principle it breaches, and what the appropriate outcome should be.

Larger-scale projects – Several business schools use larger-scale projects that might take anywhere from half a day to a term to undertake a simulated business venture in which ethics is a significant component. These involve dividing the group into competing organizations, setting the ground rules, devising appropriate commercial and ethical aims, and measures of success.

Mentoring

Those with decades of business experience are an asset that can be of benefit to others and to the organization. Not only is their expertise of value, but it is usually tempered by experience of what is practical and they potentially have a more ethical view of the world. The utilization of the wider ethical view provides an opportunity to use their enhanced understanding of ethical issues to become mentors to less experienced colleagues. This benefit to the organization is complemented by the satisfaction of sharing their knowledge. Often mentors may provide their assistance by way of being an adviser, friend, role model, supporter or confidant.

Sensitizing to ethical issues

There is much to be said for using appropriate combinations of the above techniques, since each has a special merit. Where we give such a diversity of experience it is worth recalling that early learning is more effective than later learning. Sensitization and experience early in a career set a pattern that may well be set for professional life.

Learning may involve the professionals as well as other employees within an organization. The involvement of all members of the organization is a precondition of an effective ethics policy. Among the points of involvement are those mentioned elsewhere in this work, dealing with ethical infrastructure:

- specific roles and responsibilities for ethical matters;
- a formal code;
- a training programme;
- regular reporting.

All of these are necessary, but more is required. The regularity of processes such as reporting gives ethics a recurring prominence, a prominence of no less importance than that of periodic financial accounting.

The importance of a learning strategy for an ethical culture

Given that there is a commitment to ethics, a learning programme is mandatory. As Drummond (1991) says, whatever form ethical awareness learning programmes take, their precise nature will vary from company to company. It is important that the following objectives are kept in mind:

- promote and support the organization's values and standards;
- make managers more aware of the ethical dimensions of their business decisions and conduct;
- re-educate staff in the organization's ethical policies;
- strengthen the ability of the staff to apply the organization's ethics; and
- provide a forum for managers to identify ethical issues and areas of vulnerability.

To maintain a corporation with a high ethical standard every manager should:

- behave ethically themselves;
- screen potential employees;
- have a meaningful code of ethics;
- implement ethics awareness training;
- reinforce ethical behaviour; and
- create a structure to deal with ethical issues.

Syllabus matters

Those planning a course in ethics may wish to use the 'Contents' of this (or other) books as a guide. It is recommended that any syllabus cover at least:

- the background to ethics;
- key issues (principles) in business ethics;
- international covenants and legal requirements;
- any relevant professional code;
- other relevant professional and public service codes;
- how to identify and resolve ethical disputes; and
- as much exposure to solving problems in a practice environment as time and resource allows.

Among the questions to be addressed in training are those listed below. These were taken from Eberlein (1993) and recast:

- What do business people do that is ethical, and how can this be reinforced?
- What do business people do that is unethical, and how can this be corrected?
- What do business people believe about how they should behave, and is this a legitimate part of an ethics course?
- What is the 'ethical reasoning process' by which business decisions are made?

In posing these questions it should be noted that any ethics curriculum should consider a combination of the strategies discussed above. In sensitizing to ethical issues a recurring theme is the ambiguity of the ethical position. Among the issues worth canvassing are:

- that ambiguity may permit more than one ethical solution;
- the existence of competing ethical values and principles;
- the informal business norms and etiquette; and
- the need to consult widely (including the legal context).

Essential elements of an ethical corporate structure

There are major barriers to introducing ethical conduct into organizations, which can include:

- a prevailing ethos in a business community that morality has no role in business (even when imposed by statute);
- an ineffective government unwilling or unable to address structural flaws;
- economically difficult times compelling questionable actions;

- leadership that is committed not to ethics but to profit;
- managers being measured on profitability; and
- a corporate culture focused on profitability with no concern for social responsibility.

In those places and organizations where there is a political environment that accommodates and supports ethical conduct and the leadership team are committed to making an ethical culture, then the ethical company is very possible. Having progressed through this text it would be expected that a reader would be in a position to determine what the qualities of an ethical corporate culture are. By way of summary these features are:

An ethical code. All publicly listed corporations are effectively compelled to have an ethical code. The important question is, what is the quality of the code and how does it form part of their culture? An effective code will have a number of qualities, including:

- being drafted in a collaborative manner with the principal stakeholders including employees;
- cultural differences being taken into account;
- being a 'living' document constantly tested and under review; and
- ideally it will be principles-based rather than prescriptive.

A visibly ethical leadership team. The leadership team will not only live the values themselves but it will be apparent to their employees.

Employees will be valued and seen as major stakeholders.

There is a clear ethical infrastructure. Corporations will have designated roles and processes. It is quite important that responsibilities are clearly defined and that employees are aware of what steps to take and who to approach when confronted with an ethical issue.

Selection and recruitment will be specifically targeting candidates with a demonstrated commitment to ethics. A very powerful message is sent to employees when people are promoted. Those that are promoted and their values are the models for the rest of the organization. Everyone will be looking to them to see their own path to advancement.

There are appropriate rewards and sanctions for ethical compliance. Other than promotions, there are a number of ways that corporations can reinforce or discourage behaviour such as bonuses, recognition and access to development.

Ethical training will form part of all relevant training courses, and not be an afterthought or an annexure. Ideally, it will complement ethical training that was started during the education process. Learning is a powerful force in developing ethical culture.

Ethics will form part of day-to-day decision making. All staff and managers, when faced with a decision, process it in terms of its utility to the community. Ideally, decisions will be proactive and give equal weight to social good and profitability, not just merely reject the socially irresponsible.

Ethical conduct will be the subject of reporting. A form of social and environmental accounting should be deployed in parallel with narrative reports on specific issues, problems or successes.

The importance and principal features of ethical codes

Ethical codes are meaningless pieces of paper if written and put in the top drawer. An inadequate code makes for ambiguity and uncertainty. If, for example, a code were simply to state that everyone was to act morally, with no further detail provided, then everyone would have different views, particularly in a global company where there were many cultures operating. An ethical code, like the law, will not resolve every problem but it is an important start in communicating to the employees what behaviour is expected.

Writing codes

Codes may be written in an aspirational or in a punitive style. The former is a set of propositions that are ideals (and may not be achievable); the latter is a set of prescriptions that, if breached, invite sanctions. Ethics is not about legalistic argument, nor is it about punishment; it is, at best, positive and persuasive rather than prohibitive and punitive. Among other things it fills in the interstices of the law; it is modest, not making claim to the absolute truth, and does not need a religious base. In an ideal world it would be culture free, but that may be too extravagant an expectation. At least we can try to formulate principles that transcend culture; it is the aspiration as well as the achievement that we should admire.

It is preferable for ethical codes to be active rather than passive. They enjoin us to do things and behave in particular ways rather than invite us to ignore particular things. One might mistake consensus for acceptability; one may be consistent – and quite wrong. Codes are not likely to function well if they rely on blind obedience.

The internalization of values, and their being generally accepted, are important aspects. This means that managers must pay attention not only to content but also to process for determining that content. Ideally a code should be developed and disseminated to all staff in an open, participative environment.

What is the corporate ethical uptake?

National Business Ethics Survey

Throughout this text there has been discussion and examples of how ethical codes exist in almost all large corporations. The crucial question is to what extent those values are part of corporate culture. The Ethics Resource Center in Washington has been surveying corporate behaviour for the last 20 years. In 2012 they collated the results from over 2,000 employees of Fortune 500 companies. Those results showed 59 per cent said their organization had a 'strong' or 'strong leaning to' ethical culture.

It is interesting that in a post-GFC environment where there has been legislation mandating ethical culture, there is still 41 per cent of organizations that do not have a 'strong' or 'strong leaning to' ethical culture.

SOURCE: See National Business Ethics Survey in recommended reading

The inequality of relationships is the basis of 'unethical' behaviour. Hippocrates noted this over 2,000 years ago when he recognized physicians were in a position of power in relation to their patients and could abuse that power. The misuse of power unbalances a relationship. For example, a boss who wanted subordinates to confide in him for 'therapeutic' reasons would be misusing power. The role for which he or she is untrained involves a conflict of interest that could act to the detriment of one of the parties.

It is probably true to say that the concentration of commercial or organizational power into too few hands is to the long-term detriment of both the organization and the public it is meant to serve, recalling Lord Acton's dictum that power corrupts, and absolute power corrupts absolutely. Our notion of justice is essentially one of equity. There can be little justice where power is unequal. Any code should address these imbalances.

Difficulties in business relationships often turn out to be difficulties in the relationships of key players. To love everyone is an unachievable counsel of perfection; sometimes one is obliged to have working relationships with those with whom one would rather not associate. Fortunately for business, and thanks to conventional courtesies, we have developed ways to cope with those whose personal style we find difficult.

In professional interpersonal relationships we are often obliged to work with people whom we do not admire, and would prefer to avoid. For such situations there are helpful guidelines to be found in principles such as the use of courtesy, limiting the time of interaction, and restricting the interactions to professional or commercial issues.

The ethical systems we put in place will set a precedent for future generations. Given world population growth, whatever ethical stance we adopt will have an impact on a population growing at an accelerating rate. As recently as 1905 the world population was 1.7 billion; in 1985 it was 4.8 billion and growing at 78 million per year. It is given that by the year 2000 it was over 6 billion. In 2010 it was just under 7 billion. Such 'estimates' are likely to be in error, however, since the population figures seem to be revised upward every few years. For young people growing up now, a significant proportion of all the people who ever lived will have been born within their lifetime. It is thus that ethics is important: it sets the standards and concerns that will be adopted by subsequent growing generations.

Conclusion

This chapter was primarily to provide practical methods for developing ethical cultures. It introduced the concept of ethical gradualism (an incremental approach to developing ethical culture), and progressed to issues around understanding corporate cultures and measuring ethical behaviour. It then looked at the various ways of fostering an ethical code with a focus on learning strategies. Finally, it summarized the main features of an ethical corporate culture. The chapter concluded with the importance and principal features of ethical codes. The following chapter will address how to investigate and resolve an ethical dilemma.

Focus questions

Ethics

1 How would you describe ethical gradualism? What are its important features?

2 What are the difficulties in defining corporate culture?

3 What mechanisms are available to measure corporate ethical culture and behaviour?

4 What is the difference between urgent and important? Why is this important?

5 What steps would you use to evaluate the ethics of a proposal?

6 What are the learning strategies available to foster ethical behaviour?

7 What is a MOOC? How can it be used by corporations in improving ethical conduct? Why is a MOOC to be preferred over other strategies?

8 What are the essential elements of an ethical corporate culture?

CASE STUDY   Toxic culture

Nitin has been assigned as a manager of a South American subsidiary that is performing badly. He has been specifically tasked to address the underperformance. Nitin decides that he will become familiar with people and primarily observe in the first month he is there. In that month he notes that, although there is an outward appearance of harmony, there is an undercurrent of disengagement by employees. The number of complaints from clients and suppliers is high relative to the other offices in the organization and reflects a lack of concern for service or business relationships. There is a very high level of employee absences. The quality of reports is very poor and they are often full of error. There are a number of bullying complaints from staff. There is innuendo that there have been corrupt practices with local government authorities.

Nitin's month of observation is up; what are his next steps?

Factors to consider

It would be rare in a successful manager's career that they would not at some time face a toxic culture, either in an organization as whole or in a component of an organization. Nitin made a good start by giving himself sufficient time to make his own assessments. A month may be a luxury in some situations and not enough in others. Regardless, Nitin should ensure that he has negotiated the strategy, expectations and timeframes with his manager before commencing the assignment.

Crucial to resolving the issues is correctly identifying the problem. Change agents need to be conscious that they are treating the disease and not the symptoms. Having completed his initial assessment Nitin should consider whether he has sufficient information to act or whether he should gather more. Personal observations are useful but are ultimately subjective. Nitin might consider using an expert in corporate culture or ethics to assist.

Once the causal factors are established from an assessment of the corporate culture, he should establish a strategy for remedial action. The task sounds significant, and it is likely unreasonable that his head office would expect an instant answer: it will take time. Nitin might look to the potential tasks and assign priority to what things are important and what things are urgent. For example, he may need to choose between dealing with the potential corruption issue before the customer service problem.

Issues he will need to consider could include (but are not limited to):

- investigating the corrupt practices;

- resolving the personnel issues (bullying);

- recruitment and promotion (change involves the right people);

- involving the staff in any changes;

- re-engaging staff with the ethical code;

- Looking to instil an ethos of excellence (eg customer service, relationships with suppliers, reporting); and

- installing some measures to gauge progress of the change to the culture.

An important factor to consider in the strategy is achieving progressive success; even small achievements start to have a cumulative effect. This accumulation can support future changes and act as insurance for the occasional failure. What is important is momentum.

Recommended reading

The Body Shop

The Body Shop (nd) Social and environmental reporting, *The Body Shop* [online]
    http://www.thebodyshop.com.au/about-us/social-and-environmental-reporting.aspx
Brezelton, F, Ellis, S, Macedo, C, Shader, A and Suslow, K (1999, June) Study of Corporate
    Social Responsibility, *Stanford University* [online] https://web.stanford.edu/class/e297c/
    poverty_prejudice/citypoverty/hedge_poverty.htm
Roddick, A (nd) About Dame Anita Roddick, *Anita Roddick* [online]
    http://www.anitaroddick.com/aboutanita.php

National Business Ethics Survey

Ethics Resource Center (2012) National Business ethics survey of Fortune 500 employees:
    An investigation into the state of ethics at America's most powerful companies, *ERC*
    [online] http://pdfserver.amlaw.com/cc/SURVEY.pdf

Wegmans

Heubeck, E (2012, May) Wegman's grocery list for success, *Baltimore Business Journal*
    [online] http://www.bizjournals.com/baltimore/print-edition/2012/05/25/
    wegmans-grocery-list-for-success.html?page=all.
Rohde, D (2012, March) The Anti-Walmart: The secret sauce of Wegman's is people,
    The Atlantic [online] http://www.theatlantic.com/business/archive/2012/03/
    the-anti-walmart-the-secret-sauce-of-wegmans-is-people/254994/
Staples (nd) 5 Company cultures worth emulating, *Staples* [online] http://www.staples.com/
    sbd/cre/tech-services/explore-tips-and-advice/tech-articles/google-this-5-company-culture-
    examples-worth-emulating.html

Investigating ethical breaches

09

Introduction

In the previous chapter the text addressed corporate culture; this chapter will look at the process of managing an ethical breach. It will also look at the consideration involved in assessing whether a planned action is ethical. Specifically it will address determining what is within the scope of an ethical examination, as well as investigation and evaluation. This chapter will look at the outcome types, importance of outcomes and the learning opportunities each case presents.

Key learning points

Firstly, this chapter will discuss the question of what constitutes an ethical dilemma and the value of conducting the investigation.

It then progresses to the investigation stage, specifically addressing:

- Who should deal with the breach.
- The process of dealing with the breach.

The chapter then looks at other relevant factors in investigation and evaluation addressing:

- The importance of quality decision making.
- The three quick tests.
- Promptness of dealing.
- Chatham House Rule.
- Creativity.
- Apologies as solutions.
- Whistleblowing.

Should there be an investigation?

The overreach of ethics

The 'reach' of ethics is confined to ethical issues. It overreaches when it attempts to do things beyond the ethics brief. A main difficulty here is to decide when something is not within that reach. For example, an industry ethics committee considered a research and development application. The outcome of the research was clearly seen to have political implications concerning the disposal of toxic waste. The proposed study satisfied all the rules about good research design, skilled researchers, privacy, informed consent, and the like. Committee members opposed to the dumping of toxic waste saw the proposal as providing support for the idea of the practice, and made approval very difficult. The political agenda of the committee made resistance to this proposed research an example of overreach.

Another area in which overreach is debated is the extent to which personal behaviour might intrude into reputational standing. For example, should a business person who was found to have paid less personal income tax than that for which he was liable be taken to task by the company for which he works? Do employing organizations have the right to intrude into some areas of private life? For example, should a religious charity forbid an employee from using legal brothels?

Economics of ethical decision making

In this practical frame of reference decision makers need to be conscious of the financial costs of decisions, but not bound by them. Some years ago there was an analysis of the costs of persistent petty thievery. The cost to the state of processing and imprisoning is many times the value of what is stolen, but that is no argument not to bring legal sanctions to bear. Many organizations face a similar dilemma: the cost of a minor theft to the organization may be less than the cost of the investigation.

However, a company that accepts that behaviour might find if many workers adopt the practice then it might be very expensive for the organization. The real issue is the underlying message that the company wants to make; that is, this company does or does not accept theft whether the theft is an object, a false expenses claim or a dishonest time sheet. As with crime, an ethical investigation and resolution may not be the cheapest means of dealing with a particular case, but it is something that needs to be done for reasons that have less to do with money than with high social and commercial standards and values.

What is the spirit of the rule?

Express or implied

An important feature of any adjudication process is having an action that does not strictly breach the actual language of the rule (what is expressed) but breaches the principle that lies beneath it (what is implied).

A strict interpretation of the law is often used to defeat its purpose. Throughout the text there have been a number of cases that demonstrate this: the taxation cases are good examples. The underlying principle is that everyone including corporations should pay their share of taxes. Creating complex structures and transactions may be 'strictly lawful' but goes against what lawmakers intended. When making an assessment of whether something is an ethical breach consideration should take into account what the drafters of the ethical code were trying to achieve and not become caught up in the technicalities.

How to resolve an ethical dilemma

Who should deal with an ethical dilemma?

Many corporations, particularly global ones, have well-advanced infrastructure and processes for resolving ethical issues. There is likely an ethics officer (sometimes called the risk officer) usually at a senior level, although the process will not be their exclusive responsibility. They would likely directly report to an ethics committee and the CEO. Given current standards organizations will be, at least in terms of written policy, looking to ensure all employees are engaged with the process.

From the Ethics Resource Center report noted in Chapter 8 we know that close to 60 per cent of the largest companies are committed to developing an ethical environment. While employees have an important role in terms of acting ethically themselves as well as a duty to report inappropriate behaviour, it is usually frontline managers that have the greatest responsibilities. There are several reasons for this:

- The sheer volume of issues that arise – modern global organizations are massive and produce thousands of decisions, often with ethical dimensions, and an ethics officer will not be able to deal with them all.

- Most matters are not so serious as to require escalation of the issue to more senior management.

- The frontline manager has the overall responsibility for the employees and the work which often, but not always, makes them best placed to deal with matters in terms of appreciating the situation and being able to give a timely response. This is particularly true in the global environment given an appreciation of local cultural issues will nearly always be essential and referral to head office might cause unnecessary delay.

Whatever a person's role in the organization it is crucial that they understand their own company's policies, particularly the extent of the power they hold to resolve an issue. Managers need to be alert to not taking control of matters that are sufficiently serious that they need the attention of the ethics officer, the ethics committee or the CEO. Equally they need to be conscious not to pass matters of lesser consequence along the process chain. Corporations expect managers to deal with issues in their sphere.

The process of determining if there has been or is likely to be an ethical breach

Preliminary considerations

The decision maker, whether they are a frontline manager, ethics officer, ethics committee or the CEO, will or should use a process that has a number of common fundamental features:

1 Is the incident likely to be an ethical breach? Not all breaches are ethical, as discussed previously in the 'Overreach of ethics' section above. Similarly, some events are criminal and cannot be managed 'in house.'

2 Is it a breach of the corporate ethical code? If the action appears to be a breach this should be confirmed and specifically identified using the corporation's standards. Given that most corporations have been developing ethical codes since the early 1990s it would be normal for these codes to be comprehensive (incorporating UN values in regard to human rights and basic principles like 'cause no harm'). One of the significant tests of the effectiveness of a code is how it deals with difficult cases. In the unlikely event that an action appears sufficiently serious but is not covered by the code, action should be taken to investigate and potentially review the code.

3 What is the seriousness of the breach? There are several reasons for making this assessment. If the matter is trivial then it should be dealt with quickly; if it is more serious it may need greater effort or escalation to a higher authority.

4 Who is empowered to deal with this matter? As noted above, there are often multiple layers of responsibility inside a corporate hierarchy. One of the

preliminary steps to be taken is to ask who should be dealing with this matter. This might require clarification with the ethics officer or the personnel area. It also should be noted that even if a person holds a delegation then there may also be a responsibility to report the behaviour to the ethics officer or others. Reporting is a crucial factor in 'transparency.'

5 Is there a real, or a perceived, conflict of interest? Clearly, if a person has been implicated in the breach or has a personal relationship with someone involved in the breach, then they cannot be the assessor. Equally, even if there is no actual conflict of interest, is one perceived? For example, if employees consider the accused is a favourite of the manager even though it has no substance. Perceived neutrality is a significant feature particularly if the resolution is to be accepted.

FIGURE 9.1 Decision tree – Ethical breach preliminary considerations

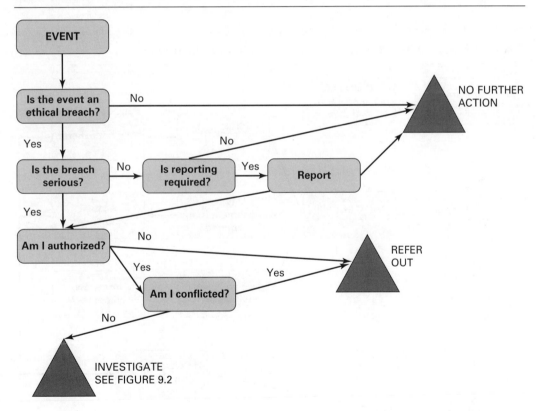

Investigation

Once it is established who the appropriate person or entity is to review:

1 A timeframe and strategy should be agreed. It is important to have a mutual understanding of expectations and how the decision maker intends the matter to progress.

2 What evidence is available? The investigator needs to gather as much material as is feasible in the circumstances including documentation and statements from relevant people. Facts and truth may not be the same thing. Untruths may be presented in various ways. One is to make a direct statement of untruth, such as 'I had no involvement', when there is sound evidence to the contrary (the plain lie). A second example is to suppress important information, failing to mention that a person had knowledge of the event. Perfect knowledge is unlikely to be available so the assessor must make a judgement when there is sufficient information to proceed.

FIGURE 9.2   Decision tree – Ethical breach investigations

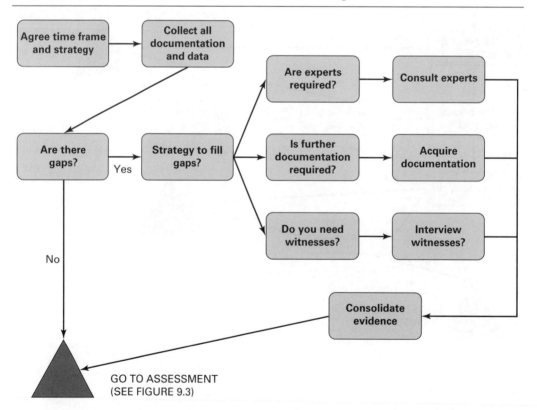

Assessment

1 How to ensure fairness. In leading up to the assessment there are a couple of crucial features to be considered. First, the accused person should be granted 'natural justice'. As noted earlier this is a right of reply to the allegations. Implicit in 'natural justice' is a clear statement of what is alleged and sufficient time for the reply. A person cannot properly defend themselves if the allegations are not really fully explained. Nor is it appropriate to call someone in without notice and not give them an opportunity to process what is happening. A right of reply may simply be a clearly written statement of the facts as they are currently seen and an opportunity to reply in writing. However, a face-to-face or phone meeting may be preferred, as more information and a better gauge of truthfulness might be available.

FIGURE 9.3   Decision tree – Assessment of ethical breach

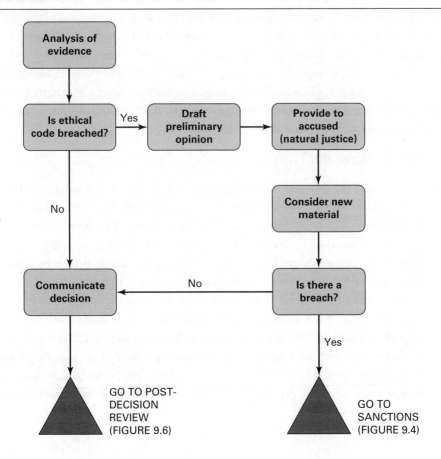

2 How is the ethical issue assessed? Contained within the corporate code
   should be clearly articulated principles against which conduct can be
   measured. For example, has there been a conflict of interest? Has the
   customer been treated unfairly? Has an employee been disadvantaged
   inappropriately? Has a community in a developing country been harmed by
   the corporate action? Are the workers of a sub-contractor in a developing
   country being mistreated? Has the environment been damaged? Have
   resources been used inappropriately?

Having gathered the evidence, given natural justice, the decision maker is in a position
to make a decision. They may find there is no further action and end the matter or
they may have found substance to the allegation. If substance to the allegation was
found, then the decision maker will need to turn their mind to sanctions.

Sanctions

What sanctions should be applied? It would be expected that where there has been
a wrongdoing by an employee, the corporation will have a range of sanctions from
warnings to dismissal. Wherever possible the sanction should be personally remedial
rather than punitive. Decision makers should also check that they are empowered to
impose the particular sanctions. Corporations will usually have guidelines and experts to assist. Within the process, though, a decision maker should not eliminate the
potential for a creative solution. There may be a better outcome to be had by looking
at all the options that are available rather than sticking too rigidly to a formula.
Creativity is discussed in more detail below.

Communicating decisions

1 How should the decision be communicated? It is crucial that a decision be
   well communicated. Whether spoken or written the decision should cover all
   the facts relied upon and the reasons for the decision. All the arguments
   provided to the decision maker by the accused should be specifically
   addressed. A common problem with decisions is that many people believe
   that 'more is better', often to the detriment of understanding.

   The decision should be as long as it needs to be and written in plain
   English so it is clearly understood. A well-reasoned decision is often an
   important factor in bringing a matter to a close and showing that the process
   has been open and transparent. The persons impacted can see that they have
   been listened to and there has been fairness even though they might disagree
   with the result. This is discussed in further detail below in the importance of
   quality decision making.

FIGURE 9.4   Decision tree – Sanctions for ethical breach

2 There is merit in organizations having or considering an appeal process. If the person is aggrieved with some part of the process (such as not all relevant considerations being taken into account) then an opportunity for review might in those circumstances assist in reaching finality.

Review of process

There is a learning experience for everyone participating in every such action. Every decision is an opportunity also for an organization to learn and improve. The matter should not stop at the finalization of the case. The matter should be discussed and examined to see if it says something about culture or process or procedure. If there is an issue then something can be done about it. Consideration should be given to:

● The corporation's ethical code (did it do what it was expected to do or is there an adjustment required?)

● A memorandum to employees about an underlying principle (that doesn't identify those involved in the initial breach).

FIGURE 9.5   Decision tree – Communicating decisions

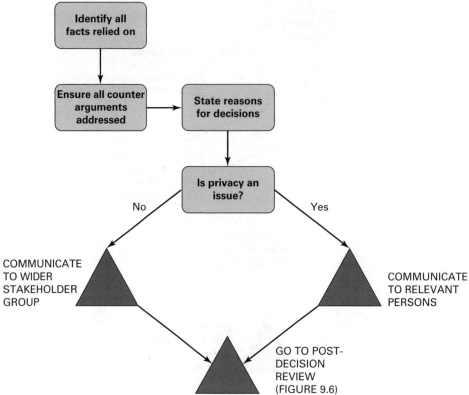

- A review of procedures. Could a mechanism be put in place that prevents the event from occurring again? A crucial principle is that staff should not put people in a position where it is easy to act inappropriately.

- Is further training required?

Ethical assessment of forward planning

It is important to note that there are two categories of ethical issues; retrospective and prospective. Organizations must deal with both breaches that have occurred and proposals of future action. While not identical there are many similarities. When reviewing a strategy the relevant decision maker should be:

- fully informed;
- understanding of the risks or benefits; and
- referring to the corporate code to assess.

FIGURE 9.6   Decision tree – Post-decision review process

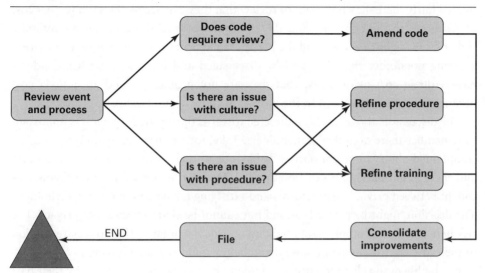

Ideally, a corporate culture is sufficiently developed to ensure that planning incorporates ethical considerations. This ethical corporation not only will be preventing harm but engaging in activities that advance the community much like Mr Matsushita (discussed earlier) envisioned.

Other factors for consideration

The importance of quality decision making

Importantly, the decision maker should aim to give the matter finality. This was touched on earlier both in the quality of the communication of the decision and promptness. Matters are much less likely to progress if the relevant stakeholders have a sense that they have been dealt with fairly. Decisions that are well presented (and well written), well reasoned, and delivered in good time are instrumental to that. Such decisions will necessarily show that the decision maker has been transparent, has given everyone involved a reasonable opportunity to present their case, has addressed every issue and has been reasonable in their conclusions and sanctions. This is very often enough to bring a matter to an end even if the aggrieved person disagrees with the outcome.

There are good reasons why the decision maker should seek finality. A good process often enhances the respect for the decision maker and the organization. It is an important statement about the ethical culture the business wants to create. In a more practical sense, if an individual feels that they have not been listened to or treated fairly there may be a right of review that they can access. This is a further cost of resources to the company and the emotional cost to those involved continues. If there is no right of review and the person remains in the organization then there is a strong possibility that they will be disengaged and inefficient. Such individuals have a direct cost in the sense that they are not productive, and an indirect cost because they are a detriment to the morale of those around them.

The discussion above has been directed towards the wrongdoer but it is important to remember there are other stakeholders. Take, for example, an employee who has complained about some concerning behaviour of their manager. There is a process and there is ultimately no sanction applied. Decision makers often find themselves caught between privacy requirements and satisfying the desires of other stakeholders. The decision might be perfectly sound but cannot be shared because of privacy. The risk here is that the complainant might go outside the organization to seek resolution to their anxiety (discussed in more detail below under whistleblowing).

It is highly desirable that a decision maker and an organization have, by their past actions, built up a sense of trust. Trust works like credit in a bank; at first people are wary because there is no value, but with each incremental demonstration of fairness and honesty, the credit builds up. Then when the dissatisfied complainant asks why, the decision maker can say, 'I am unable to give you the details because of privacy issues, but I can assure you that it was thoroughly looked into and the proper result was achieved'. If there is enough credit in the 'trust' bank account then this may be sufficient to bring the matter to finality.

In making decisions about anything there are always considerations not given in the direct context. Equitability is both a process and a proposition Adherence to the process is crucial. Dilemmas arise through ignorance, inexperience, malice and/or an undeveloped code. While we may find it difficult to either prove or contain malice we can reduce ignorance and inexperience, and we can continually develop our code. While we can develop and refine our codes, and improve the processes by which they are exercised, there is always the limitation of what a code and its attendant procedures can do. Whatever is done is certainly enhanced by constant attention to both the content and procedures.

The three quick tests

In some circumstances executives may not have time for an involved assessment. They might need to respond quickly to a crisis like Johnson & Johnson did with Tylenol. In those circumstances some instant ethical tests are needed. They are described below:

1 How would this be explained in the witness box? Imagine that you have decided on a particular course of action in response to an environmental disaster involving your company, and have implemented the response. The knowledge of the circumstances goes to a court case. Further, imagine that you are in the witness box and have to defend your decision. Would you be able to supply such a defence?

2 How would this look on the front page of tomorrow's newspaper? Imagine the same scenario as above: when the response becomes widely known, it will appear on the front page of the newspapers, across the internet and on social media sites. Would you be happy with how it looks?

3 How would I explain this to my family? In the same circumstances as above, instead of having to defend yourself in court, or appear in the papers, your family ask you to explain. After the explanation would they still be proud of you?

If still in doubt consider seeking the advice of a trusted and honest colleague. If one is not available your professional adviser (accountant, psychologist or lawyer) could fill the same role. Using a solicitor has the extra merit of the communication having full legal privilege, although the other professionals have qualified privilege. Whatever you decide, act as if the outcome were to become public knowledge.

Promptness of dealing

In ethics, no less than in any other form of adjudication, the principle of 'justice delayed is justice denied' applies. Delay on the part of the decision maker confers considerable emotional strain on those involved. It also means that witness memories become stale, that witnesses may disappear, and that reputations may be needlessly damaged. Promptness of dealing is an essential part of the process and extremely important to the perception of fairness and getting finality.

The damage of delay

The Indian court system

India has as many as 30 million cases backlogged; 4 million are High Court cases and 65,000 in the Supreme Court. An expectation that judges should hold no more than 300 cases is exceeded in some instances by tens of thousands. In 2009 the then-Chief Justice, in condemning the situation, calculated it would take 466 years to clear the backlog. By way of comparison, per head of population, Western Europe has 10 times the number of judges.

There has been widespread recognition that there is a need to address this situation and attempts have been made but these have only made marginal or very specific improvements. As a consequence economic development is severely impeded, and inequity reigns because those with access to wealth get better access to justice. Social stability is threatened.

SOURCE: See Indian justice system in recommended reading

Chatham House Rule

Chatham House is also known as the Royal Institute of International Affairs, located in London. It has been such a successful Institute that an American version was developed, and is known as The Council on Foreign Relations, based in New York. The basic rule of the Institute is that 'when a meeting, or part thereof, is held under the Chatham House Rules, participants are free to use the information received, but neither the identity nor the affiliation of the speaker(s), nor that of any other participant, may be revealed'. In essence this rule allows one to discuss any idea without any consequences of attribution (see Chatham House Rule in References).

In some circumstances, particularly where corporations invite external experts to join ethics committees, there may be value in using the Chatham House Rule. It allows the member or members to speak more freely. Parties might be reluctant to openly give their views, if those views might become public.

Creativity

A constructive look at an ethical problem will often yield a solution that satisfies the ethical code, provides guidance for the transgressor, and pleases the complainant. A significant feature here is not to be locked into the either–or mentality. The formal fallacy is called the fallacy of the excluded middle (it is either this or that, but cannot be anything else). If someone tells a business person that the options to fund a new piece of research are by either raising venture capital or by cutting back on current profits, almost invariably there is another way.

Options not considered might be to have the research and development done by an interested university, to get government-sponsored funding, to enter into strategic alliances, or to sell the research idea at a profit and then think of a new one. As with this, so it is with ethical dilemmas. The aim is to find a solution to the problem that will be creative, constructive, satisfy the protagonists, and lead to a confirmation or modification of the code (see Levitt and Dubner, 2005 and De Bono, 2010).

Apologies as solutions

We are all bound to make the occasional mistake. The question here is what to do about it. Within this question there are several significant implications, among them the perceived 'loss of face', and the legal consequences of admission of liability. Such mistakes may be acts of commission, acts of omission, or those that may not have constituted best business practice.

There is a dilemma in the admission of guilt. Any admission of negligence might lead to the implication of legal liability for the fault, particularly in Western culture. On the other hand, the admission of culpability could be disarming and generate an attitude in which informal solutions are sought and implemented. This can be particularly true of non-Western cultures. Thus one might say that, 'I am sorry it happened: if part of it is my fault I do apologize'.

Gullibility

Business people have a higher responsibility to ensure that the public are protected. In one example there is a salutary lesson derived from the Australian Securities and Exchange Commission. An advert was placed seeking investors to further develop a new animal that was a cross between a goat and a sheep (a geep). The advert indicated this new hybrid for transforming the Australian wool industry. It said that the new hybrid was the result of years of research and testing. It further went on to say that the geep had a naturally long and soft fleece, being thereby readily market-able. The new fleece contained a slightly higher percentage of wool and was just under half angora. The advert sought investors, and had a promised return of about 30 per cent. It went on to say that with a newly developed cashmere geep, the profits would be yet greater. The advert concluded with an invitation to contact, with a name and phone number given.

It is salutary to recall that, coming from a respected, government-run organization, it is not surprising that some treated the advert seriously and it brought a host of replies. Potential investors then received a warning that it was a hoax, that there was no such animal, and to be careful in future. This really demonstrates the gullibility of at least some members of the public.

There are occasions where vulnerabilities are self-induced, where the equity is unbalanced by gullibility. Another example is the instance of the Australian Securities and Investments Commission testing gullibility by putting an advertisement out on April Fools' Day in 1999. Its aim was to make investors more cautious. The pretend 'scheme' was an invitation to invest in a Swiss company set up to provide blue chip companies with insurance against Year 2000 millennium computer bug problems.

That fake advertisement yielded 233 firm investors who committed more than $4m, and a further 1,200 people who asked for more information. The Australian Securities and Investments Commission informed the potential investors, and destroyed the records. This experience should surely provide a cautionary message to those who were duped. (See Scams in References, p 230.)

Whistleblowing

The definition of ethical informing (whistleblowing) is when a present or former employee discloses information 'which the employee reasonably believes evidences a violation of any law, rule, or regulation, or gross mismanagement, as gross waste of funds, an abuse of authority, or a substantial and specific danger to public health or safety' (US Whistleblower Protection Act).

Perhaps one of the critical tests of loyalty is that of whistleblowing. Those who decide to inform over a breach of ethical principle put loyalty to principle ahead of loyalty to the organization, and perhaps to some colleagues. To be concerned over a matter of ethics can be the mark of a person of principle; it can also be the mark of an 'informer', in the pejorative sense of that term. To be one or the other depends on the principles to which the informer adheres.

The behaviour of managers is one of the greatest determinants of ethical (or unethical) behaviour: the behaviour of peers and society's moral climate also rank highly. Since we are obliged to accept responsibility for our actions we need to teach how to be ethical in what may be an unethical environment.

When an organization fails to provide such an ethical climate the employees may find themselves at risk of losing their jobs and morale may suffer, as may efficiency. An indication of trouble is when self-protective memos fly around the office and divert resources from what could have been more productive tasks. To minimize this organizations provide processes for dissatisfied employees to make complaints. They usually involve escalation through the hierarchy but depending upon who is involved there are usually also processes that circumvent the hierarchy. Many organizations provide 'hotlines' where staff can ring and raise issues of concern without retribution at the local level.

Organizations should also ensure that they protect genuine whistleblowers so that they do not suffer career or other disadvantage (there should be a person or area that ensures this principle). As has been seen ethical breaches can be very costly; if an ethical breach can be detected and appropriately dealt with internally by the organization they potentially save themselves considerable damage. Part of ensuring a flow of information is encouraging staff to come forward.

The protection of whistleblowers also provides a general deterrence to other employees. A person is unlikely to behave unethically if they know there is a high chance that the behaviour will be reported. By protecting whistleblowers all staff are effectively on notice that 'someone is always watching'.

Organizations also provide training so that individuals are aware of the processes and their ethical responsibilities. They are provided with skills to deal with their concerns. Self-empowerment in ethics may be achieved by resorting to a hierarchy of questions that the ethically troubled employee may use.

The first question is, 'Am I mistaken?' The supplementary questions are, 'Do I misunderstand the situation? Am I clear that this is an ethical issue? Do I have the relevant facts?' The second question is, 'Do I want to do something about it?' The answer may be 'No', or might need to be reviewed, and the minimum done (eg let the ethical transgressor know that you know, but do no more; or let the ethical transgressor know, and say that the matter is being ignored – on this occasion).

Here the objective is to change the ethos. It may be that the reaction to a particular issue is to use it as a lever to promote ethics in general, but to yield on the particular case. The flexibility is not on the principles of ethics but rather on retaining the commitment to principle, by applying continuous pressure to have ethical principles followed. Strong reward and encouragement for instances of ethical behaviour, social approval and admiration are powerful tools. Criticism of a milder kind (unless for an outrageous behaviour) from fellow employees is also useful.

A final avenue of self-empowerment is blowing the whistle. Before being a whistleblower readers are recommended to read 'Whistleblowers (advice to)' given in this book (see Index). What follows was derived and adopted from several sources, and in more serious and schematic form the sequence is:

1 Do I understand that it is a dilemma? If it is am I sure that it is ethical rather than another issue? Do I have the relevant information (facts, codes provision, etc)?

2 If it is an ethical problem do I want to do something about it? Is it justified in terms of importance? Is pursuing the issue likely to lead to a yet greater ethical harm?

3 If it is an ethical problem, and I want to do something about it, what is the minimum I can do that will have the desired outcome? If I want to do something about it, and I have been unable to resolve it using the organizational systems available to me, am I prepared to blow the whistle? If I decide to blow the whistle have I prepared my position properly?

The risk of unethical behaviour and whistleblowers

Jeffrey Wigand

Dr Jeffrey Wigand was Vice President of Research and Development at Brown and Williamson, a major tobacco firm. In the mid-1990s he went public with his inside knowledge of the industry, specifically how the companies downplayed the health risks and addictive qualities of nicotine. It culminated in an interview on *60 Minutes* on 4 February 1996. His whistleblowing took a severe toll on him personally, particularly the smear campaign that was launched against him. His story eventually became a film in 1999 called *The Insider*.

The consequences for the corporation were record breaking. A number of US States brought litigation against the relevant tobacco corporations that resulted in a settlement of US$348 billion.

SOURCE: See Jeffrey Wigand in recommended reading

There are various books of case studies, some from an ethics point of view, for which many cases are listed in this work. For problems with legal implications see Trachtman (2013). For accountants there is a book of case studies that outlines 10 cases, each of which is followed by a set of salient questions (Northcott, 1993).

Another very helpful source is derived from a set of tried cases that have been before a governmental body. Appropriately titled *Scams and Swindlers*, the 10 stories in the book have salutary points attached to them, each of which is spelled out concisely (Brown, 1999). A report by the US Department of State giving something of their experience is also available (see 'American scams' in references). For an overall account see Matulich and Currie (2009). It need not be thought that scams are new (see Crane *et al*, 2004, which lists scams from 1300 to 1650). Plainly the continued existence of scams and swindles is part of the human condition.

It is worth emphasizing that the subjects of whistleblowing may be as much in need of protection as are whistleblowers themselves. It is recognized that it is hard to tell a genuine whistleblower from a troubled individual, a habitual complainer, or someone with personal or malicious motives. Until the complaint is heard there is no way of even attempting to draw such a conclusion. Furthermore, whistleblowing may breach legal obligations, personal confidences, commercial or industrial secrets, or involve the destruction of old loyalties.

In recent times there have been national legislative Acts that cover whistleblowing. While it is easier to legislate for the civil (or public) service it is rather harder to do so for general business. Those contemplating blowing the whistle are recommended to these guiding principles:

- Talk the matter over with your family if lawful to do so.

- Try to solve it within the system, first informally, then formally; the system may well respond.

- Keep a diary with careful chronology; keep documents in a place of safety. Be careful not to unnecessarily expose yourself as a threat to the organization's policies.

- In diary keeping do not be self-indulgent or sarcastic; the diary may appear in later litigation.

- Be on good terms with administrative staff; their later support and testimony may become crucial.

- Identify all relevant documents before blowing the whistle; later access may be cut off.

- Identify those who may be sympathetic; try to get to know others who have blown the whistle.

- If you need the support of others make sure that it is in the form of a statutory declaration. Supporters may become non-supporters because of pressure.

- Save whatever funds you have.

- Find yourself a sympathetic lawyer.

- Check with various local (national) whistleblowers for a competent lawyer (free legal advice may be obtainable).

- Make sure that the advice you get is impartial.

Those contemplating blowing the whistle are encouraged to search online for their local whistleblowing organization.

Conclusion

This chapter has addressed the processes for managing ethical breaches as well as consideration as to how a planned action ought to be evaluated. It addressed what falls within the scope of ethical examination and how to go about the process. It looked at assessment considerations and the crucial importance of finality. Specifically it addressed the qualities of good decision making. Finally the chapter highlighted using all examinations into ethical breaches as opportunities to refine codes, procedures and corporate culture.

The following Chapter will examine problem-solving approaches.

Focus questions

Investigating ethical breaches

1 What is meant by the overreach of ethics?

2 If the cost of investigating a breach is greater than the breach, should there be an investigation?

3 What are the critical factors in determining who should investigate an ethical breach?

4 What is the significance of finality, and how would you set about achieving it?

5 Why should there be a review of every ethical investigation after the matter itself is finalized?

6 If you had to decide quickly as to a particular course of action, what test or tests would you use?

7 What is whistleblowing? If you were to consider whistleblowing what factors would you take into account?

8 What can corporations do to create a culture where individuals don't feel the need to be whistleblowers?

CASE STUDY   Investigation

Sarah has been called into her manager's office and, after ensuring that Sarah does not have a 'conflict of interest' and is properly authorized, her manager asks her to take charge of an investigation. Sarah agrees. Another manager has been accused of bullying; however, the matter is complicated. The accuser has been reported by the same manager of making travel claims greater than allowed. Morale in the section has plummeted. The corporation's ethical code specifically states that 'all colleagues, clients and contractors will be treated with decency and respect' and that 'no one should feel uncomfortable in the workplace'.

How should Sarah proceed?

Factors to consider

Investigations in a corporate environment are not solely the province of internal auditors, ethical advisers, risk managers and fraud prevention staff. Frontline managers or senior staff can be expected to perform this kind of role as required.

The manager has established that there is no conflict of interest and that Sarah is a proper person to take charge. This is clearly a highly charged matter given that there are serious allegations and counter-allegations being made. The situation is one which is very damaging and it could safely be presumed that the environment in that section would be toxic, impacting not only the people directly involved but the whole of the work group. The situation needs to be resolved as soon as possible. Sarah must balance the need to do a sufficiently good investigation in a timely manner.

An appropriate starting point is to obtain all of the relevant documentation, put it in chronological order and read it through. From this point Sarah should have a good grasp of the issues and the people involved. She should also, importantly, have an idea of the gaps, the specific pieces of information that will help her make her decision. There is a potential to get swamped by a mass of detail. Lawyers use a procedure where they lay out what they see the facts of a claim are and present it to the other side.

The lawyers for the other side go through these purported 'facts' and decide what points they disagree with. Out of 100 facts, they may be in agreement over 99 with the dispute boiling down to a single issue. The point here is to determine what is clearly known and agreed and what is in dispute.

Once Sarah is aware of the specific information she needs, she should look at the best way of obtaining it. Are there more documents? Are there witnesses that are neutral and reliable that she can interview? Is there a need to talk to the investigators looking at the complainant's alleged fraud?

Having obtained the information that is available in the timeframe she should assess that against the company's principles. Has the complainant been treated disrespectfully and made to feel uncomfortable? Sarah immediately has an issue: the complainant does feel uncomfortable; she is being investigated for fraud. Sarah needs to consider what the code means. Does it mean 'no one should be made uncomfortable for any reason', or is there an implied statement that this situation is an exception?

When Sarah concludes her opinion, she should provide a draft of her report to the accused manager and ask them if they agree or whether there is something that ought to be corrected, or something that should have been considered that hasn't been.

Having allowed the appropriate time for the accused to respond, Sarah should carefully craft a report that clearly states the reason for the decision and the facts relied on. It should also specifically address the arguments that are against Sarah's position. The report should also set out the recommended action and if there is substance to the allegation then the sanction should be shaped such that it is fair and promotes better behaviour in the future. The report should be as precise and clear as possible; voluminous reports look impressive but are an obstacle to understanding.

Finally, Sarah should consider referring any learnings. She might specifically point out the difficulty that she had with the code and request that consideration be given to an amendment.

Recommended reading

The Indian justice system

Bhowmick, S (2014, September) Justice has a mountain to climb, of 31.3 million pending cases, *Hindustan Times* [online] http://www.hindustantimes.com/india-news/justice-has-a-mountain-to-climb-of-31-3-million-pending-cases/article1-1259920.aspx

Mashru, R, (2013, December) Justice delayed is justice denied: India's 30 million case judicial backlog, *The Diplomat* [online] http://thediplomat.com/2013/12/justice-delayed-is-justice-denied-indias-30-million-case-judicial-backlog/

Jeffrey Wigand

Lyman, R (1999, October) A tobacco whistleblower's life transformed, *New York Times* [online] http://www.nytimes.com/1999/10/15/us/a-tobacco-whistle-blower-s-life-is-transformed.html

Startup Volley (2013, April), Five famous whistleblowers, *Startup Volley* [online] https://startupvolley.wordpress.com/2013/04/23/famous-corporate-whistleblowers/

Wigand, J (nd) Biography, *Biography.com* [online] http://www.biography.com/people/jeffrey-wigand-17176428#tobacco-whistleblower

International standards and first principles

10

Introduction

This chapter uses a suite of documents from the Organisation for Economic Co-operation and Development, specifically:

- guidelines for multinational enterprises;
- principles on privacy;
- corporate governance principles.

The chapter provides an example of the current state of expectations regarding ethical codes. It then considers the basic values underlying these modern expressions of ethical corporate behaviour, specifically dignity, fairness, prudence, honesty, openness and the prevention of suffering. Finally, this chapter looks at other issues to consider when looking at community values.

Key learning points

This chapter will provide the current guiding principles for modern ethical codes.
   It will then look at the community values that underpin these corporate principles, specifically:

- Dignity.
- Fairness.
- Prudence.
- Honesty.
- Openness.
- Prevention of suffering.

The chapter then discusses the related issues of:

- Relative and absolute ethics.
- The pervasiveness of actions.
- Where principles are in conflict.

OECD guidelines for multinational enterprises

For a number of years nearly all countries have had organizing bodies responsible for the development of corporate ethical codes, such as the Financial Reporting Council in the UK and the Ethics Resource Center in the United States. There are also cross-border organizations striving for greater international harmonization such as the International Financial Reporting Society.

The OECD, recognizing the importance of ethics and harmonization across jurisdictions, has developed a document: 'OECD guidelines for multinational enterprises' (see recommended reading). The guidelines, which were initially introduced in 1975, have undergone five revisions, the latest being in 2011. The current revision has been subscribed to by all 34 member nations of the OECD as well as Argentina, Brazil, Egypt, Latvia, Lithuania, Morocco, Peru and Romania. Key differences in the latest version are further recommendations on human rights abuse and greater corporate responsibility for what occurs in their supply chains. The main principles outlined in the OECD guidelines are as follows.

Disclosure

The expectation here is that corporations will provide honest information on all-important aspects of operations: financial, performance, shareholding, relationships, risks and governance. Attention should also be given to reporting in relation to factors in the OECD guidelines themselves, where relevant. Where social and environmental reporting exist they should be of a high standard. The information should be appropriate for its purpose and independently audited.

Human rights

There is an expectation that corporations will respect human rights in accordance with the United Nations framework on business and human rights, 'Protect, Respect and Remedy' (see recommended reading), which itself in turn relies on:

- The International Bill of Human Rights (see recommended reading).
- The International Labour Organization's Declaration on Fundamental Principles and Rights at Work (see recommended reading).

The principle is that corporations should not only respect human rights but should do what they can to mitigate harm in circumstances where the nation state they are operating in does not adhere to the UN principles. Corporations are also expected to ensure that where they are dealing with entities such as local suppliers, they act so as to influence those entities to respect human rights. They are also expected to provide better access for victims to compensation processes for any corporate wrongdoing. The OECD recognizes the significant power that multinational corporations hold and corporations are expected to be a positive force in respecting, mitigating and improving human rights. (See UN on victimology in the References.)

Employment and industrial relations

There is some overlap between these principles and the ILO Declaration on Fundamental Principles and Rights at Work. However, the documents are not contradictory. The main points in summary are:

- a right to freedom of association including representation and negotiation through collective bargaining;
- the elimination of child labour with an urgency on particularly abusive practices;
- the elimination of compulsory or forced labour;
- provision of non-discriminatory employment policies (for example equal treatment of women, minorities, people with disabilities, people of different races and people of different faiths);
- provision of reasonable and safe working conditions (including providing support in circumstances where workers may need to be retrenched); and
- using local labour where possible and improving their skill levels.

Environment

Corporations have been a major contributor to increased standards of living but it has come at a cost. Corporate activity has also been a major contributor to pollution, changing the climate of the world and consuming resources at such a rate that it is likely to compromise the quality of life for future generations. How corporations manage their operations so as to ensure environmental damage is minimized, climate stabilized and resources properly stewarded is crucial.

The guidelines recommend that corporations:

- collect and appropriately report on the environmental impacts (including health and safety, and potential for improvement) of their operations;
- be proactive and consider any environmental impacts of future action and mitigation strategies if required;
- not use scientific uncertainty as an excuse to not promptly and appropriately respond to likely damage;
- have plans ready for emergency situations (including prompt and effective reporting to relevant agencies);
- commit to continuous improvement of environmental management (eg reduce greenhouse gas, create products that are energy efficient and recyclable, reduce use of toxic substances and protect biodiversity);
- provide information to consumers about the environmental impacts of the corporation's products;
- ensure that employees are aware of the corporation's environmental policy and responsibilities; and
- help governments to shape public policy.

Combatting bribery, bribe solicitation and extortion

Corruption is a major threat to democracy, free markets and the social fabric of a community. The issue has become very complex for global business people because of the different values between cultures in the countries where they are operating. How bribery is managed in corporations is a core statement about that corporation's values. It is not difficult to see why employees engage in corrupt activities. It may be the only way to even enter a particular market place.

More importantly though is the often-significant short-term commercial advantage that the right bribes can bring. If one corporation's strategy involves bribes and the bribes work, then competitors and the market place are disadvantaged to the benefit of the bribing corporation. Add to that the often-fierce performance expectations placed on executives that can give great reward or brutal financial punishment and there is the recipe for corporate corruption. Specifically, corporations should:

- not offer, promise or pay bribes in any form (even small facilitation payments) or accept inappropriate benefits or advantages from partner organizations or government officers (this includes the use of third parties to act as intermediaries);
- ensure that they have appropriate programmes, systems and monitoring (financial and ethical) to detect bribery;

- have appropriate systems to monitor and report on the use of 'agents' starting with the hiring process through to the end of the relationship;
- ensure that there is an appropriate learning strategy for employees so that they are aware of the corporation's ethical code and their responsibilities;
- not make improper payments to political campaigns.

Consumers

The ethical treatment of consumers should be an important consideration for all businesses. It is the primary relationship that generates the corporation's revenue. Throughout the text there have been numerous examples of how corporations have, to their detriment, failed to properly consider their customers. Specifically, corporations should:

- ensure goods and services are safe and fit for purpose;
- ensure customers have clear and helpful information to allow them to make informed choices (including education programmes where appropriate);
- provide inexpensive, convenient and fair complaints processes;
- ensure that customer privacy is maintained;
- not use any deceptive or misleading practice (including in advertising material);
- assist authorities to address misleading advertising and practices in their industries; and
- take particular care with disadvantaged or vulnerable consumers.

Science and technology

The OECD recognizes the importance of technology to the advancement of the quality of life, particularly in developing nations. Global corporations play a pivotal role in developing and distributing innovation. This aspect is limited to some degree by intellectual property law and commercial confidentiality. However, the object is to do as much to distribute innovation within those limits. Specifically, corporations should:

- work within national policies and objectives for science in their countries of operation;
- have strategies to quickly distribute technology and knowledge;
- if feasible, undertake research and development work in all their countries of operation (including developing local staff);

- allow reasonable use of intellectual property so as to contribute to growth and sustainability in countries of operation; and

- develop relationships with local universities, other public research organizations and industry groups to contribute to appropriate projects.

Competition

This book has had a number of examples where, through inappropriate means, corporations have behaved unethically to give themselves a competitive advantage. This conduct unfairly prejudices other businesses and consumers because there is no longer a free market determining price and quality. Specifically corporations are expected to:

- act within all relevant rules and regulations of the jurisdictions in which they operate (and educate employees to their responsibilities);

- not engage in anti-competitive behaviour such as colluding with other organizations in the same market to fix prices (including tenders) and boundaries (eg agreeing to stay out of one region in return for a competitor staying out of another that they wish to occupy). This also includes inappropriately restricting output to artificially increase demand;

- co-operate with local competition authorities.

Taxation

As has been stated a number of times in this text, the payment of taxation by multinational corporations is fundamental to ethical conduct. The OECD, like many commentators and tax authorities, is not requesting that corporations pay more than their share. The focus is on paying a fair share of tax and the line has been blurred, often intentionally, as to what tax is lawfully due. Corporations, particularly internet corporations, can, by complex arrangements and structures, use differing regimes to dramatically reduce the tax paid and deny local authorities, including those of poorer developing nations, valuable revenue.

There is a degree of culpability on the part of small governments like Luxembourg who have allowed and encouraged this practice at the expense of their neighbours. There is also culpability on the part of the consulting firms that source these arrangements. However, it is not a huge stretch of imagination for a corporate executive to realize that his business is not actually based in a small European state and that it is simply called a 'permanent establishment' for tax purposes. The judgement of our business leaders should tell them that this is unethical. Global corporations' ethical codes should therefore include:

- A commitment to paying taxation not only according to the law but in the spirit of the law.
- That taxation risk be a focus for boards and governance generally. Boards and executives should ensure that they understand the tax implications of their decisions and the commensurate risks.

OECD principles on privacy

The OECD principles on privacy are also an important document in regard to ethical conduct and should be taken into account. The governing value is that every person has the right to personal privacy, except where divulgence is required by law. The OECD has set out eight principles on privacy, which are summarized below. (See OECD privacy principles in the recommended reading.)

1 Collection limitation. There should be limits to the collection of personal data. It should be done lawfully, fairly and, where appropriate, with the person's consent.

2 Data quality. Data collected should be relevant to the purpose and kept up to date.

3 Specified purpose. People should be told why the data is being collected, and it should not be used for purposes incompatible with the stated purpose.

4 Use limitation. Personal data should not generally be used or disclosed in ways the individual does not know about, except with the authority of law.

5 Security safeguards. Personal data should be given reasonable security against unauthorized access, destruction, use or change.

6 Openness. People should be able to find out easily what is held about them, what it is used for and who controls it.

7 Individual participation. People should be able to see data held about them (or be given reasons for any refusal) and be able to challenge the content.

8 Accountability. Data controllers should be accountable for complying with the principles.

OECD principles of corporate governance

The process of decision making in corporations is crucial and is tightly interrelated to how ethical behaviour is driven. Therefore, the 'OECD principles of corporate governance' should be understood in conjunction with the 'OECD guidelines for multinational enterprises'. The object of these documents is to ensure ethical corporate decision making that in turn will create effective businesses driving an efficient global market place. The OECD principles of corporate governance are summarized below. (Link to the full text version can be found in the recommended reading.)

- Ensuring the basis for an effective corporate governance framework – this principle is to clarify roles and responsibilities, and ensure corporations are operating transparently and lawfully so as to ensure a functional market-based economy.

- The rights of shareholders and key ownership function – this principle is to ensure that the structure of the corporation, its policies and procedures should protect and enable shareholder rights.

- The equitable treatment of shareholders – the corporation's policies and procedures should ensure equal treatment for all shareholders, whether they are in the minority or foreign. Importantly shareholders should have access to a system of effective dispute resolution.

- The role of stakeholders in corporate governance – corporations should ensure their policies and procedures acknowledge and work with other stakeholders, whether that relationship exists in law or has arisen by mutual agreement. Corporations should work with stakeholders to create wealth, employment and sustainability.

- Disclosure and transparency – a corporation's policies and procedures should ensure that appropriate and prompt information is supplied on matters of substance, including finance, performance, shareholding and the decision making of the organization.

- The responsibilities of the board – a corporation's policies and procedures should allow effective supervision of leadership by the board, and ensure the accountability of the board to the stakeholders.

It would be useful here to add a couple of points for consideration in the expression of principles. Both of these go to the heart of such expression. The first is that of 'necessary but not sufficient condition'. A necessary condition is just that – it is essential to bring something about. That is to be distinguished from a sufficient condition – one that suffices on its own. As an example it is necessary to have average intelligence to study successfully but that alone is not enough: a person also needs application. If capacity and application suffice they are the necessary and sufficient conditions to be successful. With respect to solving ethical problems then it is necessary to have a code and an appropriate infrastructure, good intentions, and creative solutions that satisfy agreed principles. Such conditions would be both necessary and sufficient.

The second point is known as 'Occam's razor'. William of Occam was a 14th-century Franciscan monk who articulated the principle of *lex parsimoniae*, which we now call the law of parsimony or Occam's razor. The principle is that if a person has to choose between rival explanations that have no evidence, that person prefers the simpler one. This principle has also been used in biology in Lloyd Morgan's principle of explaining animal behaviour: animal behaviour should not be interpreted as higher mental functioning if an explanation can be found in lower mental functioning. For example, was a behaviour the result of creativity or instinct? More often than not it is instinct that provides the explanation. Occam's razor is as applicable in ethical decision making as it is in other fields of endeavour.

To these comments we might also add an expression often used but not often understood. 'The exception proves the rule' does not exactly mean that: it means that the exception tests the rule.

All of these have the implication of reliability. Not only must there be agreed principles but they must be exercised in a consistent and economical manner.

First level principles

The OECD guidelines have been presented as representative of many modern expressions of what an ethical code should look like and address. These codes have been evolving for decades and use very developed language to encapsulate their principles and specialized environment. It is, however, worthwhile to look behind the corporate language to the human 'values' our communities, ethical companies, government organizations and international bodies are trying to achieve.

First-level principles are those that express the highest level of generality of standards, and act as the first reference point. They represent the topmost aspirational level of ethical behaviour. Two important points need to be noted. First is that no principle can operate in isolation; all principles are connected to, though distinguishable from, other principles. Second, there will be multiple principles in operation. The principles are known by the acronym DEPHOGS:

D = dignity

E = equitability (fairness)

P = prudence

H = honesty

O = openness

G = goodwill

S = suffering (prevention and alleviation)

Dignity

Among the most important principles of ethics is that of treating each individual as an end rather than as a means to an end. However, employment does use people as a means to an end. What is asserted here is that where there is a conflict between the issue of treating people as a means to an end, and of treating them as ends in themselves, the latter principle should prevail. We see customers as a means of making a living. In positions where the interests of the customer are in conflict with a greater profit we should treat the interests of the customer as paramount. It is for such reasons that we have product recalls, safety legislation, and offices of fair trading.

Courtesy is a significant component of dignity. As mentioned earlier, the way in which we commonly behave seems so appropriate that we are inclined to believe it to be morally correct. 'Good manners', whatever they may be, become prescriptive rather than just desirable.

An example of both bad manners and unethical behaviour would be for a professional person to betray a personal confidence. Perhaps the main point here is to note that courtesy is an essential part of treating people with dignity.

Equitability/Fairness

Equitability or fairness involves even-handedness. The essence of ethical values is recognizing and addressing the imbalance of power in relationships. We admire even-handedness in meting out judgement, and highly value the principle of equitable dealing. The power held by strong commercial enterprises is moderated by the need for courtesy and dignity towards clients, to be an essential part of work. Legal systems in democratic countries usually operate in a similar fashion. As the state has more power than the individual, that power is contained by presuming innocence of wrongdoing until the contrary is proved: we cannot be tried twice for the same offence (no double jeopardy); we may not be subject to the arbitrary deprivation of our liberty; and we require police to be accountable to a minister and to Parliament, and so on.

Ideally, a fair judgement should be between well-informed equals and it is the absence of that equity that arouses concern. If everyone were to act according to the ideal, and with goodwill, no such guidance would be necessary. Given we need such guides, with simplicity of application, this one of equity of relationships is important.

The notion of ethics is bound up with the notion of where boundaries are drawn, and what it means when they are violated. In view of the power disparity between business and the stakeholder, the boundaries need to be most clearly designated. Where such boundaries are transgressed there are significant negative consequences for the stakeholder, and the business. Among the forms of redress called for is that of healing rather than retribution.

As mentioned elsewhere in this book, the notion of conflict of interest is where a reward or belief (real or perceived) is likely to compromise the objectivity of commercial judgement. It is the institution of this inequitability in the conflict of interest that offends our sense of moral propriety.

A more sophisticated analysis of this principle involves distributive justice. There are at least three aspects to this view. One is that everyone gets equal shares no matter what (simple equitability); the second is that people get shares according to their contribution (commercial equitability); the third is that people get shares according to need (the socialist model). In commerce, shares according to contribution is the dominant mode. In practice other aspects may be evident. For example, corporate philanthropy may use the model of greatest need.

Prudence

Prudence requires business people to exercise a degree of judgement that makes the situation no worse, and should improve the circumstances. In medicine there is a concept called 'iatrogenesis'. This word means physician-caused illness. It does not necessarily mean that the physician caused the illness personally or purposely. Imagine a child with an illness requiring hospitalization. The child is placed in an environment in which disease abounds, and might catch another disease simply by reason of being in an environment in which the risks are enhanced. It is for such situations that the ethical precept of prudence is required.

How important is prudence to corporations?

Rely tampon

Procter & Gamble (P&G) was informed by the Centers for Disease Control (CDC) that tampons were potentially a factor in 'toxic shock syndrome'. Initial work showed no relationship between P&G's product, Rely tampon and the syndrome but a later CDC analysis showed 71 per cent of sufferers of the syndrome were using the P&G product.

Despite the lack of scientific evidence, P&G withdrew the product three days later at significant cost and even bought back product, including $10 million of freely provided promotional samples. They also funded an educational programme to inform the public about the syndrome and research support for CDC.

P&G judged that they exercise caution to protect their consumers and be honest about the health risk which was ultimately a better decision for their company and their brand.

SOURCE: See Procter & Gamble in recommended reading

The relevant prudent principle in the Rely tampon case is 'do no harm'. Where it is possible that harm may occur, it should be minimalized. Is the harm to be minimized overall, or is it to be exercised in favour of those more likely to be immediately affected? How will this fit with the company mission statement about being open and honest, and of protecting consumers? Whatever our decision it will be based on the consideration of prudence.

Honesty

The issues of honesty and openness are not always easy to distinguish. Such distinction as there is has honesty as straightforwardness and truthfulness. Its antonyms are lying, cheating and stealing. The concept of integrity is essentially linked to that of honesty. The term is cognate with that of being of a whole – of being integrated. To have integrity is to have a consistency of honesty that transcends particular instances. Being honest in one situation is generalized to all situations so that a person of integrity does not wear the hat of honesty in one forum and the hat of dishonesty in another. The attributes expected of a person of integrity are those of being honest (not deceitful), and of consistency of such behaviour.

Honesty is a quality that we attribute to people rather than situations. It is a quality that is associated with 'uprightness'. It is a generic term, which has two attributes intertwined. One is consistency of behaviour; the other is that of the behaviour conforming to key ethical principles. While consistency itself is not an ethical principle, it is a 'necessary but not sufficient condition'. The addition of key principles to consistency is what makes for honesty.

Openness

The essence of openness is that things should be as they purport to be, and not concealed. This principle is to be honoured in general, but not necessarily in every situation. A business person might form the opinion that a contracting party is trading while in a vulnerable emotional state, and requires support and encouragement. If the contracting party were to be open about this it makes them at once both more vulnerable and less so. More so in that advantage might be taken; less so in that the disclosure invites consideration.

Even when it is not possible to reveal, as in commercial confidences, there is openness about the reason for non-disclosure. Insofar as we may make a distinction, the two cases of honesty and openness, respectively, make that distinction.

The warning here is that if a business is overly cautious in releasing information, it may generate an impression that leadership considers itself superior to the stake-holders. This paternalistic attitude, whether in the public service or the private sector, carries social dangers. It might also be noted that it is at variance with the notion of helping to develop autonomy. The advice here is to be open and honest unless there is a compelling reason not to do so.

The converse side of the openness coin is that of privacy. This is so fundamental a point that every code of ethics enshrines it. In essence, the guide is that every person, and every organization, has the right to privacy, save for special circumstances (eg where required by law).

The Organisation for Economic Co-operation and Development (OECD), brings together countries sharing the principles of the market economy, pluralist democracy and respect for human rights. The original members of the OECD were the countries of Europe and North America. Next came Japan, Australia, New Zealand and Finland. Just recently, Mexico, the Czech Republic, Hungary, Poland and the Republic of South Korea have joined.

What is important about this organization is that it has set out some principles relevant to ethical dealing as a precondition of some trade. Thus in dealing with an issue such as privacy the OECD has considered the introduction of technologies and the impact that they have. Since the widespread use of computers to store information, its collection in databases and its ready retrieval and accessibility make it ideal for misuse. Data trade is one of the less welcome aspects of this development.

The OECD produced a set of governing rules on privacy in 2013. These principles are expressed as guidelines which govern the protection of privacy and also cover the transborder flows of personal data. There are a number of principles covering the areas of collection limitation, data quality, specified purpose, use limitation, security safeguards, openness, individual participation and accountability.

Goodwill

The issue of goodwill has been discussed on p 15.

Cheap news or misleading practice?

Native advertising

The internet has progressively created a scenario where the community does not want to pay directly for information and many services. This situation has created a complication for news providers: how to pay for a news service and provision. One response is native advertising, where marketers of products or services write 'stories' that are presented in a fashion where they are almost indistinguishable from normal news items. Those in favour say that this is beneficial to the consumer (more news for less cost) and that market research has found that consumers understand that the practice offsets the benefit of having news at no cost.

The *Economist, Forbes,* the *Atlantic,* the *Huffington Post, Time* Inc, the *New York Times* and Yahoo have adopted native advertising. Critics are alarmed at this challenge to a central premise of journalism that the writer is independent from the stakeholders in the event: what might this mean not only now but in the future? Will we see oil companies writing articles about their spills, food companies writing about their health scares or financial firms writing about their sharp practices?

Articles are being written by marketing and advertising professionals, but being presented and published as if they are written by independent journalists.

SOURCE: See Native advertising in recommended reading

Prevention of suffering

The principles of equity, fairness and dignity do address the issue of the prevention of suffering, but only indirectly. Suffering here is taken to mean suffering caused to any person or animal. It is not that we necessarily avoid suffering at all costs. Thus a surgeon causes suffering, but with consent and for a higher good. It alleviates suffering in the longer term. The suffering mentioned here has no mitigating reasons. This consequentialist view, that pain and suffering should be prevented and alleviated, should be seen in the light of other principles, such as acting with good faith, acting with consent, acting to reduce pain and suffering, and bearing in mind the best interests of the organism to whom or which suffering is caused.

The public has become acutely attuned to the suffering of people in disadvantaged countries and iniquitous positions. There has also been a significant increase in activism around the mistreatment of animals, from rabbits in cosmetic testing to orca whales captured and kept in tanks for display.

Other issues relating to principles

Relative and absolute ethics

It might be argued that there is no such thing as an ethical absolute. Codes are derivations of the human mind, and an imposition on the universe; they are invested with the different values the proponents attach to them. The need for such rules stems from a failure of goodwill. We try to capture justice by formalizing it into legal codes. Legislators have performed this service in the form of protective legislation such as truth in advertising, enforcement of contracts, safety legislation and equal opportunity laws.

It is not easy to distinguish courtesy from ethics; it is equally difficult to distinguish ethics from etiquette. The way in which we commonly behave seems so appropriate that we are inclined to believe it to be morally correct. 'Good manners', whatever they may be, take on a prescribed air and the line is often so blurred as to make distinction impossible.

The pervasiveness of actions

It is almost impossible to contain the consequences of actions. Take a relatively simple commercial example: in Australian waters there is a ban on foreign ships engaging in coastal trade (cabotage). As a 'closed shop' it protects economic interests; it also protects employment. If, however, substandard vessels were to be permitted it is likely that they would find themselves in trouble. The search for lost vessels, the rescue of crew, the refloating or wrecking of the vessel containing pollution (such as ruptured oil tanks) are all losses to the community. Here the issues broaden to the use of government resources, their diversion from other pressing applications, and the degradation of the environment, and its impact on flora and fauna.

The point is that any principle has ramifications far beyond the immediate and obvious. The lesson from this is that we should consider companies, business themes, and value systems as ongoing evolving enterprises. It is impossible to write a definitive code of business ethics because of the constant flux. Business, like all other forms of endeavour, is not a self-contained system but is pervasively affected by events outside its immediate scope.

Where principles are in conflict

One principle alone is not enough. To be open and honest alone is insufficient. Hitler was open and honest about his desire to dominate the world. Dignity is not enough on its own. Being treated with respect while being unjustly imprisoned is not morally appropriate. Where principles seem to be in conflict, the one most relevant to the case will take preference. Even within one principle there may be a conflict about its application. We might value the principle of loyalty very highly, but find the priority of its application more problematic, as in a situation where an operative has responsibility to his or her own professional code, and a loyalty to the code of the employer. Here one has to decide which is the primary loyalty.

On the conflict between principles there is a good illustration in the field of medicine. As noted above, the dual aims are to preserve life and to alleviate suffering – aims that may sometimes appear to be in conflict. A needed appendectomy on an otherwise healthy child, even with only minimum anaesthesia available, invokes the preservation-of-life principle. An aged person who is terminally ill and in great pain may require an alleviation of suffering more than the preservation of a short and painful prospective life.

Where there is more than one principle, there is a potential for conflict. One solution to the problem is to arrange the key principles in hierarchical order. Commercial confidences outrank the need to inform all shareholders about new product developments, and the research that underlies them.

Another solution is to use professional judgement, taking into account the circumstances of the case; for example, a scientist working for the defence industry sees a violation of the industry's professional code of ethics on the issue of not having informed consent of research participants, but cannot complain because to do so would involve revealing secrets of national importance. The preferred approach is not to have differential weights given to each of the principles but to consider each case against all of the principles and decide which one is the most relevant to the case under consideration. Put another way, we might say that one can be an absolutist about the principles but a relativist in their application.

How to resolve conflicting principles

Cadbury chocolates

Sir Adrian Cadbury, a Quaker, was morally opposed to the Boer War (1899–1902). Given the popularity of the war, he came into significant criticism for his views. In 1900 Queen Victoria wanted to send a commemorative tin to the soldiers fighting, the contents of which was to include a bar of chocolate. Sir Adrian was faced with a difficult dilemma. He needed the work for his employees and it was unfair that the soldiers be punished for his beliefs.

After much deliberation and considering all the stakeholders involved, he decided that he would sell the chocolates to the Crown at cost. This would keep his staff employed, provide the soldiers with chocolates and he in turn would not profit from a war he was morally opposed to.

SOURCE: See Cadbury in recommended reading

Conclusion

This chapter commenced with the OECD's guidelines for multinational enterprises as an example of where international efforts culminated. This is not to say that these will be constant; the Financial Reporting Council themselves recognize that their guiding principles are something that will continue to be developed and adapted to the changing community. The chapter then moved on to discuss the social values that underpin the ethical codes of corporations, specifically dignity, fairness, prudence, honesty, openness and the prevention of suffering. Finally we discussed other factors to consider when examining the operation of values. The next chapter provides an alphabetic ready reckoner for ethical codes for multinational organizations.

As was adduced earlier in this work, the two compelling arguments for being ethical in business are that it is for the long-term benefit of the company and, equally important, that it is the right thing to do. In concert these two arguments have substantial persuasive power.

The future and ethics

The world community is facing unprecedented challenges, a massive population, dwindling resources and huge environmental changes. If that were not sufficient our scientific knowledge is growing exponentially, finding, discovering and creating the unimaginable. It may be five years or even 10 but it is entirely possible that we might go to bed tonight and wake to find that someone has found or made something so profound that our lives will never be the same, more than has already been happening.

Something on a bigger scale: new machine intelligence, drugs that slow aging, materials so light and strong that flight is as cheap as a car, new power sources. An hour of watching TED talks on YouTube (**https://www.ted.com/talks**) is enough to make you realize how much and how quickly we are about to change. Among the many things that could occur are that these new inventions may change work as we know it. There was a time when innovation would mean the workforce moved from one kind of job to another, usually better job. This is not as certain today. Innovation may come, jobs may go and there may be nothing or next to nothing that replaces them.

Arguably the signs are already here, such as the long-term unemployment rate in some European countries. Deep structural shifts are occurring that aren't explained by cheap Asian labour or occasional downturns. What will we do when the Western world has 50 per cent unemployment? Or 90 per cent? And this is just one possible consequence of our current direction. The question is, 'are we riding on the technology express train or standing in front of it?'

The individuals that make up our global corporations will be an important, if not the most important, factor in this. Innovation does also come from independent research laboratories, but these institutes are often operating in close partnership with business. Business is a major controlling force in the laboratories, engineering workshops and design studios where these developments are occurring. It is their factories that will make the finished products and their logistics chains that will distribute to the population. No law can address these developments before they occur; the legal systems are not performing sufficiently well for issues that we have now and have known about for a decade let alone something they don't know about. We will be dependent upon the values of our business men and women. Their ethical codes are a major determinant of how we live today and the future we will live in.

We are at a tipping point for our culture and perhaps even our species and what the moral standards of our business people will be. Will they be Enron-esque: anything goes, profit is everything, big bonuses are the motivator, social responsibility is nothing, ethical codes are bits of paper to shut up government?

Or will the business people who hold our future be more like Mr Matsushita and see that their important and influential position is not their entitlement but a position of responsibility and trust, and that they have a duty to make the world a better place?

Focus questions

First principles

1   What are the main themes of the UK's corporate governance code? Why have they been included?

2   How would you describe the obligation to respect the dignity of others? Why is it important?

3   When there is an inequality in relationships, what values would you consider, if any? If a value were to apply, how would you give the idea practical expression?

4   Are honesty and openness the same? If not, why not?

5   When we refer to the prevention of suffering, does it mean that there is a moral obligation to stop all suffering? What is the breadth of suffering referred to?

6   If two principles are in conflict, openness and privacy for example, what approaches are available to assist in the resolution?

CASE STUDY   Which principle takes precedence?

Tula is a manager in a large electronics company. While sitting at her desk a female colleague and friend comes in distressed. The distress is not evident to others; it is only Tula's familiarity with her friend that causes her to notice. Tula suggests coffee and the two depart for a coffee shop. Her friend is at first reluctant to speak but after Tula promises absolute confidentiality she opens up. She confesses to an affair with her manager, a married man, someone Tula knows as well. Tula's friend is distressed because she is deeply in love with the man and she fears that he may end the relationship. As the story comes out it is apparent that the man has exposed the company to the potential of a harassment claim. Also it is apparent that her friend has been enjoying a significant amount of favouritism as a result of this affair, to the detriment of the other staff in that section. After a lengthy attempt by Tula to get her friend to take some sort of action the friend refuses.

What should Tula do?

Factors to consider

The ethical problem for Tula is that she is caught between multiple obligations:

1   she has given her word she will keep the matter confidential;

2   her employer, her company, is facing a serious risk it is unaware of; and

3   there are co-workers who are receiving inequitable treatment.

Should Tula cast confidentiality aside and confront the man or report the situation to her human relations area? She may be a person whose values are such that she cannot accept the inequity and inappropriateness of the situation. She may see a higher duty to her company and her other work colleagues. There is a risk though; a person's reliability is attached to their word. If Tula's breach of her friend's trust were to surface, people may understand and make an exception for the circumstances. But equally they may not; the trust people have in her is a valuable asset.

Tula could maintain the confidence and continue to work on her friend to resolve the situation but then the risk to the company and the inequity to others continues.

Often we see clearer than our friends the state of their relationships and the dynamics that are going on. Equally we can often see where a disastrous circumstance is headed and it is sorely tempting to intervene or take strong action. Like Cassandra from mythology, condemned by the gods to see the future but not be able to do anything about it, we often must look helplessly on as the situation unravels.

Recommended reading

Core suite of documents relating to international business ethics (OECD, UN, ILO)

International Labour Organization (1998, June) ILO Declaration on fundamental principles and rights at work, *ILO* [online] http://www.ilo.org/public/english/standards/relm/ilc/ilc86/com-dtxt.htm

Organisation for Economic Co-operation and Development (2011, May) OECD Guidelines for Multinational Enterprises, *OECD* [online] http://www.oecd.org/daf/inv/mne/oecdguidelinesformultinationalenterprises.htm

Organisation for Economic Co-operation and Development, OECD Principles of Corporate Governance [online] http://www.oecd.org/corporate/oecdprinciplesofcorporategovernance.htm

Organisation for Economic Co-operation and Development, OECD privacy principles (OECD Guidelines on the Protection of Privacy and Transborder Flows of Personal Data) [online] http://www.oecd.org/sti/ieconomy/oecdguidelinesontheprotectionofprivacyandtransborderflowsofpersonaldata.htm

United Nations General Assembly (1948, December) International Bill of Human Rights, *UN Documents* [online] http://www.un-documents.net/a3r217.htm

United Nations News Centre (2011, June) UN Human Rights Council endorses principles to ensure businesses respect human rights, *UN* [online] http://www.un.org/apps/news/story.asp?NewsID=38742#.VO1ghPmSxqU

United Nations Office of the Commissioner for Human Rights (2011, April) Guiding principles on business and human rights, *OHCHR* [online] http://www.ohchr.org/Documents/Publications/GuidingPrinciplesBusinessHR_EN.pdf

United Nations framework on business and human rights, 'Protect, Respect and Remedy' [online] http://business-humanrights.org/en/un-secretary-generals-special-representative-on-business-human-rights/un-protect-respect-and-remedy-framework-and-guiding-principles

Cadbury

Queen Victoria gift tin: South Africa 1900 (Photograph, nd) *Australian War Memorial* [online] http://www.awm.gov.au/collection/REL23561/

Chawli, N (2011, April) Analysis: Leadership drives ethics, *Business World* [online] http://www.businessworld.in/news/economy/analysis-leadership-drives-ethics/305399/page-1.html

Cadbury, Sir A (1987, September) Ethical managers make their own rules, *Harvard Business Review* [online] https://hbr.org/1987/09/ethical-managers-make-their-own-rules/ar/1

Native advertising

Garfield, B (2014, February) If native advertising is so harmless why does it rely on misleading readers? *Guardian* [online] http://www.theguardian.com/commentisfree/2014/feb/25/yahoo-opens-gemini-native-advertising

Rubel, S and Mane, S (2011) Getting in-feed sponsored content right: the consumer view, *Interactive Advertising Bureau* [online] http://www.iab.net/media/file/IAB_Edelman_Berland_Study.pdf

Procter & Gamble

McDonald, B (2014, December) Leadership reflections of Bob McDonald, *H Q Asia* [online] http://hqasia.org/article/leadership-reflections-bob-mcdonald

New York Times (1982, March) Company found negligent in toxic shock disease suit, *New York Times* [online] http://www.nytimes.com/1982/03/20/us/company-found-negligent-in-toxic-shock-disease-suit.html

New York Times (1982, August) Procter & Gamble settle a toxic shock suit, *New York Times* [online] http://www.nytimes.com/1982/08/25/us/procter-gamble-settles-a-toxic-shock-suit.html

ETHICAL CODES: READY REFERENCE GUIDE

Introduction

Given that global corporations already have codes, the following alphabetical list is intended as a ready reference guide to cross-check existing ethical codes as to whether or not these features ought to be considered and included.

Abbreviations:

- *ILO Declaration:* International Labour Organization Declaration on fundamental principles and rights at work (1998).
- *OECD Guidelines:* OECD Guidelines for multinational enterprises (2011).
- *OECD Privacy principles:* OECD Principles on privacy (2013).
- *OECD Corporate governance:* OECD Principles of corporate governance (2004).
- *UN Human rights:* (United Nations) The universal declaration of human rights (1948).

Glossary of international codes related to ethics

Accounting procedures: High-quality accounting procedures across financial as well as social reporting responsibilities where appropriate shall be used to maintain the integrity of the organization. *OECD Guidelines Chapter III, para 4, OECD Corporate governance Part I Chapter V para B.* See also 'Disclosure' and 'Reporting'

Account rigging: See 'Misrepresentation' and 'Accounting procedures'

Accuracy of statements by sales staff: See 'Consumers'

Advertising: See 'Consumers'

Animal experimentation: Activity that involves the use of animals for experimental purposes should follow the guidelines of the appropriate National Health and Medical Research

Council. In principle the code should ensure the absolute minimization of suffering and distress. See also 'Cruelty to animals' and 'Endangering species'

Annual General Meetings: See 'Board of directors'

Anonymity of contractors: See 'Privacy'

Anti-competitive behaviour: See 'Competition'

Associations: See 'Employment and industrial relations'

Auditors: Corporations' accounts should be independently audited to verify their accuracy and that information made available to the board of directors and shareholders to enable effective decision making. *OECD Guidelines Chapter III para 4.*

Beliefs or faith (discrimination): See 'Employment and industrial relations' and 'Stakeholders'

Biohazards: See 'Environment'

Board of directors: Corporations' policies and procedures should provide for effective supervision of leadership by the board, and ensure the accountability of the board to the stakeholders. *OECD Corporate governance specifically Chapter VI.*

Bottom line: See 'Profit'

Bribery: Corporations should not offer, promise or pay bribes in any form (even small facilitation payments) or accept inappropriate benefits or advantages from partner organizations or government officers (this includes the use of third parties to act as intermediaries). *OECD Guidelines Chapter VII.*

Business continuity planning: Corporations should ensure that they have contingency plans for health and safety as well as environmental disasters. *OECD Guideline Chapter V para 5.*

Note also that the speed and humanity of the response is a significant determiner of a corporation's reputation. Corporations should make a humane response (including restitution) to any disasters that might occur. They should also ensure that the company reputation is preserved by having these appropriate policies made known to the public.

Child labour: Corporations should ensure that neither they nor any person or entity in their supply chain is using child labour. They should give an urgent priority to eradicating particularly abusive situations. *OECD Guidelines Chapter V, para 1(c) UN Human rights Article 4, ILO Declaration para 2(c).*

Competition: All commercial competition should take account of the relevant laws of the local jurisdictions as well as being fair, open and honest. *OECD Guidelines Chapter X.*

Computer-based information: See 'Privacy'

Conflict of interest: A conflict of interest would occur when a relationship, an event, or material consideration would compromise the objectivity of commercial judgement. If there is a potential conflict of interest that might influence a commercial or business transaction or interest, it should be formally declared in writing to the appropriate person(s). Where declarations of conflict of interest are made, some written record should be retained.

Examples of declared interest are: directorships, a large shareholding, promise of future employment, and the employment of a close relative or friend in a position of influence in an organization that may be given business or awarded contracts by the company.

Consumers: Corporations should ensure that consumers are treated fairly and honestly, which includes goods and services being fit for purpose, no misleading or deceptive advertising, privacy being respected and special care taken of the vulnerable. *OECD Guidelines Chapter VIII*

Corporations should also provide information to consumers about the environmental impacts of the corporation's products. *OECD Guidelines Chapter VI para 6(c)*

See also 'Dispute resolution'

Copying software: See 'Science and technology'

Corporate governance framework: The infrastructure that supports the decision making of a corporation. *OECD Corporate governance Part I generally and Chapter I specifically.*

Creditors: The governance infrastructure should protect the interests of the creditors. *OECD Corporate governance Part I Chapter II para F.*

See also 'Stakeholders'

Credit privacy (and information challenge): See 'Privacy'

Criticizing competitors: Executives and advertisers in commerce and industry should avoid criticizing competitors, even with good cause. It is preferred that the merit of the corporation's own services or products be stated in a non-comparative way.

Cruelty to animals: The exploitation, painful use and slaughter of animals for non-essential purposes is to be avoided.

See also 'Animal experimentation'

Currency (of reference): Where figures are quoted within a country for any commercial transaction the currency shall be clearly stated (this applies in particular to currencies that also use the term 'dollar').

Data matching: See 'Privacy'

Deceptive information (including statistics): See 'Disclosure' and 'Accounting procedures'

Dignity and worth: All relationships, including employees, consumers and other stakeholders should be conducted in a manner consistent with human dignity and worth. *UN Human rights Article 1.*

Directors: See 'Board of directors'

Disaster management plans: See 'Business continuity planning'

Disclosure: Corporations will provide honest information on all important aspects of operations: financial, performance, shareholding, relationships, risks, social responsibility and governance. *OECD Guidelines Chapter III, OECD Corporate governance Part I Chapter V.*

Discrimination: It is unethical to discriminate against employees on any grounds. *OECD Guidelines Chapter V para 1(e).*

Dismissal: See 'Employment and industrial relations'

Dispute Resolution: Corporations should ensure that there is an effective dispute resolution process for consumers dissatisfied with products and services, *OECD Guidelines Chapter VIII para 3*, and dissatisfied shareholders, *OECD Corporate governance Part I Chapter III para 2.*

Donations: Donations should be fully disclosed to all interested parties.

See also 'Political campaign contributions'

Employment and industrial relations: Corporations are expected to respect employees and allow collective bargaining and the right to association. Corporations should also ensure decent working conditions, safe working environments and protect workers from abusive practices. They should also ensure that there is equality of treatment. Corporations should skill local staff where possible. *OECD Guidelines Chapter V, UN Human rights Articles 20, 23 & 24, ILO Declaration paras 2(a) & 2(d).*

See also 'Stakeholders'

Endangering species: Industry and commerce should take every effort to preserve biodiversity, and to prevent the extinction of endangered species.

See also 'Environment'

Environment: Corporations should not pollute, should consider environmental impacts when planning and use resources appropriately, as well as acting sustainably and openly. *OECD Guidelines Chapter IV.*

Errors (admission of): Where an error has been made it should be recognized and rectified as soon as possible. This admission or apology should be worded in such a way as to express remorse, and compensation offered when appropriate.

Exploitation: The exploitation of the disadvantaged and the vulnerable is unethical (children, minority groups, persons with disabilities, undereducated persons). This also includes workers, consumers and inhabitants of foreign countries that lack the protections that exist in developed nations.

See also 'Child labour', 'Consumers', 'Employment and industrial relations,' and 'Slavery'

Financial circumstances (personal): When organizations recruit or promote, employers are under no ethical compulsion to consider the personal financial circumstances of the employee or potential employee.

Forced labour: See 'Slavery'

Gifts: Gratuities or gifts of money, or any consideration of significant value that could be perceived as having been offered because of the business relationship or to gain a business advantage is unethical.

See also 'Bribery'

Harm: Corporations should be mindful of the harmful consequences of actions in human, animal and environmental terms. The Hippocratic notion, 'do no harm', should be the first rule of ethics.

Harmful goods and services: Where a business person or organization invests in or contracts with a business that clearly provides goods or services that are in breach of the ethical code, they shall draw those breaches to the attention of the offending organization, and take such action as is appropriate to minimize any harmful effects.

Human rights: Corporations will respect human rights in accordance with the United Nations framework on business and human rights, 'Protect, Respect and Remedy.' *OECD Guidelines Chapter IV, UN Human rights.*

Improvement: Corporations should where possible look to use and skill local staff to improve the overall standard of living in the countries of their operation. *OECD Guidelines Chapter V para 5.*

Industrial espionage: The use of clandestine operations to secure commercial information is unethical. This does not apply to gathering information in the public domain.

Information: See 'Disclosure' and 'Privacy'

Information about employees: See 'Employment and industrial relations' and 'Privacy'

Intimidation: No form of intimidation, duress, or other improper pressures should be used in business.

Job advertisements: All job advertisements should be genuine, and not fabricated to fulfil some other purpose. The guiding principle is that employment described in job advertisements should be what it purports to be.

Job selection criteria: Job selection criteria should accurately reflect the job and not have a hidden agenda.

Labelling: See 'Consumers' and 'Disclosure'

Language of commerce: The forced use of language other than the language of the nation is socially divisive and fraught with the possibility of misunderstanding. Social cohesion is fostered by a common means of communication. The primary language of commerce in the relevant country shall be the means of communication unless otherwise agreed.

In circumstances where there is uncertainty as to where the transaction is occurring, as can be the case in the borderless environment, a common language should be agreed.

Law: It is not the function of a code of business conduct to change the law. Rather, it is to fill gaps in the law, and to express the business values of the national society in particular. Importantly businesses should comply not only with the letter but also with the spirit of the law.

Corporations should assist government and therefore the community to rectify failures in the law, specifically where the law is inadequate to address the underlying social purpose. It is unethical to use threats of litigation, involving either costly cases or public embarrassment, as a means of gaining commercial advantage. The use of legal tactics to delay resolution is unethical.

Leadership: The corporate governance documents specifically look to the board of directors as a key focus in the overall management of risk in an organization; however, the practical effect is that the CEO and the leadership team have the primary responsibility. The board has oversight but it is the executive that are the drivers of the business and the conduit to the board.

Learning: Corporations should ensure that there is an appropriate learning strategy for employees so that they are aware of the corporation's ethical code and their responsibilities regarding bribery. *OECD Guidelines Chapter VII para 6.*

Corporations should also ensure that employees are aware of the environmental policy and responsibilities. *OECD Guidelines Chapter VI para 7.*

Misrepresentation: See 'Accounting procedures', 'Consumers' and 'Disclosure'

Personal information (use of): See 'Privacy'

Personal violence: Personal violence in the pursuit of business is unlawful and unethical. *UN Human rights Article 3.*

Political campaign contributions: Corporations should not make improper payments to political campaigns. *OECD Guidelines Chapter VII, para 7.* There is a view that no company should make a political donation unless the AGM approves it unanimously, bearing in mind that it diminishes profit to shareholders, though makes friends in politics.

　　See also 'Donations'

Pollution: See 'Environment'

Prevention of unethical behaviour: Corporations should ensure that their code (and ethical infrastructure) are organized in order to prevent breaches of ethics. The following features should be present:

- senior management to set a good example ('tone from the top');
- adequate ethical infrastructure be in place (see Chapter 8);
- learning strategies in ethical behaviour to be provided (see Chapter 8);
- whistleblowers be protected (see Chapter 8);
- one of the staff selection criteria to be ethical commitment;
- rewards for ethical commitment to be provided;
- social responsibility report be part of annual reporting.

Privacy: The governing value is that every person has the right to personal privacy, except where divulgence is required by law. *OECD Privacy principles Part 2 paras 7–14, UN Human rights Article 12.*

Privacy (Customer): Customers' privacy and confidences shall be maintained except where there is an overriding legal obligation to reveal. *OECD Privacy principles Part 2 paras 7–14, OECD Guidelines Chapter VIII, para 6.*

Private inquiry agents: Private inquiry agents should not be employed unless the action is approved legally.

Profit: Profit-making organizations are mindful of their obligations to maximize their profits. This motive to maximize profit should not be at the expense of keeping to the principles of ethical behaviour.

Public statements: See 'Consumers' and 'Disclosure'

Redundancies and relocation: Where redundancies occur every effort should be made to mitigate the harm, such as trying to provide alternative employment, giving ample notice, working with workers' associations and relevant government authorities. *OECD Guidelines Chapter V para 6.*

Remuneration: Any payments received by board members or principles in the leadership team should be available. *OECD Corporate governance Part I Chapter V para A(4).*

Reporting: Corporations should:

- Collect and appropriately report on the environmental impacts (including health and safety, and potential for improvement) of their operations. *OECD Guidelines Chapter VI paras 1&2.*

- Ensure that they have appropriate programmes, systems and monitoring (financial and ethical) to detect bribery. *OECD Guidelines Chapter VII, para 2.*

- Have appropriate systems to monitor and report on the use of 'agents' starting with the hiring process through to the end of the relationship to protect against bribery. *OECD Guidelines Chapter VII, para 4.*

See also 'Accounting procedures' and 'Auditors'

Safety standards: Corporations should provide a safe working environment. *OECD Guidelines Chapter V, para 4(c):*

- provide reasonable and safe working conditions (including circumstances where workers may need to be retrenched); and

- use local labour where possible and improve their skill levels.

See 'Employment and industrial relations'

Science and technology: Corporations should, within the limits of intellectual property and commercial confidentiality, adopt strategies to disseminate technology and knowledge. *OECD Guidelines Chapter IX.*

Secret commissions: It is unethical to take secret commissions or to solicit or receive compromising gifts.
See also 'Bribery'

Shareholders: Shareholders should be granted a number of rights and those rights should be protected by the corporation. Broadly these are the right to information and an effective say in material issues. *OECD Corporate governance Part I Chapter II.*

In particular, minority and foreign shareholders should receive equal treatment. *OECD Corporate governance Part I Chapter III.*

See also 'Dispute resolution'

Slave labour: Corporations should ensure that their workforce and that of their supply chains does not involve any form of 'forced labour'. They are also expected to work towards and assist with any suppression of this practice. *OECD Guidelines Chapter V, para 1(d), UN Human rights Article 4, ILO Declaration para 2(b).*

Stakeholders: Corporations should ensure that the rights of persons and organizations are recognized by law or by agreement as stakeholders. *OECD Corporate governance Part I, Chapter 4.*

Taxes: Corporations should ensure that they pay their fair share of tax and not enter into arrangements that defeat the spirit of the law and deprive governments of revenue. *OECD Guidelines Chapter XI.*

Transparency: See 'Disclosure'

Unions: See 'Associations'

Vulnerable customers and traders: See 'Consumers'

Withdrawal of harmful goods or services: Where it comes to the attention of providers of goods or services that the products are harmful, the goods or services should be withdrawn from sale and/or recalled.

See also 'Consumers'

Working conditions: Maintain working conditions that are, as a minimum, the same as that of other local employers. However, the remuneration should be sufficient to ensure that the worker and their family's basic needs are meet. *OECD Guidelines Chapter V, para 4.*

REFERENCES

American scams [online] https://www.ncjrs.gov/App/abstractdb/ AbstractDBDetails.aspx?id=242180

Ascalon, M E and Schleicher, M P B (2008) Cross-cultural social intelligence: as assessment for employees working in cross-national contexts, *Cross-cultural Management: An International Journal*, **15** (2), pp 109–30

Axelrod, T (1990) *The Evolution of Cooperation*, Penguin, London

Barraquier, A (2011) Ethical behaviour in practice: decision outcomes and strategic implications, *British Journal of Management*, **22** (suppl 1), pp 28–46

Bastien, J R (1997) Can ethics improve the bottom line? *Security management*, **41**, p 136

Bennett, B E, Jones, S E, Nagy, T F and Canter, M B (1994) *Ethics for Psychologists: A commentary on the American Psychological Association ethics code*, American Psychological Association, Washington DC

Berman, P S (2009) The new legal pluralism, *Annual Review of Law and Social Science*, **5**, pp 225–42

Brehm, S S and Brehm, J W (1981) *Psychological Reactance: A theory of freedom and control*, Academic Press, NY

Brinkman, R and Kirschner, R (2003) *Dealing with Difficult People: Twenty-four lessons for bringing out the best in everyone*, McGraw Hill, New York

Brown, R (1999) *Scams and Swindlers: True stories from ASIC*, Centre for Professional Development, Melbourne

Brown, Sir W R *et al* (1964) The Marlow Declaration, *Production Engineer*, **43** (4), pp 173–75

Burton, B K and Goldsby, M G (2009) The moral floor: a philosophical examination of the connection between ethics and business, *Journal of Business Ethics*, **91**, pp 145–54

Campbell, A H (1965) *Obligation and Obedience to the Law*, Proceedings of the British Academy, Oxford University Press, Oxford

Cellan-Jones, R (2015) Does AI threaten the future of the human race? *BBC* [online] http://www.BBC.com/news/technology-30326384

Chan, G K Y (2008) The relevance and value of Confucianism in contemporary business ethics, *Journal of Business Ethics*, **77**, pp 34–60

Chatham House Rule [online] http://www.chathamhouse.org/about/chatham-house-rule

Choi, D Y and Perez (2007) Online piracy, innovation and legitimate business models, *Technovation*, **27** (4), pp 168–78

Class Action (1991) [film] Dir. Michael Apted, USA, Interscope Communications, 20th Century Fox Film Corporation

Connor, K T (2006) Assessing organizational ethics: measuring the gaps, *Industrial and Commercial Training*, **38** (3), pp 14–57

Cormack, D (1991) *Excellence at Work*, British Institute of Management, Corby, Northants

Crane, A and Matten, D (2010) *Business Ethics: Managing corporate citizenship and sustainability in the age of globalization*, Oxford University Press, Oxford

Crane, M, Raiswell, R and Reeves, M (2004) *Shell Games: Studies in scams, frauds, and deceits (1300–1650)*, Toronto University Press, Toronto

Davies, K (2011) Regulatory reform post the Global Financial Crisis: An overview [online] www.apec.org.au/docs/11_CON_GFC/Regulatory%20Reform%20Post%20GFC-%20 Overview%20Paper.pdf

De Bono, E (2010) *Lateral Thinking: A textbook of creativity*, Penguin, London

Devlin, P (1961) *Law and Morals*, Presidential address to the Holdsworth Club at the University of Birmingham

Di Florio, C V (2011, October) The role of compliance and risk management (NSCP National Meeting), *Securities and Exchange Commission*, [online] http://www.sec.gov/ news/speech/2011/spch101711cvd.htm

Drummond, J (1991) *Communicating Business Ethics*, British Institute of Management, London

Eberlein, L (1993) The education of psychologists in ethical and professional conduct, in *Professional Psychology in Canada* (eds S Dobson and D J G Dobson) Hofgrefe and Huber, Seattle (p 201)

Elkington, J (1999) Triple bottom line reporting: looking for balance, *Journal of the Australian Association of Certified Practising Accountants*, **69**, pp 18–21

Estes, R (1996) *Tyranny of the Bottom Line*, Berrett Koehler, San Francisco

Feingold, B F (1976) Hyperkinesis and learning disabilities linked to the ingestion of artificial food colors and flavors, *Journal of Learning Disabilities*, **9**, pp 551–59

Fernandes, L (2013) Fraud in electronic payment transactions: threats and countermeasures, *Asia Pacific Journal of Marketing and Management Review*, **2** (3), pp 23–32

Ferrell, O C and Gresham, L G (1985) A contingency framework for understanding ethical decision making in marketing, *Journal of Marketing*, **49**, pp 87–96

Fight Club (1999) [film] dir. David Fincher, USA, Fox 2000 Pictures

Foreign Corrupt Practices Act 1977 (US Federal Legislation) *United States Department of Justice* [online] http://www.justice.gov/criminal/fraud/fcpa/

Francis, R D and Armstrong, A F (2012) *Meetings: Formal rules and informal guides*, Anthem Press, London

Francis, R D, Gius, E and Coin, R (2004) Ethical gradualism: a practical approach, *Australian Journal of Professional and Applied Ethics*, **5** (1), pp 25–34

Friedman, M (1970) The social responsibility of business is to increase its profits, *New York Times Magazine*, September

Furnham, A (2005) *The Psychology of Behaviour at Work: The individual in the organization*, Psychology Press, East Sussex (at p 562 *et seq.*)

Genetically modified organisms [online] http://www.loc.gov/law/help/restrictions-on-gmos/ usa.php and http://www.loc.gov/law/help/restrictions-on-gmos/england-wales.php and http://eurlex.europa.eu/search.html?qid=1425100740136&text=gmo&scope=EURLEX& type=quick&lang=en

Grensing-Pophal, L (1998) Walking the tightrope: balancing risks and gains, *HR Magazine*, 43, pp 112–14

Gurría, A (22 January 2009) Business ethics and OECD principles: what can be done to avoid another crisis? *OECD* [online] http://www.oecd.org/daf/businessethicsandoecd-principleswhatcanbedonetoavoidanothercrisis.htm

Hansen, R and Papademetriou, D G (2013) *Managing Borders in an Increasingly Borderless World*, Migration Policy Institute, Washington

Hart, H L A (1963) *Law, Liberty and Morality*, Clarendon Press, Oxford

Hartman, L P, Desjardins, J and MacDonald, C (2013) *Business Ethics: Decision making for personal integrity and social responsibility*, McGraw Hill, New York

Hegarty, W H and Sims, H P (1978) Some determinants of unethical decision behavior: an experiment, *Journal of Applied Psychology*, 63 (4), pp 451–57

Henriques, A and Richardson, J (2004) *The Triple Bottom Line: Does it all add up?: Assessing the sustainability of business and CSR*, Earthscan (Routledge), Oxford

Hofstede, G, Hofstede, G J and Minkov, M (2010) *Cultures and Organizations: software of the mind: intercultural cooperation and its importance for survival* (3rd edition), McGraw Hill, NY

Hughes, B (2015) Would you be beautiful in the ancient world? *BBC Magazine* [online] http://www.bbc.com/news/magazine-30746985

Hunt, S D and Vitell, S (1986) A general theory of marketing ethics, *Journal of Macromarketing*, 6 (1), pp 5–16

Jackson, J, Bradford, B, Hough, M, Myhill, A, Quinton, P and Tyler, T R (2012) Why do people comply with the law? Legitimacy and the influence of legal institutions, *British Journal of Criminology*, 52, pp 1051–71

Jay, A (1987) *Management and Machiavelli: Power and authority in business life*, Hutchinson, London

Kant, I (1971) The supreme moral principle, in *A New Introduction to Philosophy* (Ed S M Cahn) Harper and Rowe, NY

Kant, I (1998) *Critique of Pure Reason*, Cambridge University Press, Cambridge

Kasperczyk, R T and Francis, R D (2002) *Private Practice Psychology*, Pearson, Frenchs Forest, NSW

Koestler, A (1967) *The Ghost in the Machine*, Macmillan, NY

Kohlberg, L (1976) Moral stages and moralization: the cognitive developmental approach, in *Moral Development and Behavior: Theory, research and social issues* (ed T Lickona) Holt, Rinehart and Wilson, NY

Kohlberg, L, Boyd, D R and Levine, C (1990) The return of stage 6: its principle and moral point of view, in *The Moral Domain: Essays in the ongoing discussion between philosophy and the social sciences* (ed T Wren), MIT Press, Cambridge, MA

Kohut, G F and Corrigher, S E (1994) The relationship of age, gender, experience and awareness of written ethics policies to business decision-making, *SAMAdvanced Management Journal*, 59 (1), pp 32–39

Levitt, S D and Dubner, S J (2005) *Freakonomics*, William Morrow, NY

Lindgreen, A and Swaen, V (2010) Corporate social responsibility, *International Journal of Management Reviews*, **12** (1), pp 1–7

Lloyd, T (1990) *The 'Nice' Company*, Bloomsbury, London

Lo, S-F (2009) Performance evaluation for sustainable business: a profitability and marketability framework, *Corporate Social Responsibility and Environmental Management*, **17** (6), pp 311–19

MacLean, P (1990) *The Triune Brain in Evolution: Role in paleo-cerebral functions*, Plenum Press, NY

Majolo, B (2007) Altruism in humans: an evolutionary approach, *Journal of Anthropological Sciences*, **85**, pp 229–31

Matsumoto, D (ed) (2001) *The Handbook of Culture and Psychology*, Oxford University Press, Oxford

Matulich, S and Currie, D M (eds) (2009) *Handbook of Frauds, Scams and Swindles*, CRS Taylor and Francis, Boca Raton, Florida

McCabe, D L, Treviño, L K and Butterfield, K D (1996) The influence of the collegiate and corporate codes of conduct on ethics-related behavior in the workplace, *Business Ethics Quarterly*, **6**, pp 461–76

McDevitt, R, Giapponi, C and Tromley, C (2007) A model of ethical decision making: the integration of process and content, *Journal of Business Ethics*, **73**, pp 219–29

Milgram, S (1977) *The Individual in a Social World: Essays and experiments*, Addison Wesley, Reading, MA

Mill, J S (2007) *Utilitarianism*, Dover, NY

Moore, G E (1993) *Principia Ethica*, Cambridge University Press, Cambridge

Morris, S A, Rehbein, K A, Hosselni, J C and Armacost, R L (1995) A test of environmental, situational, and personal influences on ethical intentions of CEOs, *Business and Society*, **34** (2), p 119

Ngai, E W T, Yong, H, Wong, Y H, Chen, Y and Sun, X (2011) The application of data mining techniques in financial fraud detection: A classification framework and an academic review of literature, *Decision Support Systems*, **50** (3), pp 559–69

Northcott, P H (1993) *Ethics and the Accountant: Case studies*, Australian Society of CPAs, Melbourne

OECD corporate governance principles [online] http://www.oecd.org/daf/ca/corporategovernanceprinciples/31557724.pdf

OECD principles on privacy [online] http://www.oecd.org/sti/ieconomy/2013-oecd-privacy-guidelines.pdf

Owen, J (1983) Business ethics in the college classroom, *Journal of Business Education*, **58** (7), pp 25–62

Peters, T and Austin, N (1985) *A Passion for Excellence*, Fontana, London

Peters, T J and Waterman, R H (1982) *In Search of Excellence*, Warner Books, NY

Professional and business codes of ethics [online] http://definitions.uslegal.com/c/code-of-ethics/

Raz, J (2009) *The Authority of Law*, 2nd edition, Oxford University Press, Oxford

Reichheld, F F and Teal, T A (2001) *The Loyalty Effect: The hidden force behind growth, profits, and lasting value*, Harvard Business Press Books, Cambridge, Mass

Reidenbach, R E and Robin, D P (1991) A conceptual model of corporate moral development, *Journal of Business Ethics*, **10**, pp 273–84

Ridley, M (1996) *The Origins of Virtue*, Viking, London

Rittenburg, T L, Valentine, S R and Faircloth, J B (2007) An ethical decision-making framework for competitor intelligence gathering, *Journal of Business Ethics*, **70**, pp 235–45

Rossouw, G J and Van Vuuren, L J (2003) Models of managing morality: a descriptive model of strategies for managing ethics, *Journal of Business Ethics*, **46** (4), pp 389–402

Ruhe, J and Lee, M (2008) Teaching ethics in international business courses: the impacts of religions, *Journal of Teaching in International Business*, **19** (4), pp 362–88

Sarbanes-Oxley Act 2002 (US Federal Legislation) Known formally as *Public company accounting reform and investor protection act* (in the US Senate), and *Corporate and auditing accountability and responsibility act* (in Congress)

Savitz, A W (with Karl Weber) (2014) *The Triple Bottom Line*, Wiley, San Francisco

Scams [online] http://www.pierpont.com.au/article.php?_The-year-s-best-lest-we-forget-407

Schultz, T (2015) Byte barons, *Australian Financial Review*, 20 March, pp 1 & 4–6

Shaw, W H (2009) Marxism, business ethics, and corporate social responsibility, *Journal of Business Ethics*, **84**, pp 565–76

Singer, P (1981) *The Expanding Circle: Ethics and sociobiology*, Oxford University Press, Oxford

Stajkovic, A D and Luthens, F (1997) Business ethics across cultures: a social-cognitive model, *Journal of World Business*, **32** (1), pp 17–34

Statements of Standard Accounting Practice [online] http://www.icaew.com/en/library/subject-gateways/accounting-standards/uk-ssap

Strubler, D, Park, S-H, Agarwal, A and Cayo, K (2012) Development of a macro-model of cross-cultural ethics, *Journal of Legal, Ethical and Regulatory Issues*, **15** (2), pp 25–34

Svensson, G and Wood, G (2008) A model of business ethics, *Journal of Business Ethics*, **77**, pp 303–22

Taka, I and Folgia, W D (1994) Ethical aspects of 'Japanese leadership style', *Journal of Business Ethics*, **13**, pp 135–48

Trachtman, J P (2013) *The Tools of Argument*, Createspace Independent Publishing, South Carolina

Transparency International [online] http://www.transparency.de/ and http://www.transparency.org/whatwedo/publication/cpi_2013

Trevino, L K (1986) Ethical decision making in organizations: a person-situation interactionist model, *Academy of Management Review*, **11** (3), pp 601–17

Trevino, L K, Brown, M and Hartman, L P (2003) Qualitative investigation of perceived executive ethical leadership: perceptions from inside and outside the executive suite, *Human Relation*, **56** (1), pp 5–37

Trevino, L K and Youngblood, S A (1990) Bad apples in bad barrels: a causal analysis of ethical decision making behavior, *Journal of Applied Psychology*, **75** (4), pp 378–85

Tsalikis, J, Seaton, B and Li, T (2008) The international business ethics index: Asian emerging economies, *Journal of Business Ethics*, **80**, pp 643–51

UN on victimology [online] http://www.ohchr.org/Documents/HRBodies/CCPR/ GConArticle9/Submissions/WorldSocietyOfVictimologyDraftConvention.pdf

United Nations [online] www.un.org

UPICC principles [online] http://www.unidroit.org/instruments/commercial-contracts/ upicc-model-clauses

Vitell, S J, Nwachukwu, S L and Barnes, J H (1993) The effects of culture on ethical decision making: an application of Hofstede's typology, *Journal of Business Ethics*, **12**, pp 753–60

Waks, R (2012) *Understanding Jurisprudence: An introduction to legal theory*, 3rd edition, Oxford Uinversity Press, Oxford

Whistleblower Protection Act 1989 (US Federal Legislation)

White, J and Taft, S (2004) Frameworks for teaching and learning business ethics within the global context: background of ethical theories, *Journal of Management Education*, **28** (4), pp 463–77

Whyte, W (1960) *The Organisation Man*, Penguin, Harmondsworth

Willard, R (2012) *The Sustainability Advantage*, New Society Publishers, BC, Canada

Williams, C C and Seguí-Mas, E (2010) Corporate governance and business ethics in the European Union: a cluster analysis', *Journal of Global Responsibility*, **1** (1), pp 98–126

Williams, W (1971) *The Four Prisons of Man* Part 3: The prison of our society, Australian Broadcasting Commission, Sydney

Wilson, E O (2000) *Sociobiology: The new synthesis*, Harvard University Press, Boston, MA

Windt, P Y, Appleby, P C, Battin, M P, Francis, L P and Landesman, B M (1989) *Ethical Issues in the Professions*, Prentice Hall, Englewood Cliffs

Wines, W A and Napier, N K (1992) Toward an understanding of cross-cultural ethics: a tentative model, *Journal of Business Ethics*, **11** (11), pp 831–41

Wright, P (1992) Food for thought, *The Psychologist*, **5** (400), p 2

Zimbardo, P (2006) The psychology of power: to the person? to the situation? to the system? In D I Rhode, *Moral Leadership: The theory and practice of power, judgment, and policy*, Jossey Bass, San Francisco

Zolfagharifard, E (2015) Don't let AI take all our jobs and kill us: Stephen Hawking and Elon Musk sign open letter warning of robot uprising *Daily Mail*, 13 January [online] http://www.dailymail.co.uk/sciencetech/article-2907069/don-t-let-AI-jobs-kill-stephen-hawking-elon-musk-sign-open-letter-warning-robot-uprising.html

INDEX

Note: Page numbers in **bold** indicate section headings. This Index covers the main text pages of the book only, not the Roman-numbered preliminary pages.